SELECTED WORKS OF PEARL JEPHCOTT: SOCIAL ISSUES AND SOCIAL RESEARCH

Volume 5

HOMES IN HIGH FLATS

HOMES IN HIGH FLATS

Some of the Human Problems
Involved in Multi-Storey
Housing

PEARL JEPHCOTT

with
HILARY ROBINSON

LONDON AND NEW YORK

First published in 1971 by Oliver & Boyd

This edition first published in 2023
by Routledge
4 Park Square, Milton Park, Abingdon, Oxon OX14 4RN

and by Routledge
605 Third Avenue, New York, NY 10158

Routledge is an imprint of the Taylor & Francis Group, an informa business

© 1971 Pearl Jephcott
© 2023 Josephine Koch

All rights reserved. No part of this book may be reprinted or reproduced or utilised in any form or by any electronic, mechanical, or other means, now known or hereafter invented, including photocopying and recording, or in any information storage or retrieval system, without permission in writing from the publishers.

Trademark notice: Product or corporate names may be trademarks or registered trademarks, and are used only for identification and explanation without intent to infringe.

British Library Cataloguing in Publication Data
A catalogue record for this book is available from the British Library

ISBN: 978-1-032-33020-4 (Set)
ISBN: 978-1-032-33029-7 (Volume 5) (hbk)
ISBN: 978-1-032-33042-6 (Volume 5) (pbk)
ISBN: 978-1-003-31788-3 (Volume 5) (ebk)

DOI: 10.4324/9781003317883

Publisher's Note
The publisher has gone to great lengths to ensure the quality of this reprint but points out that some imperfections in the original copies may be apparent.

Disclaimer
The publisher has made every effort to trace copyright holders and would welcome correspondence from those they have been unable to trace.

New Foreword to the Reissue of *Homes in High Flats*

The slums of the 1920s and 1930s, alongside the ravages of war in the 1940s and the subsequent call for homes for heroes meant that the UK needed to invest heavily in housing to ensure that people had decent places to live that reflected the aspirational post-war period. In most instances, urban planners looked to the brutalist and minimalist styles of architecture that were working so well in continental Europe. Such designs enabled significant numbers of people to be housed in multi-occupancy, multi-storey concrete tower blocks that used vertical space. To build up rather than build out, using modern building techniques and materials offered an efficient and effective way to solve the problems associated with slum dwellings. Homes fit for a modern era. Glasgow and other UK cities such as Manchester, Sheffield, and Birmingham were at the vanguard of this change. Building 'up' in a high-rise meant to move away from the squalor and unsanitary conditions of inner-city tenement housing. In Glasgow, this meant sweeping away decades of problems and the wholesale modernisation of a city. Although ironically, the tenement-style houses so denigrated during this time would become incredibly fashionable, desirable, and very expensive in subsequent decades.

Given this modernisation push and Pearl Jephcott's established interest in family community and young people, it is obvious for Pearl to turn her attention to the realities of living in high-rise accommodation. Her book, *Homes in High Flats*, possibly the very first study of what it was like to live everyday lives at 'height', is typically 'Jephcottian'. Having moved to Glasgow for her book, *A Time of One's Own*, Glasgow offered a prominent locale for studying high-flat living. Yet not content with merely observing lives in high flats from a distance, Pearl moved into one of the 'slab blocks' herself to experience first-hand life in the tower block. Funded by the Joseph

Rowntree Memorial Trust, Jephcott and her team considered the social implications of domestic housing in high flats between July 1, 1966, and 1969. As part of this study, the team interviewed 60 people in the pilots and then nearly 1000 as part of the main sample. Alongside the main study, Pearl also undertook smaller studies involving interviews and observations comparing multi-storey and low-rise households, the experiences of young people aged 15 to 22, experiences of mothers with children and the views of caretakers. She undertook interviews with tenants' associations. She also documented services and facilities, lift waiting times, playgroups, and the use of gang-based graffiti. As with her other studies, *Homes in High Flats* becomes much more than a simple study of domestic housing. Pearl considers 'whole situations' as to how people are experiencing life at height. What results is a richly precisely detailed and thoroughly documented study combining interview data, discussion group data, photographic materials, maps and diagrams. It is Pearl Jephcott at her very best – imaginative, creative, lateral thinking in a way designed to document the reality of everyday life for ordinary people.

More than any of her studies, it was the use of photography that sets this book apart. For example, to highlight the loss of community that living at height brings, Pearl photographed one resident sitting in her chair to document what she could see from her window – which, when sat down, was the sky and the clouds. Only when stood up was it possible to see the other houses and signs of life below. Pearl has neatly captured the impact of social isolation that came with homes in high flats in these two photographs. Jephcott also includes pictures of children playing and laments the sparsity of provision in the high-rise flats for young people's social and leisure time. Finally, in appendix C, there is perhaps one of the first critical discussions of the role and function of graffiti. Here Pearl records the graffiti offered by Glasgow gangs of the time, including the marks made by the 'Tiny Shamrock' and floats the idea that graffiti is a mark of territory designed to intimidate or provoke.

Homes in High Flats, for me, serves another purpose. It was written when one way of life was swept away in the Glasgow tenements. This way of life was to be replaced by what, at the time, was perceived to be something better. Pearl's study captures the moment the mothers of Glasgow tenements had to change their behaviours and move away from cosy meetings on the doorstep or chats out of the tenement windows. The book chronicled the point when the everyday experiences of Glasgow's children were changed forever and are humorously accounted for in *The Jeely Piece Song*. Yet, given the passage of time, many of the high-rise flats that Pearl wrote about in this book have subsequently been demolished, making way for yet further changes to the housing stock and ways of living. *Homes in High Flats* also documents the very short-lived experiment with brutalist architecture.

Homes in High Flats is a book that speaks to a specific point in time. However, we can still learn from it as it is methodologically rich and explores challenging housing experiences, the lessons of which are still relevant today.

John Goodwin
University of Leicester
October 2022

HOMES IN HIGH FLATS

Some of the human problems
involved in multi-storey housing

★

PEARL JEPHCOTT, M.A.

*Department of Social and Economic Research
University of Glasgow*

with
HILARY ROBINSON

*University of Glasgow Social and Economic Studies
Occasional Papers No. 13*

OLIVER & BOYD
EDINBURGH

OLIVER AND BOYD

Tweeddale Court, 14 High Street
Edinburgh EH I IYL

A Division of Longman Group Ltd.

© 1971 Pearl Jephcott

All rights reserved

No part of this publicaiion may be reproduced, stored in a retrieval system, or transmitted in any form or by any means, electronic, mechanical, photo-copying, recording or otherwise, without the prior permission of the Copyright owner and the Publisher. The request should be addressed to the Publisher in the first instance.

First published 1971

ISBN: Paperback   0 05 002435 3
        Hardback   0 05 002436 1

Printed in Great Britain by
Cox & Wyman Ltd.
London, Fakenham and Reading

FOREWORD

A great deal is said and written about the problems of living in high flats, but little of it is based on real study and knowledge of these problems in a practical sense. This book seeks to remedy that situation.

Tall blocks of flats are an everyday sight in most of our large industrial cities. They owe their origin to pressures arising out of the limited space within urban areas, and the need to rehouse large sections of the population who have too long lived in homes – if that is the word – which are something of a disgrace to our contemporary society and provide standards of comfort and amenity that are far below what we might regard as reasonable. Yet although blocks of high flats may seem to provide an answer to the problem of providing new homes in a restricted space, they may be storing up new problems for the future. They involve those who live in them in a quite different environment from that they have been accustomed to, and communication between the families making up the high flat community, and between the high flat dwellers as a whole and the outside world, is almost inevitably forced into a different pattern. There are likewise obvious problems in the reliance of high flat families on lifts, in their need for play areas for children, in their desire to develop their own focal point for meeting and communication, and in the situation of older people who form an important sector of the high flat populations.

These are some of the issues examined in this study by Pearl Jephcott, in which she was most ably assisted by Hilary Robinson. As always, Pearl Jephcott has brought to this work a liveliness of mind, a degree of observation of detail that is invaluable in work of this kind, and a sense of caring and responsibility for the lives of those who, because they live in high flats, have become a group requiring special attention.

While the study owes so much to Pearl Jephcott and Hilary Robinson, it would not have been possible at all without the assistance of a great many others. The greatest debt of all is to the Joseph Rowntree Memorial Trust which provided financial support for the project over a period of four years. Especial thanks goes here to Mr. Lewis E. Waddilove, O.B.E., Director of the Trust, for his personal interest in the work throughout its entire course.

A considerable debt of gratitude is also owed to the members of the Advisory Committee specially formed to make available to the researchers a wealth of expertise in the kind of problems under investigation. The members of this Committee were as follows:

J. B. Cullingworth, Director, Centre for Urban and Regional Studies, University of Birmingham;

S. N. Denney, Assistant Chief Planning Officer, Corporation of Glasgow;

J. B. Fleming, Scottish Development Department;

Charles Murdoch, Town Clerk Depute, City Chambers, Glasgow, C.2.;

S. A. J. Oldham, Director, Parks and Botanic Gardens Department, Corporation of Glasgow;

Mrs. Muriel Smith, London Council of Social Service;

L. E. Waddilove, O.B.E., Joseph Rowntree Memorial Trust;

J. B. Wilson, William Burns (Glasgow) Ltd.;

Malcolm A. Smith, M.B.E., Housing Manager, Corporation of Glasgow.

We are most grateful for the assistance and time given by the Committee, on all of whom this task fell as an extra commitment in an already full programme.

Although the research has taken into account experience of high flat living in other parts of Britain and abroad, its main emphasis is on Glasgow, a city with considerable experience of tower blocks, as a quick scan of the horizon readily shows. Almost inevitably, such an emphasis required a special relationship between the research team and the Corporation of Glasgow – and especially the Housing Department. In this Pearl Jephcott and Hilary Robinson were most fortunate in having the guidance, advice and co-operation of the Housing Department, and again our thanks goes out to those who helped in this way. In the same way, special mention has to be made of the contribution to the study from the Scottish Special Housing Association, whose officers provided valuable assistance. Finally in this connection, a considerable debt has been incurred by the research team on account of the cooperation and participation of various tenants' associations and individual tenants. To all of these our thanks is due.

We are most grateful also to Miss D. Foy for permission to reproduce her painting in the Frontispiece and Cover design of this book.

Two other special acknowledgements are necessary: first, to the patient assistance in secretarial matters and typing of drafts, so willingly given by Miss Elizabeth Fairgrieve; and secondly to Donald Robertson whose tragic death came just as the study was completed. Donald Robertson had been involved with the project from the outset, and had assisted in its setting up as well as in giving advice as Chairman of the Advisory Committee during the course of the work. It is sad to think that he will not be here to see the finished article.

L.C.H.

ACKNOWLEDGEMENTS

Advisory Committee:
The nine members of this special Committee are given in the Foreword on p. vi.

Others:

Mrs. B. Adams, Sociological Research Section, Ministry of Housing and Local Government
Mrs. C. E. Aldington, Scottish Special Housing Association
Dr. T. Blance, Planning Department, Corporation of Glasgow
Mr. J. Boyd, Housing Management Department, Corporation of Glasgow
Mr. A. Broadfoot, Glasgow Council of Tenants' Associations
Mr. H. Danneberg, Planning Department, Burgh of Clydebank
Mrs. F. Hamilton, Glasgow Council of Tenants' Associations
Mr. F. Irving, Glasgow Council of Tenants' Associations
Mr. A. McDonald, Scottish Special Housing Association
Mrs. E. R. Paul, Pre-school Playgroups Association
Miss G. A. Robertson, Scottish Special Housing Association
Dr. K. Scott, Health and Welfare Department, Corporation of Glasgow

Miss V. Adams (Minor Study)
Mr. J. Anderson (Photographs)
Mr. G. Ashton (Photographs)
Miss H. Brown (Minor Study)
Mrs. A. I. Donald (Discussion Groups)
Glasgow and West of Scotland Photographic Association (Photographs)
Mr. D. Gower (Interviews)
Mr. W. Gillespie (Photographs)
Miss J. Holland (Minor Study)
Mr. T. Hutton (Photographs)
Mr. J. Knight (Interviews and Map)
Mrs. D. Lennie (Interviews)
Mr. I. Love (Diagrams)
Miss H. Lyon (Minor Study)
Mr. W. Mason (Interviews)
Mrs. H. McChlery (Interviews)
Miss M. McGill (Interviews)
Mr. S. Millar (Interviews)
Mrs. S. Money (Interviews)
Miss M. Morrison (Interviews)

Mrs. J. Pyle (Minor Study)
Miss J. Risner (Interviews)
Mrs. S. Scobbie (Interviews)
Miss S. Smith (Interviews)
Mr. T. Stewart (Minor Study)
Miss V. Somerville (Minor Study)
Mrs. M. Thompson (Interviews)
Mr. A. Warren (Lift Study and Interviews)

SUBJECT AND SETTING

Financed by   The Joseph Rowntree Memorial Trust
Undertaken by Pearl Jephcott, M.A., Hilary Robinson, B.Sc.(Econ.)
Subject   The social implications of domestic housing in high flats.
Date   July 1st, 1966–69.
Setting.   Glasgow. Brief visits to other examples of multi-storey housing in Britain and abroad

Information: *Main sources*   *Persons interviewed*

Main sources	Persons interviewed
Pilot sample (Clydebank)	60
Initial sample	355
Main sample	641

Minor studies involving interviews

Multi-storey and low-rise households – comparison	56
Multi-storey and deck access – comparison	30
Young people aged 15–22	44
Mothers with two children under 5	25
Caretakers	14
Tenants' associations' officers	96
Total	1,321

Other minor studies
Services and facilities
The lift
Playgroup
Graffiti
Primary school population – comparison
The disabled

CONTENTS

FOREWORD	v
ACKNOWLEDGEMENTS	vii
SUBJECT AND SETTING	ix
ILLUSTRATIONS	xiii
TABLES	xv

Chapter

1	THE BACKGROUND OF THE STUDY	1
2	HOUSING PROBLEMS AND HIGH FLATS IN GLASGOW	12
3	METHOD OF THE STUDY	26
4	GENERAL INFORMATION ABOUT THE HOUSING STUDIED	37
5	PHYSICAL CHARACTER OF THE FLATS: TENANTS' VIEWS	48
6	PHYSICAL CHARACTER OF THE ESTATES: TENANTS' VIEWS	59
7	THE SERVICES AND FACILITIES AT THREE ESTATES	65
8	THE OLDER TENANTS	70
9	FAMILIES WITH CHILDREN	80
10	OTHER TYPES OF HOUSEHOLD	101
11	HIGH FLATS AND SOCIAL CONTACTS	106
12	THE CASE FOR INVESTMENT IN STAFF	119
13	CONCLUSIONS	126

APPENDICES:

A	Basic information on examples of multi-storey housing visited in areas other than Glasgow. 1968	151
B	Number of and reasons for tenants' movement out of 5 estates	152
C	Graffiti	153
D	Facilities within ½ mile radius of estate	157
E	A note on lift waiting times and failures	159

F	Tenants' associations and kindred bodies	
	1 An analysis of 13 tenants' associations	166
	2 Cranhill Tenants' Association. Statement of Income and Expenditure	168
	3 Scotstoun House Social Club. Application form	169
G	Extra-Mural course, *New Homes and New Neighbours*	170
H	Tables	171
J	*The Jeely Piece Song* (courtesy of Scotia Kinnaird)	181

ILLUSTRATIONS

FULL COLOUR

Plate
1	Red Road, Glasgow 1969	*Frontispiece*

BLACK AND WHITE

Facing page

2	Slab blocks, Pollokshaws, Glasgow	8
3	Tenement housing, Glasgow	9
4	Aerial view, Central Glasgow and Gorbals	16
5	Tower blocks, Castlemilk, Glasgow	24
6	Tower blocks, Royston, Glasgow	40
7	One of eight slab blocks, Sighthill, Glasgow	48
8	The lift. One family and the lift is full up. Castlemilk, Glasgow	56
9	A 15th storey home, Bogany Terrace, Glasgow	72
10	An estate composed almost entirely of high flats. Red Road, Glasgow	80
11	Mrs ——. Her one person flat is on the 19th floor. Wyndford, Glasgow	88
12	Miss ——, in her chair, and the view she cannot see. Wyndford, Glasgow	104
13	Children playing, Skelmersdale and Pollokshaws, Glasgow	112
14	"The Hing", Glasgow	120
15	Traditional pavement conversation piece, Glasgow	136
16	The base of the block, Gorbals, Glasgow	144
17	High density estate, Lillington Gardens, London	152
18	Graffiti, Royston, Glasgow	153

Painting and photographs by courtesy:
Dymphna Foy, Frontispiece; A. D. S. Macpherson, 2; W. M. Gillespie, 3, 7, 15; Aerofilms Ltd., 4; O. Marzaroli, 6; G. Ashton, 5, 8, 9, 11, 12, 14; T. Stewart, 18; A. Warren, 10; *The Guardian*, 13A; T. Hutton, 13B, 16; Henk Snoek, 17B; de Burgh Galwey, *The Architectural Review*, 17A.

LIST OF TABLES

1	Local Authority and Scottish Special Housing Association dwellings built in Glasgow in three selected years, 1959, 1964, 1968	18
2	The five selected estates, July 1968	29
3	Total of multi-storey housing occupied 1967, 1968, 1969 (May)	37
4	Physical details of multi-storey housing, July 1968	38
5	Population in multi-storey estates. Main sample. July 1968	45
6	Glasgow population in relation to age. Census 1966. Multi-storey population in relation to age. Main sample. July 1968	46
7	General information. Albion/Ibrox, Castlemilk, Red Road	65

Tables in Appendix H

8	Distance of present from previous home	171
9	Dwellings in relation to storey height	171
10	Reasons for moving to present home	171
11	Length of residence	172
12	Number of persons in household	172
13	Households with dependants	173
14	Type of household	173
15	Population in relation to age and sex. Main sample. July 1968	174
16	Occupational class of adults in employment	174
17	Car (use of) and Telephone (ownership) in relation to size of household	175
18	Rent and rates (monthly) present home in relation to previous home	175
	Running costs (heating, lighting, cooking). Difference between present and previous home	175
19	Overall satisfaction	176
20	Satisfaction in relation to type of household	176
21	Expectation "Do you expect to be living here for a long time?"	176
22	Likes and dislikes re house, block and estate (as referred to spontaneously)	177
23	Overall satisfaction in relation to length of residence	178
24	Satisfaction in relation to storey height	178

25	Informant's satisfaction with lift and his assessment of other people's satisfaction	178
26	Previous home – nature of tenancy	179
27	Previous home – garden or other outside area (private or shared)	179
28	Pensioners in relation to storey height	179
29	Dependent children in relation to age	180
30	Dependent children (all ages and aged 0–4) in relation to storey height	180
31	Work situation in relation to sex and marital status	180

Chapter 1

THE BACKGROUND OF THE STUDY

Does a high flat make a good home for people in general, or does it only suit a small number of 'selected households', or has it no merits for anyone? There is no agreed answer even among those who, as the children say, "live up up up"; still less so from those who only know the towers and slabs by sight. To take some examples. "Living up here really makes you feel you are part of a great city" says one young man, illustrating his words by pointing to the spectacular pattern of lights to be seen from his 18th-storey flat. On the other hand another speaker, an elderly widow, disparaging this kind of home as cutting her off from her fellow creatures, says "I used to slip round to the shop, now I have to pay a little girl to go down." Then there is the man who finds the best thing about the place is that you are no longer entangled willy-nilly in other people's affairs, but whose opinion on that account is reversed by the housewife who has taken an outside job solely in order to escape from the depressing solitude – and she, with a husband and a couple of grown-up children still living at home, should be far less vulnerable to loneliness than someone like an elderly spinster.

The multi-storey block of flats[1] is such a dominating structure that it is easy to think of it as a handy receptacle for absorbing some anonymous cohort off the housing list rather than as a setting for the homes of real people – the place where Mr. and Mrs. Smith's new baby will be born, and that where old Mr. Brown is going to spend the last three years of his life. It is also easy to dismiss the fact that the 20-storey tower which took less than 12 months to put up will probably have a lifespan of 60 years. The grandchildren of the Smith baby could be living in that same flat in the mid 2000s. People and their homes rather than housing in the usual sense of the word are the subject of this study, and in particular the *feelings* of those who live there as to whether a high flat helps them to improve the quality of their life, that fuller life which most would like however differently they may interpret the details. One of the major difficulties in a study of this kind is that

---

[1] For the purpose of this study a *multi-storey building* is defined as one with 6 or more floors and 2 lifts, or, less often, 1 lift. The generic term used for such a building is block. The main types of block used in Glasgow at the time of the study were 'point block' (a tower built round central lift shafts); and 'slab' (a rectangular building with several places for entry). In a few instances the building consisted of joined towers or joined slabs.

though a home in a flat is familiar enough, living at a height above 5 storeys or so is not. Thus the multi-storey population is still a pioneer one, sent into a territory many of whose features are still unmapped – a condition which means that not much beyond the more surface implications of living at these new heights are likely to have crystallised.

Most of the published work on the social aspects of tower buildings and high slabs has been permeated by feelings of apprehension, especially as regards the risks to which such housing may be exposing young children and the attrition of social life that it may be inducing. The shortage of information on these and kindred matters led the Joseph Rowntree Memorial Trust to finance a three-year (1966–9) study at the University of Glasgow to be undertaken by two members of the staff of the Department of Social and Economic Research. The terms of reference were left fairly open except that the work was to concentrate on social issues, ignoring as far as proved workable those aspects of housing connected with densities, costs, architectural design and aesthetics. It was also envisaged that this study would concern itself more with practical matters relating to the day-to-day life of the multi-storey population than with the longer-distance social implications. Though it was to be based chiefly on material from one place, Glasgow, it was envisaged that a certain amount of first-hand information would be obtained from examples of multi-storey housing in other parts of Britain and Western Europe.

* * *

The traveller in almost any part of the globe can see for himself that multi-storey housing has by now become a common feature of the urban scene. The old hotch-potch of buildings hugging the surface of the earth is being more and more interrupted by rectangular giants, many of which are the towers and slabs of multi-storey housing. While the techniques devised for building high may originally have been used for the relatively impersonal needs of an institution, office or factory they are now internationally adapted to fulfil far more subtle functions, those associated with a home. Initially, too, the tall apartment block was more generally built by a private landlord for the well-to-do who could select the type of home which suited the structure of their family. Today it is used by local authorities for households with a relatively low socio-economic status. Even the small study here undertaken showed how this method of housing has spread like wildfire. Information about high flats came in almost unasked from places as far apart as Melbourne,[2] Algeria, Philadelphia, Caracas, Prague and Moscow. In the latter city the tremendous housing programme now being undertaken

[2] *High Living*. A study of family life in high flats. Stevenson, Martin, O'Neill. Melbourne University Press, 1967.

includes not only the traditional slab block but experimental 16-storey 'housing of new living'. In the high buildings there, the private kitchen has been replaced by a communal one, while even equipment like vacuum cleaners and sewing machines are provided from a common store. Another example of the use of high flats to solve massive housing requirements is in Hong Kong. Some of the vast problems connected with its difficult topography and the need to house a million refugees from China have been met there through multi-storey housing. In Tokyo, too, high flats have been built as low-cost homes for a teeming downtown area. Japan is even using multi-storey cemeteries – 'locker' tombs. Caracas shows that while high flats can quickly provide better physical conditions they can rapidly lead to difficulties, for there the authorities, in using 'superblocques' on a vast scale to rehouse a very poor peasant population, have produced social problems that have proved as intractable as the shortage of houses itself.

Background information from the dozen or so towns in Western Europe that were visited in connection with this study illustrated the extent to which the high flat has proliferated (Appendix A). In the Netherlands, where one of the early studies of multi-storey housing was undertaken,[3] the percentage of dwellings built in blocks of flats with a lift rose from 25% in 1962 to 82% in 1967.[4] In Amsterdam the very large estate now building at Bulmermeen will provide 92% of its homes in multi-storey slabs of 9 and 10 storeys. At the Overvecht development in Utrecht, 60% of the homes are in multi-storey buildings, a figure that holds for the city's current housing plans as a whole. In Switzerland the Lochergut (Zurich) and the Tcharnergut (Berne) high density housing for low-income groups both include a very large proportion of their dwellings in high-rise buildings. The same is true of many of the big estates ringing Stockholm.

In London the first use of really tall (14-storey) buildings for domestic purposes (though for the well-to-do) was at Queen Anne's Mansions off St. James's Park and as early as the 1890s. However the experiment proved premature, mainly because of the fire hazards of the time, and legislation was passed prohibiting blocks of over 10 storeys, with no extensive change taking place until the 1950s. At this date postwar pressures for new homes were intense, while new techniques in building and in fire-fighting made high-rise housing a viable proposition. Blocks on the Oakridge estate in Putney (1951) and in Glasgow at Crathie Court (1952) and Moss Heights (1953) were early examples of the flood

---

[3] *Should We Build – and Live – in Houses or Flats*, Ministry of Housing and Building in the Netherlands. The Hague. 1965.
[4] *Some data on house building in the Netherlands*, Ministry of Housing and Physical Planning. The Hague. 1968.

which swept through the next two decades. In 1957 only just over a fifth of the Local Authority dwellings in Great Britain built in that year was in blocks of 5 storeys or over; within two years nearly a fifth was in buildings at twice or more that height. The generally accepted definition of a multi-storey building is one of 5 to 6 floors, i.e. of such height that a lift is judged essential. On this definition the figures at 1968 (March 31st) were as follows: In England and Wales the estimated number of local authority dwellings in buildings at 5 storeys and over was 260,000. The Scottish figure (for June 1969 and in buildings at 6 storeys and over) was 41,055. The number under construction at those heights and over should also be noted. At April 30th 1968 it was 64,142 dwellings (at 6 storeys and over) being built by local authorities in England and Wales and 15,007 in Scotland. In London the G.L.C. alone had some 240 blocks of 10 or more storeys in occupation and another 138 were building or approved. The literature on high flats in this country has mostly concentrated on physical features, the desirability of tower as opposed to slab block, central hall access to that by corridor, a balcony as risk or asset. There has been oddly little work on the social features apart from studies undertaken by the Ministry of Housing and Local Government.[5] That has been very valuable; as was a short and early study on the needs of small children.[6] This latter, as with much of the rest of the published work, concentrated on a single feature. Relatively little has been done to look at high flats in the round so to speak. The present study attempts to go rather wider though, as said earlier, it too is confined in that it only deals with social aspects.

When comparing high-price housing in Britain with that in other parts of Western Europe, some features of its use here would seem particularly relevant to its social implications. By Continental standards the buildings here are Goliaths. Glasgow has towers of over 300 feet which is well above the level of the dome of St. Paul's, and not much below the 386 feet of the sequoias, the tallest known trees. In Western Europe the slab block, and one of 10 or less storeys, is far more often used than the tower of 20 storeys and over. Then again the providing agent is not, as in this country, confined to the local authority. This holds even where the major use of high flats is for the less well-off sections of the community. Abroad, housing associations and co-operative building organisations, trade unions and teachers' professional associations not infrequently put up a single or group of blocks on an

[5] *Families Living at High Density: a study of three central estates in Leeds, Liverpool and London.* Design Bulletin 21, Ministry of Housing and Local Govt., H.M.S.O. 1970.

"Living off the ground", Reynolds and Nicholson, *The Architect's Journal*, 20th August, 1969.

[6] *Two to Five in High Flats*, Maizels, Commissioned by the Joseph Rowntree Memorial Trust, 1961.

estate, a private firm builds another, the municipality the remainder. There, within legislative limits, both rent and conditions of tenure are left to the providing agent while each adds such facilities as its provider sees fit – shops, clubrooms, a playground, a church, etc. All this variety contrasts forcibly with the sameness of many multi-storey local authority estates in Britain. The point is important because the looks of the immediate environment and the quality of the services are probably more important to those who live in a high flat than in a home of traditional type.

Speaking in very general terms it is arguable that multi-storey housing is no temporary phenomenon but one that will persist since one of the major reasons which have led to its introduction, burgeoning populations and therefore pressure for housing, is a global problem. As far as Britain is concerned, current estimates suggest an annual average percentage increase in population from 0·5 (1931–51) to a forecast of 0·9 (1980–2000). During the next 35 years there is likely to be an increase of nearly 17½ million persons. Another change which suggests that the pressure for housing will continue is the tendency for the individual household to seek a home of its own, which of course increases the number of dwellings needed in relation to the population.[7] Pressure for houses also stems from the demand for higher physical standards as regards one's home, itself linked with affluence, better health and longer education. Quite apart from the role played by multi-storey building in helping to meet numerical demands it has certain features which meet current aspirations rather better than do most types of council housing. The high flat – all electric, dust and dirt free, within a few yards of a rubbish chute, and with no stairs or steps – is delightfully easy to run. This simplifies the housewife's job and makes it that much easier for her to follow modern trends and go out to work should she so wish. It adds bonuses in the shape of airiness, sunshine and view, matters which have always been regarded as important by those who could afford to be selective about their home but mostly have been hit and miss affairs for the poor. A high flat also has certain features which are a boon to old people, and Britain has an ageing population. One of these assets is the absence of stairs and of treacherous steps. Another is the feeling of security: you are less vulnerable to physical attack. A multi-storey home also gives something that is being increasingly sought after, viz. privacy.[8]

Another reason for the rapid introduction of high flats is that the demand for more and improved housing has been roughly contemporaneous and indeed has perhaps helped to promote the technical advances which have revolutionised building methods. Most of the

[7] *The Government of Housing*, Donnison, Pelican, p. 39.
[8] *Community and Privacy*, Chermayeff and Alexander, Pelican, 1963.

engineering problems derived from the violent structural changes inherent in vertical building have now been solved. The semi-collapse of the block at Ronan Point was due to error not to lack of basic knowledge. Industrial building, using precast concrete, prefabricated units, and sliding shutter methods, has not only facilitated the mass production of houses but greatly speeded up the rate at which they can be produced. Time is saved by using mechanical plant, e.g. the hydraulic jack in place of hand-erected scaffolding. One of the major firms involved in multi-storey housing illustrated the rapidity with which a block of flats can be produced.

> Speaking in general terms, after the foundations are complete, our multi-storeys rise at the average rate of a floor a week, with the load-bearing reinforced concrete columns, the infill panels of No-fines concrete, and the reinforced concrete floor being poured as a monolithic mass. An example of mixed development, 1,412 dwellings in 12 towers of 20 storeys plus a handful (44) of low rise houses, was built in 107 weeks. This is a building rate of one dwelling in every 3 working hours. Traditional building methods would take more than twice as long.

Other features of multi-storey housing which suit the demand for expeditious building are that it cuts down the architect's work. Whether the block is to have 6 or 26 storeys he has only one floor to design, while the use of an exactly similar plan for blocks in different localities greatly reduces his work. Another way in which time is likely to be saved is that multi-storey estates normally require less extensive sites than does traditional housing which simplifies the legal proceedings involved in the acquisition of land and property. The uniformity and the large scale of multi-storey building also tend towards the quickness and simplicity (for the buyer) of the package deal. Given the site, the big contractor or consortium can undertake every part of the work needed to produce both the dwellings and the estate down to the final detail agreed on. This rapidity of multi-storey housing is one of its greatest assets.

It is also useful in that it *may* help lessen something that harasses most local authorities, viz. acute land shortage. The actual site needed for a block of high flats can be very much smaller than that for an equivalent number of houses built on traditional lines. Provided that open space requirements are deemed to be properly met by areas outside the actual estate, then a brace of towers can usefully fill up a small, awkward, left-over site. On the other hand, and as will be argued later, the happy theory that high flats automatically save space has been shown to rest on shaky foundations. Another asset of the multi-storey, though one shared with any form of high-density housing, is that it does not necessarily increase the commuting problem. Compared with the location of most large-scale council housing, i.e. on the city's fringe, the multi-storey tends to be built in relatively central areas. From the tenant's point of view it is a great blessing to have it at the back of your mind that you can easily get to the Metropole or Town Hall or decent shops if you want to.

A very different reason for the use of multi-storey housing, but one that cannot be entirely dismissed, is that, as far as architect and builder are concerned, a soaring, potentially cloud-capped tower is a new toy and one which may confer prestige. For the local authority too, an impressive building attracts attention. It may well be a vote-catcher, an outward and visible sign that the Council is doing its job.

Scientists forecast that society is moving towards a time when food and space on the earth's surface will become far more scarce than now. Should increasing use have to be made of vertical space this suggests that the multi-storey building will continue to be built and on a magnified scale. Height as such presents relatively little difficulty even now. New York's Empire State Building is 1,472 feet from ground to top of its television tower, Hong Kong is proposing housing of 50 storeys and has a density of over 3,000 in one of its re-settlement projects.[9] Engineers are talking of towns aerial, two-mile-high affairs containing homes, schools, factories, playing fields – the wealth of facilities for civilised life which the city, "that greatest artefact of man", makes possible.

Such dreams, however, are still much in the air. It may well be that the use of very lofty buildings for housing will become discredited once the relative novelty has worn off, pressures for new homes declined, and (in the case of council housing) rents become more realistic. Education and affluence too will presumably continue to raise people's aspirations regarding the use of their leisure. Thus it is conceivable that, like the nuclear power station, the multi-storey tower might be among the embarrassingly ponderous ruins of the future. Indeed, a trend has already set in against them. It may be temporary, but in Western Europe anyhow, it is fairly widespread. In Sweden current planning policy for new areas now definitely favours lower building. A case in point concerned two suburbs in Stockholm where, although construction work had begun, the original plan was changed in order to keep building height down to 6 or less storeys. The figures for industrialised-built houses in England and Wales have begun to reflect the trend. In 1967 these represented 42·6% of all local authority and New Town dwellings where tenders were approved: in 1968 the proportion had declined to 39·2%. Birmingham is one example of a major authority

[9] *Annual Departmental Report 1968–9.* Commissioner for Resettlement Hong Kong.

which has decided not to continue with high towers but to use relatively low slab blocks. Another hint that with us the peak may have been reached is shown in the development of high-density housing on longitudinal lines with the houses strung along an under-cover access corridor, a kind of street. This new pattern has proved socially successful at the Park Hill estate at Sheffield. During the course of the study one on somewhat similar lines was built in Glasgow, with results that appeared to be useful. Blocks of only 8 storeys were included in a number of the Corporation's plans and one major estate (1,446 houses) approved in November 1967 included no multi-storey housing. A significant indication of the changing climate of opinion was shown in a 1968 Circular of the Ministry of Housing and Local Government which reduced the 'yardstick', the level at which the Ministry was prepared to subsidise multi-storey housing.[10] If an authority wished to use high flats it was, of course, at liberty to do so but it could no longer claim the previous Government subsidy based on the higher you build the better the rate. The importance of this decision cannot be overemphasised since it drew attention, reinforcing its case in terms of hard cash, to some of the known disadvantages and the possible dangers associated with the growing use of multi-storey housing.

What has caused the *volte-face*? The more important factors are referred to later (Chapter 13) but briefly they are as follows. A high flat is a very expensive type of home to build, to maintain structurally and to service. The lift for example, an essential component, is not only initially expensive but a delicate piece of apparatus to stand up to round-the-clock usage without any attendant. And its servicing charges, which frequently involve calling in a mechanic at short notice, are likely to persist until the day (60 years ahead?) the block is dismantled. This high cost of high flats compared with housing of traditional type is a powerful argument against their use in a time of financial stringency. The second argument concerns densities. It has now been proved that a very skilful use of low-rise buildings can give as high densities as do towers and slabs. Site space cannot be saved automatically if the amenities proper to the needs of the block's population are to be met. The key word is 'proper' and it implies a standard of services, shops, buildings for community use, sports grounds, etc., that are up to those which any city dweller of the 1970s has a right to expect. Multi-storey housing is also under fire because of the aesthetic risks to which it subjects the environment. Jutting, angular blocks, perhaps 250 feet high, can disrupt a townscape fatally easily. Another batch of arguments that have tended to halt the use of multi-storey housing turns on the social aspects. The implications of the rapid creation of new communities in housing of traditional type have hardly been identified, still less solved.

[10] Circular No. 36/67. Ministry of Housing and Local Government. 1968.

Plate 2. Slab blocks, Pollokshaws, Glasgow.

Plate 3. Tenement housing, Glasgow.

Add all the unknown dimensions associated with multi-storeys and the picture is still more confused. One of today's apprehensions, that we may be misusing our fantastic new powers, would seem to be exemplified in the case of high flats. They have certainly attracted a lot of attention in the popular press which suggests that they arouse strong emotions. As such they are not something to be dismissed cavalierly. In this country anyhow, the popular image of multi-storeys is nearly always a disparaging one. They are 'monstrous conceptions', 'teeming towers', 'human filing cabinets'. While the man in the street accepts in the main the soaring office block or hotel or University tower, he seems to jib at the idea that human beings, with their infinite variety of tastes, needs and capacities should be asked to make their home in a setting felt to be alien to the human condition. This general antipathy was seen at the time of the Ronan Point disaster which presumably brought to the surface misgivings that had been building up. The fact that so few jokes have grown up about multi-storey life is perhaps another small indication of popular dislike. For example, in the almost daily contact with people living in high flats that took place in connection with this study, only one anecdote was picked up about multi-storey life that was even mildly funny – that of the conscientious housewife who, accustomed at the old tenement to take her turn in washing down the common stairs, embarked on the same job from her 24th-floor home and didn't reappear for a couple of weeks.

It is now fairly well established that a policy using multi-storey housing for all sorts and conditions of households throws up practical problems. The difficulties associated with the family which has young children are particularly obvious. The small children are liable to be over-confined to their home or over-separated from it. The mother, especially if she has two or more not yet at school, is exposed to more than the normal strains associated with this stage of family life. Other practical problems concern the anonymity of the multi-storey, a point generally agreed whether welcomed or not by the individual. But social isolation is normally disadvantageous when looked at in terms of community needs, for example, those of old people. Then again, is a high flat a sufficiently flexible shell to provide the kind of home which encourages activities as distinct from merely affording somewhere to eat and sleep? Another innovation about which little is known concerns the lift, something that introduces a new element into daily life and over which the individual has no control. The common reaction is that 'they're murder'. On the other hand what a blessing not to have to haul up stairs. Another new and tricky situation which the tenant in a local authority multi-storey home has to learn to accept is that he needs to come to terms with a new personal relationship – that between himself and a caretaker.

Practical problems are not the only, nor perhaps the most important, of the social implications of this new form of home. What about its long-distance effects? For example, even when the family with small children appears to be able to cope satisfactorily, may these new conditions under which the child has to grow up affect his development adversely in ways that will not show up until later life? Again, a highly urbanised society is generally believed to have high risks in terms of social welfare, and life in a multi-storey block, with its high densities, would seem to be an intensive form of urbanised living. Studies of animal communities certainly suggest that overcrowding leads to abnormal behaviour patterns.[11] Another feature of this new type of housing, the results of which might not show up for some time, is that the block is essentially a cul-de-sac and the experience of old working-class areas rather suggests that the street which is cut off from the mainstream tends to breed social problems. On the other hand may the fact that 100 or so households live under exceedingly uniform conditions, and in a place that is so obviously a physical unit, give rise to opportunities for community development that have never been experienced before?

The complexity of such matters suggested that it would be useful to take a hard look at some of them in just one place, drawing on examples of multi-storey housing in other localities for illustrative material. That chosen was Glasgow and the study was undertaken with the full co-operation of its Corporation. The city has introduced high flats on an extensive scale and in many cases has built tower blocks that are exceptionally tall. It was thought that such features would outweigh the fact that in Glasgow the tenants' reaction to multi-storeys might not be typical. Glaswegians are, for example, accustomed to flat life, since a 60-feet-tall tenement with perhaps 12 or more homes is the traditional form of dwelling. Moreover, so much of the existing housing is still so wretched and so many people have been longing for a better place for so many years that almost anything is likely to be accepted uncritically. To take a single instance, and one deliberately chosen as far removed from the horror stories about previous homes that were continually met with in the course of this study. The family consisted of the father, a Post Office worker, his wife, and a 13-year-old daughter. Their old home had been "a right dump, a horrible place" with no bathroom, no indoor lavatory and just the one room and kitchen which meant mother and daughter had to sleep together. They had no reservations about their new life in a 2-bedroom flat on an 11th floor – "We love it".

*   *   *

To sum up. Today's world-wide need for mass housing that can be

---

[11] *On Aggression*, Lorenz, Methuen, 1966.
"Population density and social pathology", Calhoun, *Scientific American*, Vol. 206, 1962.

produced with speed has led to a proliferation of multi-storey building. Though likely to be a permanent feature, a temporary slow-down appears to have been called as far as Western Europe is concerned. In Britain its desirability as a form of local authority housing has been much questioned partly on account of its high cost, partly because of the immediate practical problems to which it gives rise, and partly due to apprehension about its long-distance social effects.

Chapter 2

HOUSING PROBLEMS AND HIGH FLATS IN GLASGOW

Anyone making a first acquaintance with Glasgow cannot fail to sense that it is essentially a big city. Linked with three river systems, built on seven hills and with distant mountains as a backcloth, it has outstandingly fine natural assets and much to commend it architecturally. Massive stone blocks are the traditional material for both public and domestic buildings. These are tall and often handsome while even back streets are wide and straight. Enclosing an area of 62 square miles and with a population of nearly a million, Glasgow is one of the 25 largest cities of the world. About a fifth of Scotland's population lives actually in the city and twice that number in the conurbation. Glasgow itself also has a considerable proportion of the country's industry. Its traditional products were large-scale ones, steamships and locomotives. Today the population is falling and much of the prosperity which was such a feature of 19th-century Glasgow has gone. Indeed economists are agreed that the one clear characteristic of the city in the last fifty years has been decline. The very magnitude of the earlier prosperity has left an unusually complex load of problems for today, particularly as regards housing.

The difficulties here have roots which stretch back to the Middle Ages when the Scottish legal system began to take shape. Ancient legal patterns still help to account for the subdivision of property and the multiplicity of owners which hamper current housing policy. Until the middle of the 18th century Glasgow was still small and attractive. One writer of the 1760s thought it among the most beautiful small towns in Europe. A generation later Dorothy Wordsworth's perceptive eye was struck by the largeness of the town and "its appearance of business and bustle". She likewise commented on a characteristic that seems to have persisted, viz. the city's friendliness. Talking with the women she found busy at their washing beside the river she noted them as "very civil".[1] As recently as fifty years ago some of the city's central areas, now warrens, had reasonably decent housing. These are sadly different pictures from that of today's popular image of Glasgow which mostly echoes that put so delicately by a Continental 'Go to Britain' brochure

[1] *Recollection of a Tour in Scotland, A.D. 1803*, Dorothy Wordsworth, Ed. Shairp, 1874.

– "Beautiful and gay the city may not be, but . . ." The drastic changes created by the Industrial Revolution followed their familiar pattern in Glasgow. Expansion was based chiefly on the Clyde's shipbuilding and on the demands made during the railway boom for locomotives and rolling stock. The population drawn into the city, Irish peasants and cottars from the Highlands, was an exceptionally poor one coming from what are still among the remoter areas of Western Europe. The social changes involved in this must have been far more radical than any of those connected with the massive population shifts of the last half century. As in other Victorian cities there was a long lag before administrative machinery was set up to meet the needs of those who, in human terms, were required to pay the price of the Industrial Revolution. The grossest problems were probably associated with their housing. Though some improvement was made from the 1880s onward, e.g. in the Saltmarket area, it was not until 30 or so years later that the Labour Government of 1924, introducing subsidies for local authority housing, began to give the Corporation something like adequate powers to tackle the city's housing problems.

Current housing needs have to be coped with in an unusually complex framework. If decline in the economy is to be halted, renewal on almost every front is not merely desirable but vital. It includes the replanning of large expanses of the city's central area within a ring road. A new tunnel under the Clyde is to be supplemented by two new and elegant bridges over it. An instance of the scale of industrial development now judged necessary is a £2·1 million scheme on $6\frac{1}{2}$ acres near the centre of the city at Anderston Cross. This will include multi-storey warehouses and factory buildings providing 600,000 square feet of industrial floor space together with 1,455 multi-storey flats, 346 low-rise houses, a new church, etc. New offices, shops, hotels, factories, greatly extended provision for education and recreation, and massive rehousing have to jostle with each other for cash, land and manpower, all of which are scarce. The size of the city's loan debt, £265 million in 1968, indicates that the overriding problem is finance. A very rough budget of the costs that rebuilding is likely to require between now and 1990 has been put at around £1,000 million. It is a daunting prospect. On the other hand if Glasgow is to flourish, or even to hold its own economically, socially and culturally, the key is modernisation. And here housing is probably the heart of the matter.

The characteristic Glasgow house, acres and acres of them, is a tall stone tenement blackened by the years. Of all the homes, 85% are in purpose-built flats within this type of structure. It normally has 4 storeys and is some 60 feet high. A Continental type of housing, it is extremely solid and well built with fine woodwork, lofty rooms and handsome windows. It has been referred to as being in its heyday "a vernacular architecture that is unmatched for urban permanence and dignity anywhere in the world". But it was constructed 80–100 years ago and its life has practically expired. Interiors are often broken down beyond repair and they lack basic facilities. Even in the tenement's prime the approach to the individual flat (normally three of them on each of the building's four floors) was a dreary affair. It comprised a doorless, draughty passage from which rose 50–60 stone, uncarpeted stairs. This passage led through to a back court. Surrounded by such tall buildings, this was a sunless place and has often degenerated into a mud and puddle-filled shambles.

The extent of Glasgow's current housing problem was highlighted in an exceedingly valuable, fact-filled survey undertaken for the Corporation in 1965 by Professor Cullingworth.[2] The first interesting point about its findings related to the pattern of ownership. Of the city's 326,000 dwellings, only 19% were owner-occupied, the remainder being divided into tenancies from the local authority (43%) and from private landlords (38%). The very high proportion of Council-owned dwellings should be noted. It reflects the fact that Scottish local authorities in general own a higher proportion of housing than do those in England and Wales. As regards type of dwelling, tenements were found to represent 85% of the total, compared with the Scottish average of 46%. The low standards of the city's housing was shown in such facts as the following: 30% of all the households had one bedroom only compared with the Scottish figure of 18%, and a further 46% had only two. Thus many people were living at extremely close quarters inside their home. An example, not untypical of many others met with in the course of this study, was that of the young woman who mentioned more or less casually that she had been one of eight children who with her parents had lived in a 'room and kitchen'. The level of amenities was also exceedingly poor. Over a third, 38% of all the Glasgow dwellings, had no fixed bath or shower. Nearly 22%, compared with Scotland's 13% and Great Britain's 5%, had no internal w.c. and 41% no "hot water at 3 points". Deficiencies on this scale sound almost incredible for the 1960s and for one of the world's major cities. If the amenities were poor, it was some compensation that rents, again as in Scotland generally, were low though this was to some extent offset by very high rates. *A Profile of Glasgow Housing* showed that private tenants were paying an average annual net rent of £25.10., Council tenants £32.5. Other facts concerned the economic level of the Glasgow population. The average total income of the households, £16.10., obscured the fact that as many as two-thirds had a head whose weekly income was £10 or less. Information from other sources supports this finding about relatively low

---

[2] *A Profile of Glasgow Housing*, Cullingworth, University of Glasgow, Social and Economic Studies, Oliver & Boyd, 1965.

incomes, e.g. the city's high unemployment rate. In September 1967 the U.K. figure was 2·4% and that for Scotland 3·8%; for Glasgow it was 4·5%. Car ownership, yet another indication, is also low. In 1968 less than 1 in 10 of the Glasgow population owned a private car compared with 1 in 4 or 5 in Birmingham and Manchester.

A city with a relatively poor population and one faced with the need to bring itself up to modern standards in so many fields is obviously hard put to find the necessary funds. The financial problem is intensified in the case of housing because of the high proportion of homes which are Council-owned and the low rents. Some indication of the scale of the difficulty is that the current (1969) figure for the housing debt is some £228m. with an annual deficit of £7 million. This means that any abnormal costs present a serious threat to the rate of rehousing. Cases in point were the £30m. damage caused by the hideous storm of January 1968, and the high sums needed to adapt any blocks which, in view of the Ronan Point collapse, were judged to be structurally at risk. Financial stringency has held up rehousing for years. For example the introduction of substantial Government subsidies for Council housing first came into operation just when Clydeside was suffering from the economic stagnation of the late 1920s and early 1930s. Though the city's rehousing in these interwar years was extensive, much of it was mediocre in quality. World War II held up progress again and by 1947 the total stock of houses built by the Corporation had only reached 63,000. The really big drive did not come until the 1950s when three peripheral housing estates were built, each with a population of about 40,000. A postwar target – 5,000 new dwellings per annum – was achieved between 1953 and 1957 and again in 1966 and 1967. But even this proved insufficient to meet a live housing list that in 1968 seemed to have gelled at about 47,500 applications, of which 26,000 were on a priority list.[3] In other words today's challenge can be described less as one to raise existing standards than to halt a decline. It is a considerable feat that, despite its problems, the Corporation has built some 150,000 houses in the last half century. The quinquennial average of municipal dwellings completed by the Corporation and Scottish Special Housing Association (see page 18) was 5,325 (1949–53); 5,286 (1954–58); 2,986 (1959–63) and 4,927 (1964–68). The city's current plan for redevelopment is claimed to be the largest urban renewal scheme in Europe. One of its main features is massive work on 29 large sites. In April 1969 this was taking place on 14 of them. A low rent policy of course adds greatly to the financial burden. Moreover, the Corporation shoulders almost the whole of the housing programme itself since private house building for sale has been negligible. The figure for the 3-year (1966–8) average

[3] *Annual Report* 1968, Corporation of Glasgow Housing Management Department.

was a mere 75. Few sites have been available for the private builder because the authority's own housing programme has been so urgent. The high rates associated with this concentration on Council housing have pushed the higher income groups outside the city boundary, while those on the housing list have little incentive to look out for a place themselves. The chances of finding a suitable house are remote, and in any case prices are so high compared with the rent of a Council house that the latter is a financial bargain.

What has been the repercussion of all the above on Glasgow's attitude to multi-storey housing? The reasons which have popularised its use in other parts of the world have of course operated in Glasgow but certain of the arguments in its favour have been particularly compelling. In practically every field of modernisation the city's overriding problem is land shortage. The need to leave an extensive acreage of flat ground for industrial development in a terrain that is full of small hills is one problem. Another is the amount of old housing at high densities which has had to be sacrificed to new roads. Some 7,000 houses are to be given up for this alone. Most of the sites still available are small and in many cases basically unsuited to housing. They may be on the steep (1 in 7) slope of a drumlin, or alongside a railway, or beside a cemetery, or over-close to a factory. The extreme pressure for sites is illustrated in the case of two of the city's large multi-storey estates. In one a major geological fault runs through what is roughly the centre of the site. At the other the piles for its 8 blocks (20 storeys) had to be specially treated to counter the chemical action of the soda waste on which the estate was built. Until such time as the city's boundaries are redrawn in line with a regional policy, pressure for land will become even more intense. As far as housing is concerned, one obvious solution is to build high.

Another of the arguments in favour of multi-storey housing that is highly relevant in Glasgow's case is its rapidity. The Corporation has a moral obligation not to delay the replacement of homes that are intolerable. It also has to rehouse with the minimum of delay families from the many dwellings which may not be in really poor condition but must come down to make way for the gigantic construction schemes. The large consortia which undertake multi-storey housing offer the kind of package deal which speeds up the rate at which an authority can make its decisions. Their estimates are readily understood, comprehensive, and reliable as to time and costs.

A third matter which has told in favour of high flats is the continuing necessity to rebuild at high densities. The city's gross density rate (30 p.p.a. for 1961) exceeds that for Liverpool (27 p.p.a.) and is far above that of Birmingham (19 p.p.a.) or Edinburgh (14 p.p.a.). But the more revealing picture is that for net residential densities. High density is a feature of old tenement building when, as in Glasgow, four uniform

Plate 4. Aerial view, Central Glasgow and Gorbals.

floors of flats are stacked neatly on top of each other. When the tenements themselves are tightly packed, as was the case with most of those built in the late nineteenth century, the density may rise in extreme cases to 500 p.p.a., while one of 150 p.p.a. is common. This means that in general less than two-thirds of the original population in the old housing can be rehoused on the site even at densities that by modern standards are very high. Thus multi-storey building, with its own high densities, would appear an obvious solution to one of the major problems that face the Glasgow planner though, as will be argued later, this is liable to involve the sacrifice of satisfactory amenities.

The decision to use multi-storey housing on a large scale has also been influenced by the city's heavy financial commitments. While both the costs for the initial construction of high flats and their maintenance are higher than those for low-rise building, multi-storeys were originally able to claim a higher Government subsidy than that available for a low-rise dwelling of corresponding size. The sum available for this additional long-term relief was £30 per flat for 60 years. As said earlier Government policy regarding subsidy changed in 1968 but by this time the city had already built or planned some 150 blocks.

Another and different type of reason which may have influenced the Corporation in favour of high flats is that its earlier housing policies aroused much adverse criticism. Glasgow is not unique in finding that new housing does not in itself necessarily lead to improved all round standards but some of its experiences have been particularly unfortunate. Too many areas of its interwar housing have degenerated into near-slums to judge from their external appearance and shady social reputation. "If you say to anyone that you live in .... you'd think you had horns." The huge peripheral estates to which about 10% of the city's population was decanted after the war have also been denigrated. Adverse comment has been made on their location in that they require such large numbers of people to live perhaps as far as 7 miles from the city centre, involving them in high transport costs and employment problems. The Corporation has also been under fire for niggardliness and years of delay in providing leisure and cultural facilities for these enormous 'environmental vacuums'. A committee which reported on housing management in Scotland presumably had Glasgow's postwar housing particularly in mind when it wrote of being "grossly disappointed at what we found".[4] One answer to the above criticism was to introduce an entirely new form of building.

To pile like on like, as in a multi-storey, seems vaguely akin to the character of Scottish architecture. Way back in the 16th century Edinburgh had 10-storey tenements. This tradition of flat life has

[4] *Housing Management in Scotland*, Report by a Subcommittee of the Scottish Housing Advisory Committee, H.M.S.O., 1960.

undoubtedly made it easier than would be the case in an English setting for the Corporation to sell the idea of high flats. Even today, when so much of the city's housing is in tenements that are obsolete, the term 'tenement' does not necessarily imply a decayed structure. Nor has it dubious overtones socially. Pretty well all classes but the very wealthy are prepared to live in a tenement flat. Many people prefer a home that is on one level, and to share a common stairway and be without any garden or yard of one's own is not regarded as much of a disability.

Despite the above inducements to build multi-storeys it should be emphasised that the Corporation did not originally intend them for family use. But social and political pressures for improved housing were so intense that this policy fairly soon went by the board and the flats were offered to pretty well anyone on the housing list provided household size and the various priority qualifications were suited.

The first tenants moved into Glasgow's first Council home in a high flat in June 1952. Multi-storey housing provided either by the Corporation or the Scottish Special Housing Association[5] grew relatively slowly for some years but in the early 1960s the pace increased. In 1959 the number of dwellings built in multi-storeys as compared with those in traditional low-rise housing was only 1 in 50; in 1964 it was 1 in 1; and by 1968 6 multi-storey flats were built for every low-rise dwelling.

In terms of individual blocks and referring merely to the increase

Table 1[6]

Local Authority and Scottish Special Housing Association dwellings built in Glasgow in three selected years, 1959, 1964, 1968.

Date	Multi-storey	Low-rise	Total
1959	60	2,998	3,058
1964	2,383	2,407	4,790
1968	3,857	642	4,499

[5] Under the Housing (Financial Provisions) (Scotland) Act, 1968, as amended by the Housing (Scotland) Act, 1969, this Association, in part financed by the Treasury, may be empowered by the Secretary of State for Scotland to build houses in districts designated by the Secretary of State.

In May 1969, S.S.H.A. multi-storey flats in Glasgow numbered 2,650 in 37 blocks. S.S.H.A. tenants have to be nominated by the local authority from its housing list but the Association manages its own property. Unless stated otherwise any further references to the city's multi-storey housing includes that provided by the S.S.H.A.

[6] Certain discrepancies between the figures in this study and those given in the annual reports of the Housing Management Department of the City of Glasgow are due to the fact that two estates with buildings of 6 and more storeys which it was thought desirable to include in the study are not treated as multi-storey buildings by the Housing Management Department.

which took place during this study, the figures were as follows. At February 1967 there were 92 blocks in occupation; at July 1968 (the date on which most of the statistical material used here was based) there were 143; and at the last count, in May 1969, the figure was 163 (Table 3, p. 37). The rapidity with which multi-storeys have been introduced should be stressed because of its relevance to the social effects of so new a form of home. Then, too, the blocks are exceptionally high (well over three-quarters of them having from 11 to 31 storeys) which might be expected to produce social repercussions.

The Corporation's Housing Management Department employs much the same methods for its high flats as for its 121,500 low-rise homes. Administration is undertaken from one central office and this same building is the headquarters of the Glasgow branch of the S.S.H.A. The Corporation, but not the S.S.H.A., has 11 district offices situated throughout the city. Each serves a maximum of about 12,000 households. The tenant pays his rent and conducts most of his business with his local office. It will be noted that the Corporation does not employ rent collectors. The S.S.H.A. used to do so but has now abandoned this policy for those houses built in Glasgow after 1966: houses built before then still have their rents collected. The Association's tenants deal only with one central office. Apart from caretakers, neither the Corporation nor the S.S.H.A. employs full-time staff working directly from the estate. Such men as technicians for the lift or gardeners (from the Parks Department) are called in as needed. The caretaker is required to make his home in an ordinary flat, generally on the first floor, in one of the blocks for which he is responsible. He works only in connection with the multi-storey blocks though there may be low-rise housing on the estate. The proportion of caretakers to blocks is normally 2 men to 3, or possibly 4, blocks. At March 1969 the total of caretakers was about 100, of whom 22 were S.S.H.A. employees. As the only resident representative of management these caretakers play a key role in the social as well as the physical well-being of the city's multi-storey population.

The Corporation allocates all types of dwelling from its waiting list on eight priority categories. The principal ones are for households living in a building which is structurally unfit, below standard in sanitary conditions, or in an area being cleared for redevelopment. If one of a household's members requires to be rehoused for medical reasons, this also gives priority. Applicants may express preference as to location and type of house they would like and there is a rough and ready rule that they can turn down three or so offers. No one who definitely dislikes the idea of a high flat is forced to take this type of home; but the pressures to move from bad housing are so strong that people are reluctant to do anything which they feel might prejudice their chances of a better place. The prospective tenant for a multi-storey has no choice

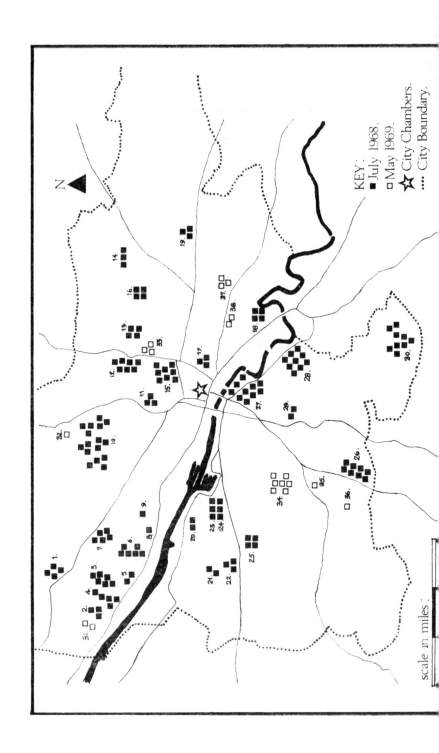

Fig. 1. (above) Map locating multi-storey blocks in Glasgow: July 1968 – May 1969.

Multi-storey blocks. July 1968 and May 1969.

Occupied July 1968 (Main Sample).

Geographical area Map No.	No. of developments	No. of blocks	Geographical area Map No.	No. of developments	No. of blocks
1 Blairdardie, W.5.	1	4	19 Cranhill, E.3.	1	3
2 Kelso Street, W.3.	1	3	20 Langlands Road, S.W.1.	1	2
3 Lincoln Avenue, W.3.	1	6	21 Queensland Drive, S.W.2.	1	2
4 Kirkton Avenue, W.3.	1	5	22 Moss Heights, S.W.2.	1	3
5 Blawarthill, W.4.	1	2	23 Albion, S.W.1.	1	3
6 Scotstoun, W.4.	1	6	24 Ibroxholm, S.W.1.	1	3
7 Broomhill, W.1.	2	5	25 Mosspark Drive North, S.W.2.	1	4
8 Crathie Court, W.1.	1	1	26 Pollokshaws, S.1.	5	8
9 Fortrose Street, W.1.	1	1	27 Hutchesontown/Gorbals, C.5.	3	10
10 Wyndford, N.W.	6	16	28 Toryglen+Toryglen North, S.2.	3	9
11 Woodside, C.3.	1	3	29 Battlefield, S.2.	1	2
12 Carron Street, N.	1	7	30 Castlemilk, S.5.	3	9
13 Springburn B, N.1.	2	4	Total	49	143
14 Red Road, N.1.	1	3			
15 Sighthill, N.1.	2	8			
16 Royston, N.1.	2	4			
17 Ladywell, C.4.	1	3			
18 Summerfield, S. E.	1	4			

Additions July 1968–May 1969.

Geographical area Map No.	No. of blocks
31 Northland Drive, W.4.	2
32 Maryhill B., N.W.	1
33 Red Road, N.1.	3
34 St. Andrew's Drive, S.1.	7
35 Pollokshaws D, S.1.	1
36 Kennishead, S.W.3.	1
37 Parkhead, E.1.	3
38 London Road, S.E.	2
Total	20

as to what height above ground his home shall be, nor its position, e.g. north or south facing. He ballots as regards height but does not do so until he actually comes to the block in order to sign his tenancy agreement and get his keys. Should he dislike his draw he can try to swop floors with someone else but has to do so on the spot. He cannot exchange floors later on without considerable difficulty. Until quite recently the possibility of transfer from one Corporation house and district to another was very limited. In general a tenant did not expect to be accepted for transfer from a multi-storey house for five years. Mutual exchange, permitted if both houses are within 23 miles of Glasgow, has also been relatively infrequent. Recently the Corporation's policy on both transfer and exchange has become far more flexible and the numbers taking advantage of this have been much increased. The target is now 5,000 per annum. A gross shortage of dwellings exacerbates problems connected with transfer and, as in so many areas, Glasgow is short of small dwellings. In 1968, for example, there were 10,500 applicants for a smaller home, compared with only 4,500 for a larger place. Transfer as such does not, of course, lessen total demand. Waiting time for getting a fresh home is considerably influenced by the applicant's willingness to move to any part of the city. In the case of certain much disparaged districts the time may be as short as 18 months even though, as said before, the current (1969) housing list is 49,000.

The essential features about Glasgow's use of multi-storey housing may be summarised as follows. The city's economy is such that it has no choice but to engage in massive reconstruction if it is to hold its own. This holds for a variety of fields, the most significant being the need for modernised housing. High flats have certain characteristics which meet Glasgow's requirements particularly well. The city is extremely short of land, and towers and slabs do not inevitably require such extensive sites as are needed for low-rise dwellings. Thus they simplify the problem of rehousing at high densities which is crucial for a city where the existing ones are often abnormal. They are also a rapid method of building, and there are urgent social, economic and political reasons why there should be the minimum of procrastination about improved housing. First introduced in 1952, they have not proved openly unpopular with their tenants. This could be because previous homes have often been so deplorable and also because flat life is traditional to the city. The extent to which Glasgow has used this new form of housing (15,000 flats by May 1969) suggested that it would make a useful setting in which to look at their social implications. On the other hand it is very possible that certain features of the Glasgow situation may invalidate generalisation.

* * *

Before giving facts and figures about the flats it may be helpful to have a little information about a few of the people for whom this new form of housing is 'home'. The following pen pictures were taken from information that tenants gave at interviews held with a 5% sample of the flats occupied at July 1968. The interviews in question were drawn at random from those held with people living on 5 of the estates which, as will be shown later, were selected for special study.

The first home contained a man in his 40s, married but now living alone on the 3rd floor of one of the five blocks of an outlying estate. He had got the flat because his old home came into a redevelopment area. Since he worked at jobs which took him all over the country (a friend employed by the same firm drove him to work) he saw little of the estate or block; but after $3\frac{1}{2}$ years in this high flat he had come to the conclusion that it suited him well. The place was easy to clean whereas the couple of rooms he had rented previously had been in bad condition. His rent and rates had risen from £2·40 to £6·60 a month but this did not seem to bother him. He hoped to stay on in the place. He did, however, volunteer the comment that a high flat like this was no life for the kids. Too many of them just hung around the entrance to the block.

The household at the second flat, a retired couple, had moved in two years ago from a 4-apartment council house about a mile away. This new home, four floors up, had 2 apartments. Monthly rent and rates, £9·32, were about £1 higher than previously, running costs much as before. They found the Corporation all right as a landlord – "You get your repairs done". The husband, 72 and an ex-manual worker, liked the whole thing fine and was glad not to have a garden to bother about. Both stressed the comfort. The wife, eight years younger than her husband, had certain reservations about multi-storey life. Anyone could come up the stairs on to the veranda and look or get in – "I would not stay a night here on my own". She also missed her old neighbours, especially when she first moved in. There was not the same friendliness about this type of home. You could live here for years and never meet anyone.

At the third home the family with their two youngsters, a girl of 7 and a boy of 5, were up on the 25th floor. They had been here a year and a half, after being 9 years on the housing list. They thought the flat itself first class, particularly after the very poor two-roomed place they had moved from and where they had become officially overcrowded. They very much appreciated having a bedroom to themselves, the lovely living-room and, in particular, the bathroom. Moreover, the estate was not too far from their old neighbourhood so that the husband did not have to change his job and his wife was able to keep on her part-time work. Rent and rates were a bit steep, rising to £12·26 next month. They had, however, a major trouble. Their 7-year-old had always been frightened of the lift. They had taken her to various doctors and to a psychologist. The latter said she'd grow out of it but "a fortnight ago I took her on the lift and as soon as it stopped (at the third floor) she dashed out and we had to walk up again". This was their chief problem. They also disliked other things about the place. They felt there were too many families with children in the block, e.g. there were eight kids besides their own on just this one floor. Shopping was unsatisfactory. You either had to use the vans, with their extra pennies on everything, or pay an 6p bus fare. The school, too, was a ten minutes bus ride and at peak hours the buses filled up before they reached the estate. They had asked the Corporation for a transfer but thought their chances so poor that they were planning to leave Scotland next year.

The next family had 3 members, husband, wife and a daughter of 18, all in jobs at a good level. They too had moved from another Corporation house, but roughly the size of this one. The new place was much more central and they reckoned this one of the best things about it. Rent and rates had risen, from £7·97½ to £10·72½, but running costs were lower. They enjoyed sitting out on the balcony and were glad to be no higher than the 9th floor because at a pinch you could walk up. They had made some good friends since coming here. All told they thought their type of family well suited to a high flat.

The last of these five, randomly-chosen households, a couple in their late 40s, had now lived in a high flat for 5½ years. Their previous home had been single rented room, at £2·60 a month and 3½ miles away on the other side of the city. Both husband and wife were in what sounded like good jobs. Although they ran a car, they emphasised that one of the best features of the new place was its central position. The flat was great, nicely shaped, got all the sun and was well built. They compared the view (you could see Loch Lomond) with that in the old tenement where all you saw was another tenement with someone looking in at you. The people in their block liked to keep their houses nice. The lifts were good, you could get down in 50 seconds. So was the caretaker. On the other hand the entrance was poor, with the paint chipped and no tiles. The garage doors were defaced. They recognised that the

Plate 5. Tower blocks on peripheral estate, Castlemilk, Glasgow.

Corporation could only do so much towards keeping the estate in order and that this largely depended on the tenants. Though this couple plainly found a multi-storey home suited them, they said "no" when asked if they expected to stay on for some time. Were they perhaps forerunners of the up-and-coming family who, when housing pressures lessen and personal standards rise, will no longer be satisfied with a multi-storey home?

Chapter 3

METHOD OF THE STUDY

Glasgow's housing problem is of such magnitude that any investigation which may bear on it is less likely to take the form of an academic exercise than to be an attempt to provide material on which action can be set in motion expeditiously. It must be emphasised that this study was not concerned to say if high flats are a good buy for Glasgow, nor did the research staff deal with the key question – had this type of home social implications other than those connected with new housing of traditional type? Rather they concentrated on collecting facts relevant to social issues, and on close consultation throughout the three years of the work with the tenants themselves. At the date the study started very little information was available about the social impact of the city's new flats. A small inquiry on how the tenants were reacting was undertaken in 1965 by the Junior Chamber of Commerce but it only concerned one estate. Apart from this, no assessment appeared to have been made. Nor was much in the way of composite factual information available from the Corporation. This meant that during the first six months of the study (July to December 1966) a great deal of fact-finding had to be undertaken at the 80 or so blocks then in occupation. Collection of basic material had to be continued throughout the study since during its three years the number of blocks doubled.

Six months' preliminary work was undertaken before any interviews were held with tenants and these first personal contacts were not made in Glasgow but in the neighbouring burgh of Clydebank (population 50,000). Sixty pilot interviews were held there with a 5% sample of those households living in high flats. The interviewers, chosen with a good deal of care, included an architect, a sociologist, a social studies student and a tenants' association committee member as well as the two research-staff. The result of this pilot suggested that the right questions were being asked as to facts but that those on the tenants' views were not sufficiently precise. The interview schedule was revised to try and establish more exactly any changes in their life that the tenants themselves ascribed to this new form of home. For the initial interviews in Glasgow itself a 5% sample was drawn of the 7,732 multi-storey homes in the 92 blocks (provided by the Corporation and S.S.H.A.) which were in occupation at February 1967. The interviews, undertaken by Market Research staff, were held in the following May and June.

Since it was apparent that the number of multi-storeys was going to increase throughout the study it was plain that more recent information would be needed for the final report than that derived from this initial sample. Thus a second one, the main 5% sample of this inquiry, was undertaken in July 1968. This was based on the 14,658 high flats then occupied.

	Total households	5% Sample	Households which gave effective interviews	Households not contacted	Households which refused interview
Initial Sample (February 1967)	7,732	374	335	8	11
Main Sample (July 1968)	14,658	692	641	41[1]	10

[1] High figure thought to be due to difficulties related to shift work and pre-Christmas activities.

The interviews, again undertaken by Market Research staff, were held in the following November and December. In this main sample certain questions from the first one were repeated exactly, others in a modified form.

The 'views' material from the initial Glasgow sample was supplemented by that obtained in day-to-day contacts between the staff and people knowledgeable about individual estates (officials from the Housing Management and Planning Departments of the Corporation, staff of the S.S.H.A., caretakers, clergy, health visitors, teachers). It suggested that the following topics might be fruitful for intensive study. (*a*) The kind of environment, in terms of facilities and services, that high flats need. (*b*) The suitability of different types of household for life in a multi-storey. (*c*) The problems relating to children. (*d*) Any trained staff that high flats, as an unfamiliar type of housing, may require. (*e*) The special functions and problems of tenants' associations when operating on a multi-storey estate. Additional subjects which were not much in evidence in the earlier stages of the study but which assumed importance as contacts with the tenants lengthened, included problems that seemed inherent in the multi-storey block during the initial months but often sorted themselves out with time. Difficulties associated with delay in the provision of amenities and services for the estate also came more to the fore as the study proceeded. So did the influence of the block's demographic structure on its social character. Another matter that had been more or less taken for granted in the early stages of the study, the alleged loneliness of multi-storey life, was thought worth exploring since the more one came to know the tenants, the more divergent were their views on this. The addition of the above subjects to the original five meant that the study broadened rather than deepened.

The early stages of the field work also indicated that it would be sound to concentrate on a limited number of estates (Table 2). This would enable the staff to make sustained relationships with individual households, increasing their chances of finding out which aspects of multi-storey life had most bearing on the tenant's satisfaction or otherwise. If the staff could get to know an estate reasonably well it should be that much more possible to see what aspects of its physical character appeared to favour or hinder its growth as a community. With these aims in mind, five estates were selected for special study. They were in various parts of the city and thought to be not too 'untypical' of the estates as a whole. Each of those selected for special study had at least one feature judged relevant to the topics chosen for intensive study. During the study the two research staff went to live (for $6\frac{1}{2}$ weeks in all) in a multi-storey flat on four of these five selected estates.

The first one, Castlemilk, was $4\frac{1}{4}$ miles south-east of the city centre.[2] It was situated on the edge of a large (40,000) postwar council estate. The multi-storeys were a string of five towers (19 storeys). They had no low-rise houses actually associated with themselves but looked down, across a main road, on to modern tenements. The five blocks backed on to a steep slope of unfenced and wooded hillside, with fields and farms beyond. Fronting them was another sloping area of common land with old pine trees and a bit of a burn. The semi-rural setting was judged very favourable for the child living in a high flat (once he was old enough to go out by himself) and Castlemilk was selected for special study largely for this reason. Wyndford, the second estate, was about 3 miles north-west of the city centre and close to a busy shopping street and such places as an Employment Exchange and Child Welfare Clinic. At the date of the main sample it comprised 16 blocks (8 to 26 storeys), and an unusually high proportion (748) of low-rise houses. Situated on the site of old barracks and surrounded by a high and handsome wall, the estate was visibly self-contained. Socially it was believed to be settling down rather well. This, and the fact that it was a S.S.H.A. estate, were the major reasons why Wyndford was selected. Albion, the third estate, was about $2\frac{1}{2}$ miles from the city centre but to the south-west. It had three blocks (19 storeys) but no low-rise housing. Near the docks, it was a hemmed-in estate and close to an arterial road. Alongside was the home of the Rangers Football Club, a greyhound

---

[2] Strictly speaking the name 'Castlemilk' is applied to the whole of this area. For convenience it has been used in this study solely for the multi-storey blocks in Mitchell Hill Road.

Table 2

The five selected estates, July 1968

	Wyndford	Royston	Albion	Castlemilk	Red Road*
Distance from city centre	3 miles NW	1 mile N	3 miles SW	4¼ miles S	2 miles NE
Terrain	Sloping	Sloping	Level	Steep slope	Sloping
Size (acres)	33.3	8.5	2.8	15.2	21.6
Density (p.p.a.)	152	181	320	119	212
Estimated population when estate completed	5,000	1,500	1,000	1,800	4,700
Date first m/s block occupied	1963	1961	1966	1964	1966
Blocks and dwellings					
Multi-storey Blocks	16	3	3	5	3
Dwellings	1,000	351	285	570	552
Low rise ,,	748	102	–	–	–
Total ,,	1,748	453	285	570	552
Blocks/Access					
Central	15	3	3	5	2
Linear	1	–	–	–	–
Other	–	–	–	–	1
Dwellings/storey height					
6–10 storeys	270	–	–	–	–
11–20 storeys	280	351	285	570	–
21–30 storeys	450	–	–	–	312
31 storeys	–	–	–	–	240
Dwellings/number of apartments					
1 apartment	155		57	95	–
2 apartment	112	117		95	208
3 apartment	733	234	114	380	104
4 apartment			114		240

Population/age (as in main sample)

Age	Total sample					
	%	%	%	%	%	%
0–4	7	4	0	8	15	10
5–9	7	5	5	5	16	21
10–14	6	3	10	13	4	8
15–64	70	68	68	64	56	55
65+	11	20	17	10	8	5

* Figures relate to that part of estate occupied at July 1968.

course and industrial building. The fourth estate was Red Road. Though only 2 miles north-east of the city centre it was curiously cut off from the main stream of city life. The surroundings of the estate included a clutter of largely derelict works, a Local Authority old people's home and extensive interwar 2-storey council housing. One very small shop and a church were the existing 'services' in the immediate vicinity of the estate. At the date Red Road was selected for special study only 2 of the 8 massive blocks planned had become occupied. But both were already showing signs of social problems since the lifts were proving most inadequate. They were of the standard, 8-person size, but had to serve an unusually large number of storeys (31) and an unusually high proportion of child-users. Since all 120 of the flats in each of these two blocks were 3-bedroom homes, they mostly contained children. The lack of shops and the poor transport added greatly to the tenants' difficulties. The last estate, Royston, was even nearer to the city centre, only about a mile away, but to the north. It was built on rising ground above a main road and in an area of interwar council housing, decayed older tenements and small declining shops. The estate consisted of 3 blocks (20 storeys), 102 low-rise houses and a few new shops. It was chosen as one of the city's earliest (1961) ventures in high flats. Since the novelty of this new type of home should have long worn off, this might make it a useful contrast to the city's high flats in general.

To the man in the street one block of flats looks much like another as a setting for one's home. Though the blocks themselves had more distinctive features as regards their internal layout than their exterior appearance might suggest, one of the major things affecting their desirability in the tenants' eyes was the character of the estate as a whole. The 49 estates occupied in February 1968 were found to have marked physical differences. In some instances the tenants could draw on existing facilities – shops, schools, halls, playgrounds, clinics, churches, etc. – which were almost at the foot of the blocks. In other cases the local provision was minimal. Some estates had serious transport problems. An examination of the facilities readily available was therefore undertaken at three of the five selected estates listed in Table 2, p. 29, viz. Albion, Castlemilk and Red Road. A list was completed and mapped of the major services and facilities located within a half-mile radius of the estate's centre. No attempt was made to compare the estates as regards the extent and quality of the provision: rather attention was paid to types of deficiency that common sense suggested ought not to have been countenanced, and about which the tenants were consciously frustrated. Since the necessity to use a lift so affects the flat dweller's accessibility to the outside world, it was thought desirable to study certain aspects of the lift's use at these 5 estates. An architect who had already examined problems of lift breakdown and waiting time at another estate undertook a study on the latter point at each of the five selected estates. Details of the methods he used are given in Chapter 5 and Appendix E. An altogether different matter, but one about which many tenants were disheartened, was vandalism. They were most anxious that this new setting for their home should not revert to the sordid ones so many had had to live with in the past. An honours psychology student undertook a small study of one aspect of scruffiness, viz. wall defacing. He did this at Royston, trying to identify those responsible and to see if the graffiti showed any common characteristics. Were they, for example, used on particular types of surface? Further details of the methods adopted are given in Appendix C.

Since much of the existing work on the social effects of high flats has concentrated on problems connected with the children, it was intended that this study should concern itself largely with other matters. But the first six months' contact with people living in the flats, irrespective of whether or not they had children themselves, showed that this was a subject uppermost in many minds. The same impression was given by the formal interviews of the initial sample. This suggested that it would be unrealistic to look at the social implications of multi-storey housing without including matters connected with the children. 'The children' were therefore included in the subjects chosen for special study. It would obviously have been valuable to set up control groups of children living in high flats as compared with those in low-rise homes and possible methods of doing so were explored in some detail with senior members of the Medical and Education Departments of the University and of the Corporation. However, in view of the methodological problems, they did not think this study had the necessary resources and advised against it. The policy finally pursued was to look at the children's life from a variety of angles. Almost every type of schedule that was used throughout the study included questions relating to them. Information about children was also obtained from a few primary schools. At one of these an honours psychology student compared the total population of 257 boys and girls with that of the 47 who lived in three near-by 20-storey blocks. She used written and verbal tests, drawings, etc. to assess the two groups. The staff of this and of another primary school attended by the children of these particular blocks also made their own assessment of the two sets of children regarding attendance, academic level, etc. Another angle on the children, relating to the use they made of the playgrounds and open space around their blocks, was collected by 20 social studies students who in the early days of the study made a rough record, at 21 estates and at set hours, of the number and approximate ages of children playing on places of different types. As regards the children not yet at school, a certain amount of information was obtained by a graduate social studies student who examined the alleged loneliness of a multi-storey life for young mothers. She contacted 25 mothers on two estates, some living in a high flat, others in a low-rise home. The mothers in question each had two children not yet old enough for school. Useful information was also obtained through very small discussion groups, involving about 18 mothers in all and held at four of the five selected estates. The groups were kept informal and the mothers appeared to have so many pressing difficulties about their children that they talked readily. At Royston a group of mothers initially numbering about 7 decided as a result of informal discussion that they would try to start a pre-school playgroup themselves. As this seemed a useful situation in which to observe whether tenants would take effective action about a specific need, the group was kept under fairly close observation for over two years. Another angle on the subject of children and multi-storey housing came from the children themselves. Four primary schools with some, or in one case all, their pupils living in multi-storey homes, wrote and drew material on what makes a good place to play, etc. No attempt was made to compare the two sets of writers, but their writings and drawings helped to show how the children themselves viewed some aspects of life in a high flat.

The fact that living high was a relatively new experience for the great majority of the tenants posed difficulties since their views and problems might be strongly influenced by unfamiliarity. When this study began only 8 of the blocks had been up for 10 or more years and two of the three estates involved were untypical. One, built in 1953, was almost confined to elderly people; at the other, built in 1952, the tenants were rather above the economic and social level of the city's multi-storey population as a whole. However, it seemed useful to look at this second estate in some detail since all its flats were 4-apartment ones, i.e. by now they would be likely to contain adolescents and young adults who had spent a considerable part of their childhood under multi-storey conditions. Another social studies graduate student undertook a short investigation of the 15–22-year-old population of this estate, interviewing 44 of the 127 in this age group. She concentrated on how they thought life in a high flat had suited them as children, and whether they would choose to live in one when they got married.

No specific study was set up to examine the reactions to high flat life of selected types of household, apart from certain ones relating to families containing children, and one concerned with a dozen individuals who were seriously disabled. But the material from the two 5% samples and that from all the minor studies was always looked at with household type in mind. This was particularly so as regards older people.

As already pointed out, this study did not concern itself with the testing question of whether a high flat has social implications which differ radically from those of a home in low-rise housing. On the other hand there was continual anxiety about much of the material as to how far 'multi-storeyness' might be affecting the situations analysed. But any attempt to use control groups was hamstrung by the difficulty of finding estates with (*a*) enough dwellings of similar size in both their multi-storeys and their low-rise housing to provide sizeable groups; (*b*) enough households in the two types of dwelling who had lived there sufficiently long for patterns and views to have become relatively stabilised. Thus only one study was undertaken on the above lines, and even here the maximum number of matching sets that could be found was only 30 (and these were not all on one estate). In it attempt was made to see whether, on the same estate, differences in the physical character of multi-storey and low-rise dwellings influenced just a few and fairly obvious matters connected with the tenant's day-to-day life, and his views on a few and fairly obvious subjects. For example, how did frequency of contact with neighbours compare, or opinions as to whether the home was good value for money? Thirty low-rise houses of 2, 3 or 4 apartments chosen at random on three estates were matched for size with 30 high flats on the same estates. The two sets proved to be broadly similar as regards family size, work situation, head of household's occupation, and length of residence. In age structure, however, and this plainly was relevant, the high-flat families had a larger number of dependent children. Another relevant matter was that, due to the difficulty of finding matched households, 7 of the 11 blocks concerned were only 8 storeys in height which meant that 16 of the 30 flats were found to be situated below the 6th floor. At this low height the lift does not exercise so much control. The study was preceded by 12 pilot interviews on other estates and the interviewers were chosen with particular care. They were a psychologist, a sociologist, an architect and a doctor's wife with children of her own. The latter interviewed the 4-apartment households as those most likely to contain children. The response rate was good, 56 of the 60 households co-operating. It was also satisfactory that the man's point of view was well represented; the numbers of men and women interviewed were about equal.

Another attempt just to glance at comparative material was made at a new, high density (149 p.p.a.) estate planned somewhat on the lines of Sheffield's Park Hill. At Glasgow's Balgray Hill four-fifths of the 1,100 dwellings are in 6-storey terraces stretching along a hillside. They include split level maisonettes and flats, and range in size from a single apartment to a few homes with as many as six rooms. High towers (25 and 26 storeys) form the rest of the estate. Their flats have either 2 or 3 apartments and there are only 4 flats on each floor. These towers certainly gave an impression of aloofness and their immediate surroundings seemed to have fewer people about than the semi covered-in deck access 'streets' of the terraced houses. On the other hand the towers had proportionately fewer children. Could one substantiate the impression that there was less life about the towers than the 'streets'? Another social studies graduate student did a small study on this subject, interviewing tenants at 56 flats in the two types of housing, but confining the homes to those which had only two apartments so that there were not likely to be children in either group.

The research staff's initial contacts with the blocks very soon indicated that the caretaker was a key figure, an impression which was sustained throughout the study. They supplemented their day-to-day contacts with caretakers by a formal interview with one of them at each of 14 estates. These were held towards the end of the study when a good deal of insight had been gained into the caretaker's role. The estates were selected as likely to have dissimilar problems from the caretaker's point of view. Discussion centred on what matters regularly troubled him as regards maintenance, how he viewed his supervisory functions, and the kind of services and amenities he personally would like to see introduced.

A different set of people closely linked with this new type of housing were the officers of tenants' associations. In the early days of the study chance contact with the Glasgow Council of Tenants' Associations suggested that these organisations might be a useful source of information. With its help the research staff got in personal touch with every association connected in any way with a multi-storey estate and tried to continue the contact throughout the study. They had innumerable contacts with officer bearers and ordinary members, attended business meetings and took part in some of the associations' bus runs, dances, etc. They ran a conference (attended by 65 people) on the part that tenants' associations may play as agents in promoting community development, and followed it up by getting the University's Extra-Mural Department to run three courses, 'New Homes and New Neighbours' (Appendix G). Two honours students in the Department of Politics made a study in some detail of 13 of the associations, interviewing all 96 of the office bearers about their particular function, their previous experience of voluntary work, and how they envisaged their association's future.

*   *   *

The Rowntree Memorial Trust which financed this study asked that brief examination should be made of the social implications of multi-storey housing in places other than Glasgow. Those eventually selected for visits (lasting about 12 weeks in all) are listed in Appendix A. The topics concentrated on were the same as those chosen for intensive work in Glasgow. At the very beginning of the study a member of the research staff also had the privilege of spending three weeks in the Sociological Research Section of the Ministry of Housing and Local Government. A number of visits were made to London because of the scale and variety of the use made of multi-storey housing by both the G.L.C. and the boroughs. The Park Hill and Hyde Park experiment at Sheffield was another obvious choice for any study of the effects of layout on social contacts. Liverpool's severe housing problems suggested that the use of high flats there might be very relevant to their use in Glasgow. As regards the Continent, the staff were advised to visit Stockholm because of its early use of high flats, the high standards of the facilities associated with its new housing, and its imaginative provision for children's play. The Netherlands' long-standing interest in the social aspects of planning made it another particularly suitable place to look at experiments in connection with multi-storey housing. It was an official of the Netherlands Ministry of Town and Country Planning who advised a visit to a Swiss example of multi-storey housing, the high density, mixed development estate of Tcharnergut in Berne. Before the above visits took place senior officers in the Housing and Planning Departments of the authorities concerned, and in some places sociologists and welfare workers, were asked to advise on the most suitable examples of multi-storey housing to visit, bearing in mind the topics chosen for special study in Glasgow. In general the estates were first visited in the company of such people as housing officers, architects, sociologists, and community development workers. In some cases the research staff re-visited them later on, unaccompanied. A limited number of contacts were made with tenants themselves, some of them committee members of tenants' associations or their Continental equivalents. The Netherlands visit had useful repercussions since on two occasions Dutch students in architecture and sociology, 27 in all, who were visiting examples of housing in this country, were taken round some of Glasgow's estates and into homes by members of tenants' associations. Exchange of visits between tenants also took place between the London Association of Housing Estates and the Glasgow Council of Tenants' Associations.

Methodological difficulties were numerous even though the study was not an exercise in academic sociology. The continual increase in the number of blocks occupied meant that the essential basic stuff of the study was always changing. This affected the use to which the two samples could be put. While the factual material was broadly similar in character, whatever the age of the blocks, that relating to the tenants' views was not, since the main sample contained a far higher proportion than the initial one of people who had only recently been exposed to multi-storey life. Another difficulty was that both the samples were small, only 5%. But if two were to be undertaken the funds did not permit them to be on a larger scale; and it was thought desirable to have a second set of interviews otherwise the figures would be hopelessly out of date when the report came to be written. Another problem concerned the setting up of control groups. Large numbers of the population on the estates were so new that they had to be excluded when investigating any subject in which length of experience of multi-storey life was judged to be essential. It was satisfactory that there were high response rates in almost all the studies involving interviews. That for the initial sample was 95%, for the main one 93%. In the small but important multi-storey and low-rise study, 56 of the 60 households co-operated. It was also useful that a good deal of the material in both the formal interviews and informal contacts was provided by men. They represented 38% of the total in the combined figure for the initial and main sample. The point is stressed because so much of the existing material on the social aspects of high flats represents only the woman's views. Another satisfactory aspect of the methods adopted was the extent and ease of the casual contacts made between the tenants and the research staff, some of them persisting from the beginning to the end of the study. Most of the tenants were extremely co-operative and indeed seemed pleased to be consulted on the pros and cons of multi-storey life. "We didn't know anyone at the University bothered with us."

Chapter 4

GENERAL INFORMATION ABOUT THE HOUSING STUDIED

The basic Glasgow material on which the study was based is given in Table 3. This shows the number of multi-storey flats and estates which were in use at various stages of the work. More detailed information of the position at July 1968, when the main 5% sample of this study was drawn, is shown in Table 4. Unless stated otherwise any figures quoted henceforth will refer to this date. By May 1969 an additional 8,300-odd flats in some 73 blocks were occupied, under construction or had been approved. Even should this total of 24,000 homes in high flats not increase much, it can be estimated that roughly 1 in 14 of Glasgow's 976,000 citizens will shortly be living under multi-storey conditions.

Table 3

Total of multi-storey housing occupied 1967, 1968, 1969 (May)

Date	Dwellings	Blocks	Estates containing m/s & l/r housing	Estates confined to m/s housing	Total
February 1967 (Initial Sample)	7,732	92	18	7	25
July 1968 (Main Sample)	14,658	143	28	21	49
May 1969	15,632	163	–	No information	–

The location of this new form of housing is worth noting. Though by no means confined to redevelopment at high density in the heart of the city, 45% of the blocks occupied at May 1969 were within 2½ miles of the City Chambers and certain ones within 5 minutes' walk. It is also of interest that earlier figures, those of the main sample of July 1968, gave 36% of the households as living within a mile of their former home (Table 8). The sites were very diverse in character and scale. Some blocks looked down on to a pastoral scene with cattle grazing almost literally at their base; others overlooked derelict works, busy railway lines, graveyards. A small estate of just two blocks might be perched on the crown of a steep hill, a large one occupy 8 level acres in a curve of the Clyde. Some were on virgin land where practically all services and amenities had to be introduced; others, in built-up areas, could draw on near-by shops and existing bus services. If the site was very steep and/or confined, it was difficult to introduce amenities like playgrounds beyond the statutory minimum. As many as 21 of the 49 estates

Table 4

Physical details of multi-storey housing. July 1968

Estates (in geographical areas)*

Estimated population of estate	No. of estates	Blocks in estate	No. of estates	M/s or mixed housing on estate	No. of estates	Date 1st block in estate occupied	No. of estates
0–1000	7	1–3	14	M/s only	14	1952–9	3
1000–2000	9	4–6	9	Mixed housing	16	1960–4	12
2000–3000	8	7–9	5			1965–8	15
3000–6000	3	9–11	1				
6000–8000	3	12–16	1				
	30		30		30		30

Blocks**

	Height	No. of blocks	Access to flat	No. of blocks	Balcony	No. of blocks	Flats per floor	No. of blocks
Point blocks 107	6–10	23	Linear (corridor)	23	Balcony	114	2	3
							3	4
							4	32
Slabs 23	11–20	80	Central (hall)	120	No balcony		5	3
						29	6	65
Other 13	21–30	38					10	2
							12	9
	31	2					10†	11
							12†	14
							14†	7
							28†	1
		143		143		143		

† = split level

* The 49 estates, though sited in only 30 geographical areas, are listed separately in Corporation reports and are normally regarded by their tenants as separate estates.

** Including joined point blocks.

Table 4 (continued)

Flats

Size of flat	No. of flats	Size of flat	Rent and rates per month
1 apartment	742	1 apartment	£5.40–£7.52½
2 ,,	4,257	2 ,,	£6.16½–£9.70
3 ,,	8,716	3 ,,	£7.65–£11.70
4 ,,	943	4 ,,	£9.30
	14,658		

Estate	No. of Blocks	Height (storeys)	No. of blocks at this height
Crathie Court	1	6/7/8	1
Fortrose Street	1	8/9	1
Wyndford	7	8	13
Carron Street	3		
Kelso Street	3		
Wyndford	1	9	·1
Moss Heights	3	10	7
Toryglen	4		
Ladywell	1	12	1
Blairdardie	2	13	2
Hutchesontown	4	14	6
Blairdardie	1		
Ladywell	1		
Ladywell	1	15	19
Blairdardie	1		
Wyndford	5		
Carron Street	4		
Langlands Road	2		
Pollokshaws	4		
Toryglen	2		
Cranhill	3	18	8
Broomhill	5		
Pollokshaws	1	19	1

Table 4 (continued)

Estate	No. of Blocks	Height (storeys)	No. of blocks at this height
Royston	3		
Lincoln Avenue	6		
Scotstoun	6		
Blawarthill	2		
Albion	3	20	43
Hutchesontown	2		
Castlemilk	9		
Sighthill	8		
Battlefield	2		
Queensland Drive	2		
Ibroxholm	3	21	7
Mosspark Drive North	4		
Toryglen	1	21/22	1
Woodside	3		
Toryglen 2	1	23	11
Summerfield	4		
Pollokshaws	3		
Hutchesontown	4		
Toryglen	1	24	10
Kirkton Avenue	5		
Royston	1	25	3
Springburn	2		
Springburn	2	26	5
Wyndford	3		
Red Road	3	26/27/28	1
Red Road	2	31	2
		Total blocks	143

were confined to multi-storey housing and even where low-rise was introduced it was generally much in a minority. The 'typical' low-rise home was a 4-storey walk-up tenement. An example of a large (40-acre) estate built almost entirely in high flats was at Sighthill which had 9 uniform slab blocks (19 storeys). In one part of the city 5 new estates

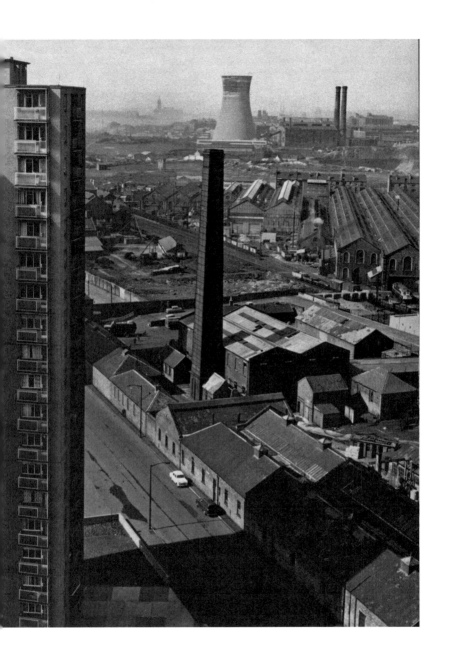

Plate 6
Tower blocks in central area, Royston, Glasgow.

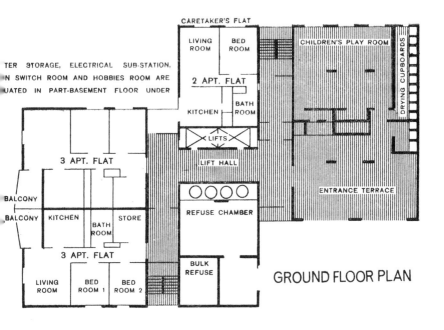

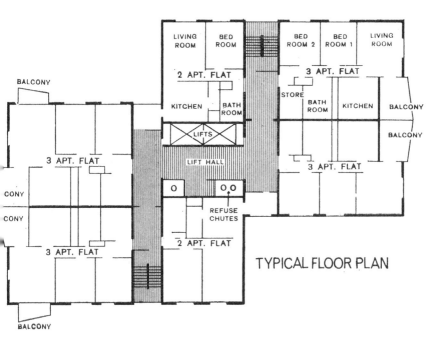

Fig. 2. Royston (20 storey block). Typical floor and ground floor.

with 26 blocks, mostly over 20 storeys, had brought some 10,000 high-flat tenants into a district previously containing a considerable proportion of small semi-detached and owner-occupied houses. As regards size, and speaking generally, it can be said that about half of the 30 geographical areas where multi-storey housing predominated, or was the sole component, had a population of over 2,000. In three cases it rose to 6,000 or more. The difficulty of defining the estate's boundary meant that it could be very misleading to quote density figures. But on the whole they appeared to be high. Whereas any density over 75 p.p.a. must be regarded as considerable, many of the Glasgow estates had a figure in the region of 150 p.p.a. At the Red Road estate they rose to 212 p.p.a.

The blocks themselves varied in design, method of construction, materials and height. Colours included off-white, buff, sandstone red and a lot of elephant grey. By Continental standards and those in other parts of Britain, Glasgow's multi-storeys were exceptionally tall. Forty of the 143 occupied in July 1968 had 21 or more storeys and 44% of the flats were above the 10th floor (Table 9, Diag. 2). The most dominating looking of the estates, Red Road, had 6 blocks of 31 storeys, 1 of 26

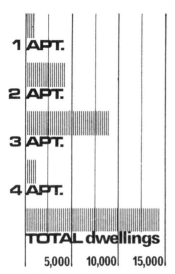

DIAGRAM 1
MULTI-STOREY DWELLINGS
IN RELATION TO NUMBER
OF APARTMENTS. JULY 1968
Corporation of Glasgow and
Scottish Special Housing Association

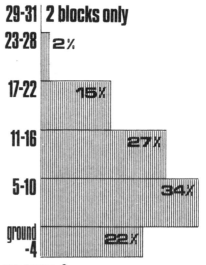

DIAGRAM 2
MULTI-STOREY DWELLINGS IN
RELATION TO STOREY HEIGHT
Main Sample. July 1968.

FIGURE 3.

and another at varying levels – 26, 27 and 28 storeys. Practically the whole of this estate's population of nearly 5,000 was housed in these exceedingly high blocks. Of the city's 143 multi-storey buildings 107 were point blocks, not slabs. Here the door of the individual flat opened directly on to the lift hall of that particular floor: in the slab block the door opened on to an internal corridor, itself leading off the lift hall. In just a few blocks, 'split-level' or 'scissor-planned', the flat had two storeys with its own straight and steep internal staircase. Features of the floor hall in a typical block were the metal sliding doors of the two lifts and the wooden ones leading to two concrete safety staircases running from roof to ground. In the point block the typical floor had 6, or rather less often, 4 flats; in the slab it might have 12 or more. The block was wired for T.V. reception and for private telephones but had no telephone box of its own. A shared rubbish chute was normally

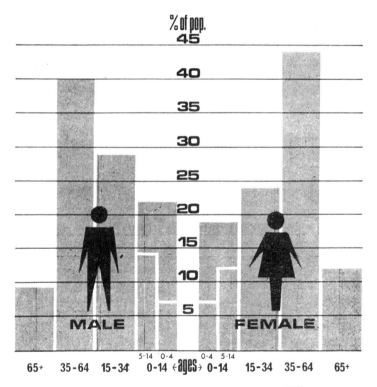

DIAGRAM 3 POPULATION IN RELATION TO AGE AND SEX
Main Sample. July 1968.

FIGURE 4.

available on each floor and some form of shared area for clothes drying, semi-open to the wind. Communal laundries were infrequent. Apart from servicing rooms for the lifts the pumps and the rubbish chutes, a limited number of storage cupboards, and in some cases a caretaker's workroom and/or office, few of the blocks contained any rooms other than the above. Just one estate had incorporated in the original plans certain rooms for the tenants' social use.

Sixty per cent were 3-apartment homes, i.e. they had 2 bedrooms. A feature of this new housing with important demographic and social implications was that none had more than 4 apartments (Table 4, Diag. 1). Maximum overall floor area for a 2-bedroom flat, the typical one occupied by a 2-child family, was 665 square feet and might be considerably less. The actual figure for one flat (2 bedrooms but no balcony) was 565 square feet and its lift hall, shared by four identical flats, was 372 square feet. The typical flat, 61% of them, had a living-room, a separate kitchen, 2 bedrooms, a bathroom-cum-lavatory (with no external window) and a very small storage room. Eighty per cent had a balcony, in general one for the flat's own use and perhaps 3 square yards in size. Floor-to-floor height was normally rather less than 9 feet. Cupboards were generous, windows large and reversible for cleaning. Most of the flats were all-electric. Heating methods varied but under-

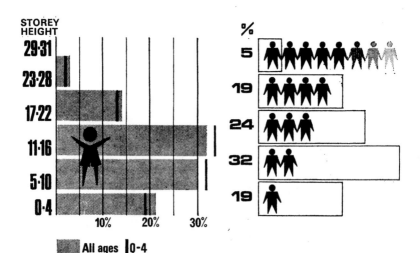

FIGURE 5.

floor heating was relatively common. For a 3-apartment Corporation flat the 1968 average monthly figure for rent and rates was about £10. This was rather higher than that for a comparable low-rise Council home and rather lower than that for a S.S.H.A. high flat of comparable size. The 1969 gross figure for building costs of the kind of 3-apartment flat referred to above was roughly £5,500.

Table 5

Population in multi-storey estates. Main sample, July 1968.

Age structure	Household size (persons)	Household type	Occupational class of all wage-earners	No. of years in current home	No. of years on housing list (where applicable)*
%	%	%	%	%	%
0–4 yrs. 7	1 person 19	Adult (16–65) 46	Professional 1	0–1 yrs. 62	0–5 yrs. 8
5–9 yrs. 7	2 person 32	Pensioners 14	Non-manual intermediate junior grades 27	2–3 yrs. 27	5–10 yrs. 9
10–14 yrs. 6	3 person 24	Households with dependent children (one or more 0–14) 27	Personal service 17	4–5 yrs. 6	10–15 yrs 15
15–19 7	4 person 19	Other type, mixed elderly etc. 12	Foremen Supervisors 4	5+yrs. 5	15–25 yrs 16
20–34 20			Skilled 19		
35–49 20			Semi-skilled		
50–64yrs 23	5 or more 5		Unskilled manual 21		25 yrs. 8
65+yrs. 11			Not employed 22		No inf. 44
			Other 3		
TOTAL 100	100	99	100	100	100

* Related only to the 136 informants who gave 'homeless or overcrowded' as their reason for being allocated a flat.

As stated by the tenants themselves, the first of the two main groups of reasons why they had been offered this new home was that they were on the housing list – homeless, overcrowded, etc. This held for 37%. Another 31 per cent had had to move because their house was needed for redevelopment purposes (Table 10). The main sample showed that 62% had been in the flat for less than 2 years, and 43% for under one year. A mere 5% were old-stagers in that they had been there for 6 or more years (Table 11). Another point of interest was the marked absence of larger households due, of course, to the absence of large-sized flats. Table 12 shows that households with 5 or more persons numbered only 5% whereas the 1966 census showed that 20% of the city's households were of this size. Though the dates are not strictly comparable the comparison is valid enough. On the other hand the 2-person family was rather over-represented in the flats, comprising 32% of the households compared with the Census figure of 27%. Sixty-four per cent of the household had no dependent member, adult or child (Table 13). The average number of persons in flats of various sizes was as follows: 1 person for a 1-apartment flat; 1·6 for a 2-apartment; 3 for a 3-apartment; and 5 for a 4-apartment. Another point about household size that was relevant to social issues was that in 19% of the households the tenant was living alone, and a high flat is believed to be an isolated home. Finally it was noted that 27% of the households had one or more children aged 0–15 inclusive (Table 14).

The following table shows that the age structure of this new population was not markedly different from that in the city as a whole.

Table 6

Glasgow population in relation to age. Census 1966. Multi-storey population in relation to age. Main sample, July 1968

Age	City of Glasgow 1966 %	Main sample 1968 %
0–4	10	7
5–9	9	7
10–14	8	6
15–19	8	7
20–34	19	20
35–49	18	20
50–64	17	23
65+	10	11

The 35–64 age group was rather over represented, 43% compared with the Census figure of 35%. So was the 50–64 group, 23% compared with 17%. On the other hand the proportion of children aged 0–14 was

somewhat lower than that for the city, 20% in the flats, 27% in the Census. For the 0–4 group it was 7% and 10% respectively. An interesting point here is that this multi-storey population did not echo the emphasis on youth that is characteristic of most new housing.[1] It should also be pointed out that individual estates might have very different patterns in their age structure (Table 15). As regards household type, that with all its members between the ages of 16–65 was the 'typical' one, 44% of the total (Table 14).

No questions were asked as to the household's income since this might have told adversely against the free flow of talk that was so desirable if people were to say how they really felt about this new kind of life. But the following material gives some indication of socio-economic levels. The 'typical' tenant was a manual worker, 53% of the jobs recorded being in manual work, with only 19% in white-collar employment and nearly all of that at a junior level (Table 16). However, the fact that rent and rates were rather above those for other council dwellings of corresponding size, suggested that high flats might attract a rather better-off population. Moreover, the poorer household and even the one eligible for rebate might have excluded itself because it could not face the cost of the new goods and chattels felt to be socially essential for such a stylish kind of home. Then again, the absence of larger-sized flats automatically kept out the really big family which by and large is the poorer one. Another small indication that the multi-storey population was not too badly off was the number of households with a private 'phone, 29% compared with 32% for the city (Table 17). The many friendly contacts made with people at their homes also suggested that most of them were probably not too hard up. It was rare to see a shabby object and many households had obviously refurnished at considerable expense, e.g. had put a smart new fire surround into their living-room. Popular opinion supported this hunch about the socio-economic level of this new population. It was "a wee bit class" to live in a high flat. You had moved up in every sense.

[1] Cf. *The Needs of New Communities*. Ministry of Housing and Local Government. H.M.S.O. 1967.

Chapter 5

PHYSICAL CHARACTER OF THE FLATS: TENANTS' VIEWS

"I love my home"

"I love my home". Ask pretty well any Glasgow housewife and her husband how they find life in a high flat and, dismissing the chronic grumblers, the majority will say something on the above lines. They were "very well satisfied", or "we seem to be happy enough", or "for us it's ideal". The place was "way beyond what we were used to", or it was "grand here, quiet and peaceful, nothing upsets you". One tenant who felt that just everything about the house and its situation satisfied her, quoted her husband as saying that he only started to live when they came here. It was noticeable how few people referred spontaneously to such potential sources of *dis*satisfaction as the structural safety of these soaring buildings. The Ronan Point tragedy occurred during the study but it did not seem to perturb these tenants about their own safety. Nor did Glasgow's furious gale of January 1968, although some high flats had their windows sucked in, people saw their furniture moving across the bedroom, and in some blocks the lights and lifts went off. There was little sign of fears about fire. People tended to be careless, not scrupulous, about keeping escape doors unbolted. There seemed to be few apprehensions about using a lift, as distinct from the very common complaints about its service.

This impression of satisfaction was confirmed by the material obtained in the formal interviews of the two samples. In this case the interviewer deliberately pinned the tenant down by inquiring separately as to how he or she found their flat, then their block, and then their estate, while at a later stage the interviewer came back to the subject with this question: "*On the whole* are you satisfied with living here or not?" The great majority of the tenants, some 90% of the combined samples, said "yes". About the same proportion (86%) of the main sample also said "yes" to a question on whether they expected to live in this high flat for a long time (Tables 19, 20, 21). Overall satisfaction came out again in the intensive interviews of the multi-storey and low-rise study (p. 33). Though the number of households involved, 56, was too small to use statistically, it was noted that only 2 of the 28 high-flat households gave an impression of dissatisfaction when asked "How do you like

Plate 7　One of eight slab blocks, Sighthill, Glasgow.

living here?" On the other hand 11 did say that, given the chance, they would move down to one of the estate's low-rise houses of similar size to their own. Some further reactions are given in Table 22.

The extent to which tenants who had sampled multi-storey life decided to move out would seem to be one obvious test of satisfaction. The possibility of comparing a year's transfer figures from the Authority's high flats with those from its low-rise housing was examined but discarded when preliminary examination of the figures indicated that a comparison of bald rates was likely to be misleading. However an analysis was undertaken on the five selected estates for the year ending December 31st 1967. The figures, provided by the Housing Management Department and the S.S.H.A., showed that the number of moves from the 1,943 flats concerned was only 86 (Appendix B). But it was plain from the reasons given by the tenant and as amplified by the officials of the District Housing Office that this figure did not represent a free choice. It was strongly affected by the city's absolute shortage of housing, the relative costliness of privately owned property and to some extent by the Authority's rulings on transfer. Nevertheless it is a fair assumption that the figure would not have been so low had people been radically opposed to multi-storey life.

Overall satisfaction must obviously be related to rent, rates and running costs. At the date of the main sample and dismissing rebate, no one was paying less than £6 a month and very few as much as £13 or over. Though these figures are low by English standards, they were almost always much steeper than in the tenant's previous home where 61% had paid under £5 per month (Tables 4, 18). Despite this and the continual protest about rent, people gave the overall impression that they considered their flat good value for money. This plainly was one of the clues to their positive reactions to living high.

It would be unfair to dismiss this overall satisfaction without referring to an important exception and one which held whether the speaker was an elderly bachelor, one of a middle-aged couple, or a young mother. This was that a high flat was "nae use for the bairns". Dissatisfaction on this aspect of multi-storey housing came out in both informal talk and the statistical material. For instance, when answers to the question "On the whole are you satisfied?" were broken down by household type the only household which showed marked difference from the norm was that which contained a child under 5. Of the 89 households concerned, nearly half were dissatisfied.

Could this overall impression of satisfaction have been largely a question of novelty? It was impossible to test this statistically because at the date of the main sample only a handful of households, just 5%, had been in a multi-storey home for over 5 years. But taking those households which had lived there 5 or less years, overall satisfaction held steady up to the fourth though with some decline in the fourth/fifth year. But even this was not marked (Table 23). It is also relevant that, as said earlier, Glasgow has certain features which may well predispose people to multi-storey life.

The tenant's views on his flat

Many families were enormously set up, almost awed with their high flat when they first saw it and they continued to point out its physical attractions even when they had been there for some years. Its brightness, airiness and modernity were a fantastic contrast to the gaunt and gloomy places so many had lived in previously. To have a bathroom outweighed even the dream kitchen or the under-floor heating. A mother pointed to her 3-year-old who, accustomed to being washed in the sink, would splash about for ever in this lovely shiny bath. They showed the snow-white toilet next to the bath and some recalled the horrors they had known, maybe a murky, unlighted den off a stone passage outside the house. The snugness of one's home matters a lot in a Northern climate, and comfort was a word constantly in use by people of all ages, children as well as pensioners. The flat's cleanliness was another thing they talked of. The place was practically dust free and shoes brought little dirt into the home since the approach was via lift hall, lift and across the polished tiles of the floor hall. They also considered that health should benefit from the cleaner atmosphere though there is considerable uncertainty as to how far the air really is purer. Evidence about the possible effects of height above ground in relation to air pollution from smoke, sulphur dioxide, etc. suggests that in periods of high wind almost any variation is possible. Decrease of pollution with height is most evident in periods of general calm.[1] The tenants themselves also pointed out that when the children played outside the block they got more sunshine here than they did in the old streets where the 60-feet-high tenements cast such long shadows. The powerful electric lighting about the block's entrance and of all the common areas was cheerful compared to the wan and minimal bulbs on the stairs of the old tenement. Then too the flat was so convenient. There was no coal to get in and no grates to clean. The low ceilings and swivel-hung windows saved lugging a stepladder about, and you tipped your rubbish into a chute instead of having to hump the bin up and down stairs. "You can do the week's wash, get Billy up, have dinner ready and be done for the day easily between 9 and 12." Another satisfactory feature of the flat which almost every adult referred to spontaneously was the view. In the old home they had so often looked out on to a dreary street

[1] *The Investigation of Domestic Pollution*, 1958–66, H.M.S.O. 32nd **Report of the Warren Spring Laboratory.**

or the broken-down washhouses of a back close. "Now we look out and see shrubs and things." Even should the nearer prospect be dullish, the distant one was nearly always fine and it could be breathtaking – a sweep of perhaps 15 miles, or even a glimpse of Arran, 40 miles away.

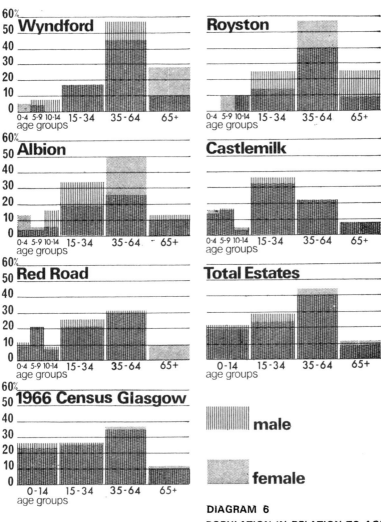

FIGURE 6.

DIAGRAM 6
POPULATION IN RELATION TO AGE
Five Selected Estates. Main Sample.
July 1968.
Total Estates. Main Sample.
1966 Census Glasgow

"I could sit a couple of hours looking at the lights," said an elderly man.

The actual height of their block, the sheer drop, did not seem to worry the tenants. Perhaps because those who were nervous about such things had excluded themselves. On the other hand, there seemed to be some feeling that 10 floors or so was the desirable limit. At a pinch one can walk up this number of flights and it is just possible for adult and child to maintain a brief bawled conversation with each other.

A recent investigation by the Ministry of Housing and Local Government, "Living off the Ground", makes the point that the very high block of, for example, 22 storeys is less favoured than that of medium height.[2] It was also noted that at Wyndford, which had blocks of 8, 15 and 26 storeys, the local people hardly regarded the 8-storey blocks as 'multis'. The height at which the tenant's own flat was situated aroused less comment than had been expected, as many as 88% saying they were satisfied (Table 24). Had there been strong preferences here, prospective tenants would probably not have accepted the luck of the ballot so readily. Families with children had rather more positive views on height but even here only 26 of 176 households who had a child under 16 were dissatisfied. It was noted that 6 of these had one or more children under 5. The one floor that was generally unpopular was that at ground level. It collected dirt, there was the risk of break-in, it was noisy; one was for ever bothered by callers who wanted information about the block and by children who were too short to reach the lift buttons.

On the whole the tenants did not complain much about noise that was due to the structure of the building though the odd flat might be at risk, e.g. one next to the lift mechanism at the top of the block, or one alongside the great bins into which the rubbish chutes hurl their contents. Noise might also be a problem in the block so designed that a corridor was situated above a bedroom. The main troubles about noise were due to the propinquity of such things as a playground, a set of garages or, less often, a busy railway line. On the whole, however, Glasgow's multi-storey blocks would seem to be less vulnerable as far as noise is concerned than is the typical tenement street-side home. This relative quietness is a particular asset to a population which is likely to include shift workers. And it benefits any closely-packed community since noise is such a fertile ground for ill-will between neighbours.

The majority of the flats, 67%, had a small balcony perhaps 3 yards square. Casual observation did not suggest that people made much use of balconies for sitting out. They were, however, appreciated by those who liked to grow some plants, and it was handy as a place for putting the pram out. But it was just an anxiety if there was a small child in the

[2] *Op. cit.*

family and mothers tended to lock the door and lose the key. Even for the child who could be guaranteed not to climb, it was too small for much in the way of play. He couldn't run, bounce his ball, or pedal his trike there. All told the balcony's chief practical use was probably for storage and a little discreet clothes drying. On the other hand it gave a sense of freedom and a breath of fresh air. It was also a vantage point, a kind of 20th-century gazebo, for getting a look at the outside world. Despite this, and in view of the general lack of enthusiasm about the balcony, might it be sounder, in a northern climate, to put the equivalent space into a glass-sided room for shared use by the households on one floor?

The tenant's views on his block

The tenants showed no really strong preferences about the types of block used in Glasgow – point, joined point block, and slab. Just a few blocks, split level or scissor-planned and thus necessitating an internal staircase for the flat, were generally unpopular. The stairs made extra work and were inconvenient since the living-room and the door to the flat were on different floors. The block with central hall access gave rise to fewer complaints about noise from passers-by or overhead than one with a corridor access. People disliked any internal corridor which was long, skinny and institution-like. Households whose homes were grouped round a central hall seemed to value this on social grounds, though the actual siting of the flat in relation to this hall did not arouse much comment. If the flat was in a corner and cut off by a smokescreen door it was a little isolated, but this was not regarded as important. On the other hand the size of the flats on one's floor, and therefore the size and age structure of one's neighbours, was often referred to. For example, if all the flats had 3 bedrooms then all were likely to contain children and all might be tolerant of letting the kids use the hall to play in. The floor which had nothing but 1 or 2-roomed flats, and therefore few young households, was quiet certainly but might be rather dull, according to one's point of view. On the whole the tenants preferred the floor where the flats were of different sizes.

Facilities for laundry aroused a good deal of adverse comment. Just a few blocks had communal laundries on the ground floor, the only suitable place because of the weight and noise of the equipment needed. There was no overt demand for the communal laundry and no strong evidence that it had the social assets ascribed to it in the case of some of the high flats in, for example, London and Sheffield. The tenants' real problem was not the washing as such, which could readily be done inside the flat or at a laundrette, but getting things dried. There were many nostalgic memories of "our lovely old drying green". The blocks had various types of drying areas for shared use that were semi-open to the air. These might be up on the roof, or at the base of the block, or on intermediate floors. Or each floor might have a locked electric drying cupboard with a meter. Some had an electric cupboard inside the flat. Most tenants approved the Councils' ruling that balconies should not be used for (visible) drying – "you can't have towers draped in underclothes". On the other hand even if the flat had its own drying cupboard this was insufficient for a sizeable wash, and shared facilities gave endless troubles over theft, vandalism and rows with other users.

A shared duty which seemed to work reasonably smoothly and about which the housewives of each floor mostly made their own plans, was cleaning and polishing the hall, seeing the rubbish chute was tidy and washing down the safety stairs. They were prepared to do these common chores though they did comment that it could involve quite a lot of work. If a housewife did not pull her weight they looked to the caretaker to take the necessary action. He himself had to clean the lift, the main lift hall and the surround of the block. Tenants were very critical if he failed to keep these common areas up to the high standards which the great majority maintained in their own flat and floor.

Another facility that could involve shared use but which mainly worked all right related to cars. Compared with other major cities, private car ownership is still low in Glasgow. Only 22% of the multistorey households said they owned or had the use of a car (Table 17). Normally there was room for parking, and if the owner could leave the car within eyeshot of his own flat that suited many people. Vandalism in connection with cars was infrequent. Any lock-up garages, at 62½p a week, were often under-occupied. Thus the major problem was one for the caretaker who had to see that the estate's own cars and those of visitors did not intrude on to access areas which must be kept clear for ambulances, fire engines, etc.

One matter about which people complained frequently was the absence of a public phone box in the block. Over two-thirds (71%) of the households had no phone and the figure was much worse in the case of the 1-person household which, by and large, was that of a pensioner, i.e. someone who needed easy access to a phone. Public phone boxes were far from numerous on most estates, e.g. there might be only one box for nearly 1,000 households, and in any case public boxes are so frequently out of order. Moreover on a council estate the phone is still used largely in connection with some personal stress which means that it is more than usually frustrating not to be able to get at one.

The last main facility on which every tenant had something to say concerned the lifts in his block, two metal-lined boxes (3′ 6″ × 4′ 9″ × 7′) with a maximum load of eight persons. The effect of the necessity to use a lift on the siting of facilities is discussed later (Chapter

7). The following paragraphs give the tenants' personal reactions. Life in a multi-storey block has been compared to that on an island where the boat service to the mainland is occasionally suspended for an unknown period or, more often, has spells when it is reduced and uncertain. All of a sudden a lift becomes essential to life and in the case of older tenants they may never have been in one before. Irrespective of age, nearly all had personal sagas to tell which showed what a key part was played by the lift. While no one dismissed the benefits of not having to haul up tenement stairways they gave a strong impression that a lift-ridden existence added to the strains of daily life. This was so even when the lifts in their own block were relatively reliable. This general atmosphere of worry about the lift was probably reflected in the fact that though 62% said they themselves found it satisfactory, they reduced the figure, to 37%, when asked if *other* people did so (Table 25).

All-told it was probably the unpredictability of the thing that was its most maddening feature. When, as in certain blocks, the service was known to be inadequate there was also the constant anxiety "Shall I get on?" But even on the estates where the lifts were relatively reliable there was no rational basis on which to decide whether to wait or walk it. The real crunch came at night when nerves were frayed. This, too, is the time when, as Richard Church points out, some deep-seated need, a primitive anxiety to reach shelter and safety, inflames us all with "an instinctive urge to hurry home".[3]

Complete breakdown due to an external cause such as an electricity failure or a strike is one of the hazards that faces the lift user. Glasgow's 1968 hurricane cut off the electricity in certain blocks. At Red Road some families had the alarming experience of walking down to the ground floor, the children terrified because unfamiliar with the shadows cast by a candle. A few months later a strike of maintenance men meant that, in a number of cases, one of the block's two lifts was out of action for up to three weeks. One mother told how she had to lug a pram and toddler up 18 flights; on another estate a man walked up and down to a 17th floor four times in one day; in another case an invalid had stumbled down 9 flights, unaided but for her two sticks. The lifts also vary in their basic reliability, in the efficiency of their firm's servicing, and in the caretaker's ability to deal with the minor troubles he is authorised to handle. Any block with a high proportion of children is especially vulnerable. There is always a critical stage, the early days of the block's occupation, when both the children of the block and those of the vicinity 'play the lift', using it like a super yo-yo. Trouble also tends to occur when the load is heavy, i.e. when school comes out, and during the holidays. Another strain is caused by the small child who can only reach the button by jumping, using a stick, etc. One real sinner,

[3] *The Voyage Home*, Church, Heinemann, 1964.

in that he holds up the lift, is the milk boy who props its door open with his crate while he collects from perhaps 16 flats. Or on a quiet floor footballers have been known to use the lift cage for a goal!

The necessity to use a lift can have odd repercussions on the tenant's daily life. Somehow one needs to be tidy if going in the lift. Thus it deters people from popping out in their slippers for the odd bit of shopping, or seeing what the kids are up to. Or again, there is the pensioner who, if he has to use the lift, won't bother to take a turn round the estate before the evening sets in. The occasional whiff of fresh air, and the occasional brief spell away from the rest of the household, are useful in terms of health and temper: but they have gone as far as the 'typical' flat-dweller is concerned. That the lift may even dictate the pattern of the tenant's day was shown in the case of the mother who never went out in the afternoon because of the risks of the early evening queues which meant she could not be sure of getting back in time. She was also liable to incur black looks if her pram stopped others from squeezing on to the lift, a matter that did not make for good relationships within the block. The lift's uncertainties had other repercussions. People spoke of the difficulties doctors had in getting to their patients because of lifts not coming, or out of order, and of workmen who went away disgusted with their jobs not done.

It was not easy to determine which the tenants found the more frustrating, total breakdown or time spent in waiting. An architect[4] who made a study of these two points at a 24-storey block at the Summerfield estate, using a multi-pen recorder connected to the lift mechanism, listed the lift's movements for five consecutive weekdays in June 1968, at 7–8 a.m., 10.30–11.30 a.m. and 5–6 p.m. These pen recordings showed that a high percentage of the waiting times were within an acceptable (90-second) limit. His findings suggested that at this particular estate it was breakdown, not waiting time, which was the main nuisance. He interviewed the block's tenants and their experiences supported his finding. He also made a larger study, but on waiting time only, at one of the blocks on each of the five selected estates referred to in Table 2. Employing student observers with stop watches in the lift halls, he got figures on the total use of the lifts between 4.30 and 5.30 p.m. on five consecutive weekdays, December 9th–13th, 1968. This showed that the number of people using the lifts during this one hour on the five consecutive days was 2,230. The large number is worth noting since for all practical purposes these users had no alternative method of reaching the place they wanted. The serviceability of the lifts varied greatly. Assuming a 90-second wait for the user, his chances of getting a lift

[4] Material on lift usage kindly provided by Mr Anthony Warren, Department of Architecture and Building Science, University of Strathclyde. See also Appendix E.

Plate 8

The lift. One family and the lift is full up.
Castlemilk.

within that time ranged from 94% (Wyndford) to 33% (Red Road). On the other estates the figure was 70%, 76% and 77% respectively. Waiting time for a 90% chance, i.e. the period one has to wait 9 out of 10 times for arrival of a car, varied considerably, ranging from roughly a minute and a quarter (Wyndford) to nearly eight minutes (Red Road). At the three other estates it was about 2–3 minutes. The number of persons in the lift, its mean car load, also differed. The lift's official capacity was in all cases 8 persons and in the great majority of the journeys the mean was much below this, rarely exceeding 2 persons. But at Red Road the mean was never less than 6 persons; in one case it rose to nearly 12; and in another to just under 14 persons which is nearly double the official maximum.

What would reduce the problems connected with the lift? Its initial cost is worth emphasising, some £1,300 *per storey* at a rough estimate.[5] Expenditure is to some extent limited by the rulings of the housing cost yardstick. But this, determined on a density and occupancy basis, takes no account of the age structure of the block's population and experience shows how much this can affect wear and tear. Secondly, maintenance is a recurring expense so it is worth experimenting with anything that might lessen the cost.

The following suggestions might be worth exploring. In view of the increasing use of self-operated lifts by large numbers of people, a tougher version should be designed. In particular it should be made more child-proof, e.g. have buttons at a lower level, armoured buttons, and armoured door-closing gear. The Authority should satisfy itself that the maintenance service operates with the minimum of delay. This would also help dispel fears about getting trapped between floors for a long time. Blocks especially subject to trouble, e.g. those with a high proportion of children, should be given an extra-rigorous maintenance service.

If the lift supply has proved grossly inadequate to the needs of the block's population, as is the case in two of the 31-storey blocks at Red Road, might it be possible to attach an additional lift? In Switzerland examples were seen of blocks where, as a fire precaution, the lifts were confined to external ones.

The drill about the proper use of a lift should be firmly established early on. During the initial stages of a block's occupation it would be sound to employ someone whose job included keeping an eye on the lift and lift hall. In these first months the caretaker has too many other responsibilities. Good storage facilities for prams, cycles, trunks, wheeled toys, etc. would lessen congestion on the lift. Lavatory facilities near the base of the block (needed for a variety of reasons) might lessen

[5] Figure based on cost for 2 inter-related lifts for a 19-storey block, calling at all floors and collecting calls on downward journeys only.

misuse of the lift cage. This is particularly troublesome at the weekend when men coming back from the pub use it as a toilet, drunks are sick, etc. The lift plays such a vital role in the tenants' lives that all aspects of its use ought to be not just tolerable but positively satisfactory.

Some of the more nebulous problems connected with the lift, e.g. annoyance over even a brief delay when one is so nearly home, would be lessened if this place where one has to wait about was less boring. It is also poor psychology for this hall, the threshold of home for perhaps 300 people, to be the unwelcoming affair that it is in some types of multi-storey. Since the doors into the lift hall are constantly being opened, should not some form of wall heating be provided? And one solid seat would be a boon. So would anything that gave the place some individuality, showing that this is 'our' block, not just any old one. There is also a strong case for having a board with the names and flat numbers of the block's occupants. How many callers give up and go away because they cannot locate a particular household; and how much unnecessary door-knocking is entailed? S.S.H.A. blocks use such a board but Corporation tenants are said to be opposed to it. Is this really anything more than a lingering memory of primitive beliefs about a man's name being bound up with his life, i.e. something to be kept secret? Perhaps the matter should be thrashed out with the appropriate tenants' association.

The lift hall, which everyone uses and where people often have the odd minutes for chat, is likewise a strategic spot for disseminating information through notices. And again it is poor psychology to confine these to admonitions – "Don't put rubbish . . .", "It is the tenant's duty . . .", "No loitering". The phone numbers of major welfare services, statutory and voluntary, would be useful. As with all the notices they should be in bold enough lettering for older people and the short-sighted to be able to read them. If there is a tenants' association it should have its own board. Since buying and selling is an excellent way to get people acquainted, it might be worth experimenting with a board for small 'want ads'. The immediate riposte to all this is that notices just get torn down. But has there been much experiment with the tenant-sponsored variety, as distinct from the negative, impersonal ones of the Authority? That vandalism is not an insuperable difficulty is shown by the way in which some groups of tenants humanise the lift hall on their own floor by putting down rugs, curtaining windows, hanging plants, etc. Perhaps one or two of the less child-filled blocks might take the plunge about some of the above ideas.

Chapter 6

PHYSICAL CHARACTER OF THE ESTATES:
TENANTS' VIEWS

"It's awful to let it go"

"The average person," said one tenant, "only worries about his flat. The estate never bothers them. So long as they have a bathroom and a bedroom of their own they couldn't care less what it's like." The evidence from the study did not support this view. Though, on balance, the flat mattered more than its setting, people were much concerned about the quantity and quality of their estate's amenities and also about the danger of the place getting down at heel. They quoted earlier Council housing where, for years, the tenants had led a kind of frontier existence and which in some cases had become a social byword. A young wife with a year-old baby and living on the 19th-floor of one of the pleasanter estates took a fairly typical line.

> I like the house. I really do. I like having all the mod. cons. It is quiet. Out of the way. I don't mind the height. And I like having my own house better than living with someone. There are play areas for children but they are all stone. Would be better with grass. And I can't put the wee one out to play on his own. Someone must be there to watch him. I find the sink in the kitchen rather small for doing washing. Some of the newer houses have the floors tiled and walls papered for the people to go in. I don't see why they couldn't all have the same.
> The lifts are quite often off. Once or twice I have had to walk up. They are a bit better now. The kids have started to paint on the walls which annoys me. I feel the houses and blocks could have been finished better. The entrance could have been tiled. The neighbours are very nice although I rarely see them. When anyone is ill a stretcher has to go upright. Same with a coffin. I think the lifts should be bigger.
> It is handy for town. No bother with transport and there are plenty of shops here and it is only 10 minutes from the centre of the city. There is a mothers' club at the clinic. One afternoon they take the kids and you can sit and knit or blether without them. The kids from this block have to cross the access road to get to the

swings but traffic takes a short cut through to Cumberland Street. I feel the playpark should have been enclosed in the scheme. And people come from other places to the nurseries and they aren't taking any more names until next September. Even when my one is older I couldn't let him out as I couldn't get down to him in time if anything was wrong.

In general the location of their estate was regarded favourably since it tended to be fairly near their old home and not too far from the centre of the city. Nor much comment was heard about the desirable size for a multi-storey estate. The fact that the smaller ones were often built on a vacant lot within a built-up area helped to popularise them because the tenants could at once draw on the services of the area. On the other hand the very small estate was often on a steeply sloping site which meant it might not get more than the statutory minimum in the way of play areas, parking space, etc. A site of this kind often involved a lot of climbing, flights of 30 steps, or long diagonal slopes. When ways were slippery old people, invalids and mothers with prams dreaded them. A hilltop site also added to the discomfort from the blustering winds that are liable to surge around a multi-storey wherever it is situated. Studies such as those carried out in a wind-tunnel at the Birmingham School of Architecture show that wind speeds around the base of a tall building may be increased to from two to three times the incoming velocity.

Good transport and reasonably easy shopping were so important to the tenants that these two matters largely determined whether they found their home satisfactory or not. As regards transport, there were endless complaints that no extra buses had been put on to meet the needs of an additional population and that this situation had faced them not just in the early months of the estate but maybe for several years.

Another frequent criticism, and especially so at the larger virgin sites, was the delay in provision of the butcher–baker type of shop quite apart from such things as a chemist, hairdresser, laundrette, hardware store, and post office. In general shops were not built till the housing was finished so that in the larger estate hundreds of people might spend years under semi-camp conditions. Two estates, with some 700 and 500 homes respectively, illustrated the extent of delay. Though both had been occupied for over 5 years they still had no shops nor apparently any likelihood of them. It was a 15–20 minute walk to shops and the bus service was indifferent. At a third estate, where the first block had been occupied for over three years, the 1,000 or so households had a walk that took even the brisker people at least 8 minutes to reach any bus or shops – and the latter were few in number and run-down affairs.

Tenants also complained about the increased cost of shopping. Even when the estate had its own shops these were relatively few, had captive customers and charged accordingly. Moreover, since rents for these new premises were high, the shops were often branches of multiple stores. These did not give the convenient, round-the-clock service of the small, family-run shop. The mobile van had cashed in on these shopless estates but it, too, was more expensive than the ordinary shops, its stock was limited and it had no fixed hours. You shopped under pokey conditions, often had to queue in the rain and altogether found it an indifferent substitute for the kind of service that anyone living in a major city has the right to expect. These Glasgow tenants may have been particularly vocal about shopping inconveniences because the tenement housing to which they had been accustomed often had shops at the foot of the building. You just popped down your own stair to them. Other relevant points both as regards shopping and transport are that these housewives, like most working-class ones, reckoned to shop daily, did not deal with the kind of firm that has a delivery service, and had no car for their own use even among the relatively small number of households which possessed one.

Another matter which the tenants brought up when talking of the satisfactoriness or otherwise of their estate was the need for more places they could use for activities in common – playgrounds, sports facilities, rooms for committee meetings, halls, etc. Their emphasis on these as well as the fact that shops – the market place – have a social value, showed they recognised one of the justifications of urban life, viz. that it meets a deep-seated human need for gregariousness. This matter is discussed later (Chapter 11).

These high-flat tenants were also exceedingly concerned about the looks of their estate. They had so often come from such decayed streets and such dreary districts that perhaps they had unduly high hopes of the new environment – "We'll be able to sit out in the grounds." They were less critical of dull layout, "All the same wherever you turn", than of poor upkeep. And very many were genuinely grieved about deliberate vandalism. Problems in this field are not peculiar to multi-storey housing but the point is that this high-flat population seemed to be aiming at improved standards.

The highly artificial character of the layout of the multi-storey estate demands extra careful upkeep. Since costs here are bound to be high (they are estimated as perhaps equal to that of capital cost if taken for a 20-year period) the planners argue that equal subsidy should be given to both. Problems connected with maintenance can be eased if the initial design of the estate cuts out too many level and exposed areas and concentrates on ones that are semi-concealed. Artificially moulded grass-grown spaces, and playgrounds and car parks screened by a fence of tough shrubs (laurel can be unexpectedly cheerful) help to keep the place tidy. Sizeable trees are an enormous asset, as can be seen in estates where some of the old timber has been preserved. The Parks' Department's splendid tree-planting policy throughout the city of course includes the multi-storey estates. It was noticeable how even a dozen saplings alongside a block helped soften its rough texture and hard lines. Trees also lessen air pollution, give shelter to humans, and bring insects, birds and bird song. Their soft lines and flickering shadows are a relief after the hard angles of the towers and slabs. They likewise give the seasonal variety in colour and shape that is so needed when the earth is clamped down under stone, tarmac and concrete. A bit of lightheartedness might not be a bad idea. How far would a sturdy Virginian creeper climb if faced with a multi-storey! More seriously, why not have some red hawthorn trees at Red Road? Or revive, for this ultra-modern housing, the old custom of the Celts of planting a rowan tree near the house?

> "Rowntree and red thread
> Keeps the devils from their speed"

The tenants were inclined to ascribe any misuse of their estate to vandalism, and to dismiss the wear and tear that is inevitable if there are children about the place. There were, however, endless examples of deliberate damage at many of the estates. They included breaking railings down (for weapons?), tearing out telephone equipment, wrenching the handles off fire safety doors, breaking into the meters of drying cupboards and even smashing the lights on the estate's Christmas tree. There were also quantities of graffiti.[1] They included scrawls up to four feet high; in purple, black, yellow, white and green; and on corridors, garages, ceilings and floors. In fact they could be almost anywhere except, oddly enough, on the door of the individual flat. They were rarely smutty in content. Mostly they related to an individual name or to that of a gang – "S is a stoat", "Up the Fleet", "Young Young Partick", "Jesus Saves, Cadder Kills". Occasionally they harked back to ancient hostilities – "1690" and "F . . . the Pope". Graffiti are said to have long been a feature of down-town Glasgow and a study of today's versions might throw interesting light on modern Glasgow. Meanwhile the point is that vandalism in general costs a mint of money (£195,000 for damage to the city's schools alone in 1967–68) and it is a real distress to those who, as in the case of so many tenants, have to endure its sight every time they go in or out of their own home. Moreover, it puts a stop to so many of the experiments that might be of value to the estate. A case in point relates to the need for a temporary building for small meetings while the estate is shaking down. But any-

[1] See Appendix C.

thing like a wooden hall has to be dismissed, "It would just get vandalised".

Before discussing possible action the following comments may be relevant. The pressure for housing is so great that homes are occupied long before the estate is finished and patterns of rough usage get established because they do not, as yet, matter. Then again, many of the children have been accustomed to semi-derelict property and another stone hurled through a window is neither here nor there. Moreover, the areas where adults expect to be responsible for their children's behaviour have not been firmly established either in the block or on the estate. In the old home each family knew what part of the world outside the home was, roughly, theirs. And the matriarch who had no hesitation about stopping misbehaviour and whose authority was widely respected likewise seems to have gone. Finally, and perhaps more important than any of the above, the city is so short of amenities for young people that any new provision is at risk.

In the Netherlands a small charge for the estate's upkeep is added to the actual rent. It could be that this acts as a weekly reminder that misuse may touch the tenants' own pocket. This is said to be particularly useful in the early years of the estate. Another idea that might be worth experiment would be to try to associate a particular part of the estate with a particular block on the theory that what you own you look after. Some form of low fencing would be needed to define its boundaries and something of interest – a seat and a bit of special planting perhaps. The Winstanley estate of Wandsworth Borough Council found it useful to have caretakers patrolling from 6 to 10 p.m. Could a tenants' association co-operate with the caretaker on a regular job of this kind? And could there be discussion groups between caretakers, the children of the local schools, members of the tenants' association, and officials of the district office of the Housing Management Department? The slant would not be on vandalism but on how we, co-operatively, can improve our estate. At the same time it would be sound to take a good look as to what recreational facilities are available for the youngsters in the surrounding areas. If these are meagre and the housing is unusually poor, there is a strong temptation for them to work off some of their frustrations by wrecking anything that, like a smart new multi-storey estate, contrasts so strongly with the conditions under which they themselves have to live.

The Glasgow tenants' views on a home in a high flat as regards its physical character can be summarised thus. With certain exceptions, notably the family with young children, they found it satisfactory. They thought highly of the flat itself but had many reservations about its setting, particularly as regards long delays in the provision of basic facilities. They were also most concerned that the estate's upkeep should not be allowed to deteriorate. It is important to emphasise that these reactions may have been strongly influenced by such local conditions as these. (*a*) A flat in a 4-storey tenement is not an alien experience. Eighty-three % of the initial sample had lived previously in a tenement-type home. There was no comparable figure from the main sample but only 9% had been in owner-occupied homes (Table 26). Eighty-three % had not had a garden (Table 27). (*b*) Though rent and rates were much higher than in the old home, running costs had not increased markedly (Table 18). Housewives compared their present "one electricity bill and you know where you are" with the fluctuating sums spent on coal, coke, paraffin, gas and electricity in their former home. (*c*) In many cases this had been of poor standard. Figures from the initial sample showed that nearly half the households had come from either a 'single-end' or a 1-bedroom home. (*d*) Many had waited years for a better place. Figures on the 136 households which gave 'homeless or overcrowded' as their reason for being allocated a flat showed that 52 had been on the housing list for over 15 years (Table 5). "We watched the multis grow and each of us dreamed of occupying one some day." (*e*) Well over two-thirds of the households in the sample were adult ones, i.e. were not immediately concerned with problems connected with children (Table 14). (*f*) The fact that people had so often come from bad housing may have made them reluctant to complain about disadvantages that were trivial compared to those they had lived under in the past.

Chapter 7

THE SERVICES AND FACILITIES AT THREE ESTATES

The tenants' complaint, that in many cases the services and facilities on their estate were below standard, was supported by what the research staff knew of the estates as a whole and more particularly of the five selected for special study. The criticism was so widespread that a special study was undertaken at three of them. An examination was made of the extent and quality of the provision actually on the estate and that readily available within a half-mile radius, i.e. within easy walking distance. It was listed and mapped. Another matter examined was whether the necessity to use a lift affected the nature of the services needed. The estates chosen were Albion-cum-Ibrox,[1] Castlemilk and Red Road. Each had a population within a range of roughly 2,000–5,000. They were in different parts of the city and except for their educational provision which was relatively standardised, they had marked disparity as regards transport, shopping and facilities for recreation and cultural activities. They were described briefly in Chapter 3 but the following table gives some additional facts.

Table 7

General information. Albion/Ibrox: Castlemilk: Red Road.

	Albion/Ibrox	Castlemilk	Red Road[2]
Distance from City Chambers	2¼ miles	4¼ miles	2 miles
Date 1st block occupied	1966	1964	1966
Number of blocks	6	5	8
Number of dwellings (m/s+l/r)	648	570	1,356
Multi-storey dwellings as % of total	90%	100%	98%
Acreage	9	15·2	21·6
Estimated population	2450	1,800	4,680
Estimated child (0–15) population as % of total	26%	36%	39%
Density – p.p.a.	204	119	212

[1] Treated as one unit for this particular study since they were less than a third of a mile apart and in much the same type of locality.
[2] Figures expected when estate is completed.

Albion-cum-Ibrox

These six blocks had good *transport* since they were alongside an arterial road. Five Corporation bus services were available and there were two underground stations within half a mile. As regards *shops*, Appendix D shows that the tenants could draw on a wide range. The same held for *public services*. *Recreational provision* included a large (175-acre) public park within the half-mile radius, though its use for the flats' children was limited since they had to cross a main road to reach it. They had minimal playgrounds on the estate itself. One of the city's large new sports halls was within the half-mile. The Rangers' football ground was near-by, bringing thousands of people into the vicinity for short spells. A modern pub stood alongside one group of blocks. No provision was available on the estate itself for *group activities*; but since there were 7 schools and 9 churches within easy walking distance it was normally possible to obtain meeting places.

Castlemilk

The five towers at Castlemilk were disadvantaged in many eyes in that they were 4 miles as the crow flies from the city centre. Three bus services were available but no other public transport. Two quite small groups of shops were within a 10-minute walk and in one case were on bus routes. A good shopping centre could either be reached by bus or by a 20-minute walk. But this latter necessitated a return journey that was steeply uphill and culminated in another sharp climb to the blocks themselves. The estate backed on to 72 acres of wooded banks open to the public so that outdoor *recreational provision* for the children was judged unnecessary. Though there was no pub within the half-mile there were a couple of cafés and a fine community centre became available for the whole area three years after the blocks were built. Two points need emphasising. Except for schools and the dozen or so shops within 10 minutes' walk, practically all the facilities listed in Appendix D involved either a bus ride or a 20-minute walk. Secondly the high-flat population was a minor part of the 40,000 people served by the facilities listed in Appendix D.

Red Road

Before commenting on Red Road these points should be made. The estate was not typical since all of its 8 blocks were exceedingly high. Secondly, almost the whole of the population was housed in high flats. Thirdly, it was commonly acknowledged that the lifts in two of the blocks were inadequate. Lastly, all the flats in these particular blocks had 3 bedrooms which gave an unusually high proportion of children. *Public transport* available within a half-mile radius was practically confined to bus services and these were not on a major route. Few additional services were put on as the estate's population increased. At the date of the facilities listed in Appendix D, which was three years after the first block was occupied, no *shops* had been built. One dim little shop was in existence before the estate was begun but apart from mobile vans the whole of the tenants' shopping either involved a bus journey or a peculiarly dreary walk of over three-quarters of a mile. Even when one reached the shops they were limited in character. They did not, for example, include a drapers, a shoe or furniture shop, a dry cleaners or a hairdressers. As regards *health services* there was no doctor's or dentist's surgery within the half-mile radius and the nearest clinic was more than a mile away. Outdoor *recreational provision* was extremely limited except as regards opportunities for football. No playground had any mobile equipment and there was no pleasant bit of enclosed space for toddlers and their mums. Except for rooms in schools and two small churches which were heavily booked, there was no place within the half-mile where any kind of *group activity* could be held. The initial plans included two schools, a group of shops and considerable provision for play. But by May 1969, and two and a half years after tenants had occupied the first block, only one school had been built and two formal playgrounds had been constructed. In the many visits which the research staff made to the flats at Red Road they rarely came away without feeling depressed, particularly at the thought of children being required to grow up there.

Comment on types of provision as seen at the three estates

Transport. Since bus service frequency is not normally adjusted until a pattern of demand has been established, the early tenants on a big estate may suffer an unsatisfactory service for years. Temporary changes to the service should take place as the population grows.

Shops. In fairly central areas and when the multi-storey population was only between 1,000–2,000, the new estate was satisfactorily serviced by existing provision. However, the new population bolstered up shops which were basically inefficient so that the flats' population had only a poorish service. When the estate was an outlying one or had only meagre existing facilities the tenants were seriously disadvantaged in terms of convenience, time and cost. In such cases mobile vans took advantage of the lack of shops: but this did not provide a substitute for shops proper since they had limited stocks and were not suitable for more than the occasional purchase.

Health and Welfare. Appendix D shows that two of the estates had no provision within the half-mile radius.

Education. The education services, especially as regards primary schools, were introduced more quickly than any other facilities. It was very unfortunate that the new primary school at Red Road was a denominational one since its premises were an obvious place for group facilities and its staff could have played a valuable part in helping to integrate the estate.

Recreational provision. All three areas were relatively near open spaces but this did not obviate the case for imaginative provision for play near the child's home. The only really good facility was for football. No estate had any semi-sheltered play area. It might have been useful to install a mobile lavatory to test whether, as mothers said, this was a genuine need. When the estate's population was too small to support a pub or restaurant, then cafés, snack bars, chip shops, etc. should have been provided. None of the three estates had shops cheek-by-jowl with the flats and in two of them much of the tenants' shopping involved a considerable walk or a bus ride. They also lacked the many features of the traditional urban scene that facilitate casual human contact. Nor had they places really near at hand where any kind of communal activities could take place. And none had any kind of public library service. Thus they tended to be not merely inconvenient but dull places in which to live.

Staff. Some of the troubles caused by the shortage of facilities would probably have been mitigated if local authority staff trained in social welfare and community development had been available. In consultation with the tenants they could have established priorities of need.

Delay. Redevelopment can increase a population a hundred-fold in a matter of weeks and certain types of facility plainly cannot keep pace. On the other hand years of delay in providing such things as a toddlers' play space or a bus shelter are socially inexcusable.

The necessity to use a lift as this affects the provision of services and facilities

The assumption that the facilities needed by estates follow similar patterns to those required in high-density housing of traditional type fails to take account of the effect of the flat-dweller's necessity to use a lift. The tenants' own comments were given earlier (Chapter 5) but additional points must be made.[3] The effective distance from the top flat of a 31-storey (280 feet high) block can, at times, be far greater than the block's actual height. For example, assuming a lift rate of 300 feet

[3] Comment kindly provided by Miss Jean Forbes, Department of Social and Economic Research, University of Glasgow.

a minute and a delay at rush hours of 20 minutes, the time distance by lift for someone who has to get from top to ground is 20 × 300 feet, or 6,000 feet. Again, assuming a walking rate of 15 minutes a mile (a speed unlikely to be reached when climbing stairs) it takes 12 minutes to get from the ground to a top-floor flat. Thus in terms of time distance on foot the block is not 280 feet but ¾ mile in height! These are extreme examples but the necessity to use a lift adds a dimension to the daily life of everyone whose home is above the 5th or so floor. Dismissing waiting time connected with actual break-down (which is not infrequent and often necessitates calling in a mechanic who does not live locally) that generally held to be acceptable is about 90 seconds. However it is never possible to rely on this since many factors, e.g. heavy usage at rush hours or furniture being moved into the block, may lengthen it. It is, however, less the length of the wait, though one of 20 or more minutes is by no means uncommon in some blocks, than its unpredictability which is the constant irritant. The uncertainty is particularly frustrating when the user is in a job which has fixed hours which means he travels at peak periods. The problem is intensified when he has to rely on public transport. In his case this necessity to use a lift puts him at a positive disadvantage as regards time-keeping, bonuses, etc. Whoever the user, this need to take a lift affects almost all his activities that take place at ground level. It makes shopping more laborious so that the shop to which the housewife goes daily should be extra easily accessible. It also argues the case for G.P.O. services to be extra near at hand. The introduction of high flats suggests that the G.P.O. should re-examine its regulations governing its services. This is especially so in the case of public telephones. In this connection it is worth noting that the police do not patrol a multi-storey block. The fact that the medical world is questioning whether multi-storey life puts additional strains on life suggests that such services as a branch health and welfare clinic should also be easily accessible. A mobile library service which could be stationed at the very foot of the block would be particularly useful since multi-storey life tends to keep people like pensioners and the mother with small children so housebound. This is a facility which could easily be set up in the very early days of the estate. The lift also adds to the many problems which stem from the physical limitations of the flat and the general lack of opportunities for social contacts in multi-storey life. This argues the case both for extra generous provision for recreation and for it to be easily accessible. The matter is discussed further in Chapters 8, 9, 10. A final point to mention is that in general the planning of a multi-storey estate demands more care as regards services and facilities than is the case with traditional housing. Really effective afterthought, difficult in any type of estate, is particularly so in the case of high flats because of the restricted nature of the site.

Chapter 8

THE OLDER TENANTS

"If only someone would knock on the door more often"

This chapter and the two succeeding ones examine Glasgow's high flats in terms of how they suited households of different 'types'. Take, for example, the elderly couple. Was a high flat just a place where they lasted out the end of their days, or did this type of home make it that much more likely they would really live them? The prospect of moving to a multi-storey was no theoretical matter for the Glasgow pensioner since figures from the study showed that at July 1968 11% of the flats' population was aged 65 or over which was the same percentage as that for the city (Table 15 and Census 1966). Of all the households 14% were those of pensioners only (Table 14). Translating this into individuals, it represented some 2,200 women and 1,300 men. Since nearly every block had a certain number of small-sized flats there were pensioners in most blocks and in some of them a considerable number. At Balgrayhill, for example, the 4 multi-storey towers (25, 26 storeys) each had as many flats with only 2 apartments as it had of larger ones; and at Wyndford 4 blocks (26 storeys) contained nothing larger than a 1-bedroom flat.

Apart from the small number of older people living in blocks built chiefly for pensioners, how in general did the older tenants like the life? The answer is that the type of households classed as 'elderly' showed much the same amount of overall satisfaction (94%) as did the adult households in general (Table 20). When individual schedules were examined these too gave an impression of contentment though these older people did make a good many references to problems. The following examples of their comment are taken from the schedules of five interviews picked at random from those households of the initial sample which comprised or contained a pensioner. The first was that of an elderly widow living with her daughter; the second, that of a couple in their mid-70s. Both said they were very content. At the next household a husband and wife in their late-60s said that in general things were very good. The road to the shops and lack of a public callbox were really the only drawbacks. A different story came from the next household. Here the occupant, a widower of 80 and in the flat for three years, had definitely "never taken on with it since I came. You are frightened to burn the fire and the rent is so dear . . . I just didn't want to come but I'll finish my days here." There was another unhappy tenant, a widow of 82, in the final household. "I had nowhere else to go, and I'm too old to bother about shifting again. I wish I was back in my wee room and kitchen where you were able to meet people and you knew everybody round about. Here you don't know a soul and nobody bothers about you."

Another angle on pensioners' reactions came from the casebooks of a social work agency. These too suggested that on the whole multi-storey life was pretty satisfactory. There was, for example, the spinster (68) who had moved from a single, service room to a 17th-floor flat. She was delighted with it, had sold her heavy, old-fashioned furniture, purchased modern stuff and seemed to have one problem only, the high electricity bills. The agency's account of the reactions of another household, a couple in their mid-70s who had previously lived in a room-and-kitchen in badly deteriorated property with an outside w.c. was as follows:

> After 57 years in the same house, and a great longing for a new one on the wife's part for many years (the husband was averse to change), they were eventually rehoused on the 13th floor of a multi-storey. The health of both deteriorated dramatically and they lost interest in living. Loss of contact with familiar things, with routine, with known faces, left them with a sense of suspended insecurity which the new luxury of mod. cons. did nothing to dispel for a time. Anxiety over the cost of maintaining the new-fangled flat was a cause of great tension. The wife, however, . . . now finds to her surprise that she is managing the monthly payments of rent, electricity and gas. The couple were taken to visit a friend in their old district a week or two ago, and have now lost all sentimental longing for going back. . . . Looking forward now to meeting people when the weather is warmer in the courtyard below where seats are provided.

Though views were diverse the above material suggested that on the whole these older people found multi-storey life suited them. This was certainly the impression which the research staff gained from their many informal contacts with pensioner households. At the same time, and as will be argued later, it was essential that safeguards should be provided. It is, of course, an almost insoluble problem to construct any valid standard against which to weigh 'satisfactory' as regards someone else's life. The generally accepted test as to whether old people are reasonably well in the widest sense of the word seems to be related to how far they feel themselves still part of the community. Or have they opted out? In the case of the pensioner in a high-flat, 'community' mostly means any relations with whom they keep in touch and the other households on their own floor. Bearing these broad matters in mind, what had multi-storey life to offer them?

"I have no doubts" (about living in a high flat) "I am very very comfy" was how an elderly widow expressed it and the comfort of the home was something they talked about continually. The place was so easy to keep warm, there was hot water, the toilet was inside the house, and to have a bathroom and an elegant one at that was sheer delight. There were no steps to trip over and the absence of stairs was a boon after a lifetime of hauling up and down the old tenement. This was especially so for the stouter woman of whom Glasgow has many. Moreover, since old people tend to lose height as well as agility, they appreciated the fact that the shelves, electric light bulbs, windows, etc. of the new flat were easier to reach than those of the high-ceilinged rooms of the old tenement home. This easier housekeeping also meant they did not have to rely so much on other people and thus they felt more independent. After the murkiness of so much of the old housing they enjoyed the brightness of the flat. And they greatly valued the view.

Glasgow has no policy about keeping pensioners to any particular floor as regards height though one in four were found to be living between ground and sixth floor (Table 28). The pensioner households who were consulted in the main sample had much the same views on floor height as those of the adult households in general, i.e. they were content with their existing floor. At some of the multi-storey estates visited in London, e.g. those of the G.L.C. and of Wandsworth Borough, pensioners were given the lower floors if housed in high flats at all. On the other hand at a block of 130 pensioners' flats visited in Lucerne they were said to prefer the higher floors. Perhaps the fact that the Glasgow pensioners were so accustomed to tall buildings, and that they now had a lift, made them relatively easy to please as regards floor height. They were, however, bothered about noise and it was noted how often the word 'peaceful' came into their talk. Since they spent much of their life indoors and mostly went to bed early it was important that their flat should not be situated where there was noise from a playground or the lift or a rubbish chute. Another point they spoke of often was security, a matter of real concern in Glasgow. Provided their flat was not one where an external balcony could give access through a window they felt physically safe in a multi-storey.

The physical proximity of the other homes on one's floor and the tenants' tendency to regard their floor as a unit may mean that the older tenant gets better care from neighbours than in traditional housing. It is helpful if the floor contains households of various sizes and ages. One thoroughly unsuitable location was in a top (22nd) floor

Plate 9 A 15th-storey home, Bogany Terrace, Glasgow.

which necessitated a climb of 30 stairs beyond the lift. This floor had 5 flats, 3 for a couple and 2 for a single tenant. Provided there are reasonably reliable people on the pensioner's own floor they need not be "what you'd call neighbours", with all this phrase implies. But however helpful those living alongside, there is a strong case for trying to move older people in some sort of local group, or with a related household. A case in point at one of the Hutchesontown blocks was an elderly lady who had a flat on the same floor as that of a married son and his two children. She was on the 16th floor and rarely went out but she had the run of both homes, the boys nipped in and out, and the two households were of mutual help. The Corporation has done a good deal of quite local rehousing in this particular area and the research staff certainly gained the impression that the high flats here were less anonymous places than those in many other parts of the city.

Another matter about which the older people talked, and especially those living alone, was the difficulty of summoning help. Only 15% of the 1-person households had a phone (Table 17), no block had a public call box and there was considerable variation between blocks as to how far tenants felt they could ask their caretaker to use his phone. The possibility of getting help from the other households on one's floor was limited. The number of flats on the floor was often small (it might be as few as two in a split-level block) and people were out a lot. In any case one might not be capable of getting to the hall door. Nor was there always a party wall on which one could try to tap. Two cases which occurred within a few days of each other and in just one block were as follows. A lady of 71, an arthritic, found herself unable to get out of her bath and was trapped there from 9–12 p.m. She was badly bruised in her efforts to get up and obviously had a most alarming experience. Three weeks later she was still shaky. In the other case the pensioner had fallen in the evening and lain all night on the floor of her flat. Quite apart from physical harm, a great deal of anxiety would be relieved if some method of calling help was provided. The various systems which operate in group dwelling schemes for old people imply staffing problems which inhibit their use for the ordinary multi-storey block. But perhaps an alarm light from flat to base of block could be installed. This would at least indicate the floor where help was needed. Or would it be feasible to adapt to multi-storey use the alarm system installed by the Reliance Telephone Company at, to quote an example, a group of old people's low-rise homes in Rutherglen? A bell from each home connects to that of a volunteer, one of the more able-bodied among the estate's residents. When this rings an indicator tells him who is calling, he goes across to the flat, finds out what is wrong and if necessary telephones for the relevant help. This simple service is used extensively, especially in winter. The volunteer is given a free telephone from the

Authority, the system is not costly to install, and the Medical Officer of Health regards it as very satisfactory.

The first few months of the new home could be particularly difficult for the pensioner. Moving house, an upset to anybody, is doubly so to those set in their ways, with no spare cash for emergencies and when the new surroundings have so many unfamiliar features as a high flat. The ballot as to which floor their flat would be on, followed by that hurried first sight of the place that was likely to be their home for the rest of their lives, was the first of many strains. Notes made on a ballot that was believed to be fairly typical read as follows:

> The prospective tenants began to assemble in the base of the block about 9 a.m. By 9.40 or so some 70 people had arrived, mostly middle-aged. Latecomers crowded in during the next half hour and it must have been difficult for them to hear the proceedings. Two officials, one from the Corporation, one from the S.S.H.A., addressed the tenants briefly, introducing the caretaker, reminding people about not keeping pets, the need to avoid bulky packages in the chutes, and other domestic matters. The senior officer, a young man, then took a roll call – "John Brown?" "Here": "Mrs. McDonald?" "Present". He then described the balloting method, explaining that mutual, on-the-spot exchanges were permitted. Tenants with special health priority would have the choice of flats on the first three floors. These would be balloted for first. A ballot slip, $\frac{1}{2}'' \times 2''$ of flimsy typescript on which was the flat number and its floor, e.g. 24D, was drawn by each applicant as his name was called. There was a great deal of talk, noise and excitement and the official had to ask for order several times. The actual drawing occupied perhaps 40 minutes. Each tenant (as called out) then went up to the first floor to sign the necessary documents, collect his rent book and a bunch of six or so keys. He then moved to a neighbouring room where an official of the Electricity Board asked him about types of payment, etc. The above took perhaps ten minutes. He then made his own way to whatever flat he had drawn, unlocked the door and had his first exciting sight of what was to be his future home. At 11.30 there were still 20 or so tenants who had drawn their number but had not yet started on the other proceedings.
>
> The officials, about 8 in number, together with an 'unofficial' sales girl from some dairy who was taking orders for milk delivery, were pleasant in their handling of the tenants. But the atmosphere was tense and worried. The place was crowded and people on the fringe had difficulty in hearing. Some were standing as long as $2\frac{1}{2}$ hours. One invalid with a stick was helped out of the crowd and

given a chair in a draughty passage. An hour later she was still sitting there. The noise, press and difficulty some had in reading what was on the vital slip, and the long waiting made for a distracted atmosphere. It was not a good introduction to a new home and, in many cases, a new landlord.

Another thing to which pensioners had to get accustomed was the lift. In general they seemed to cope with this pretty well and it was exceptional to find someone like the widow (75) with a middle-aged son who was so nervous of it that she had not been out since she moved to the flat nearly two years before. Once installed, they had to learn to cope with numerous unfamiliar but essential objects, the chute, new electric equipment, a new type of window to open, new keys, a new place in which to dry their laundry. The elementary problems of any new home, like changing a light fitting or fixing a hook, might be major ones for them. They would also want to come to some sort of terms with the other people, perhaps twenty new faces, on their own floor. And they were inevitably involved in one new relationship, that with the caretaker. The cost of this new home was another anxiety. Even though one might have a rebate it could be alarming just to think about the enormous increase. For example, the rent paid by the widow and daughter referred to earlier (p. 70) had risen from £2 to £7·25 a month; that of the 80-year-old widower from 55½p to £6·82. The horror tales of alarming electricity bills which go the round of any new block were particularly frightening to old people. They had already met expenses connected with new furniture and had they previously lived with, or near, relatives who helped them with their washing, this was another cost. If they had no helpful relatives or friends to turn to they might worry on about such things for months. All told there would seem to be a strong case for the Authority or some voluntary agency to provide staff whose job it would be to help the older tenant settle into the new life. Might it be possible to adapt to their particular needs something on the lines of an experiment made by a Citizen's Advice Bureau in conjunction with the Camden Borough Council at their Dorney Tower high flats? The C.A.B. set up a temporary office in the block as soon as it was occupied, to offer their help to tenants, to try to develop the C.A.B. as a neighbourhood service, and to see if a baby-sitting scheme might speed up the rate at which new tenants got to know each other. Reviewing the situation, the C.A.B. felt the experiment had justified itself as regards its two first objectives but not the third.

How did a multi-storey home suit that crucial matter, the need to keep pensioners independent by enabling them to do their shopping? Compared with the old street the estate's roads were traffic free which lessened the small crises that face old people every time they need to cross an ordinary road. The argument for having services and facilities *on* the estate was particularly important for these older tenants who had neither the energy nor money to go far afield. A good bus service helped with shopping and meant they did not feel too cut off from their old neighbourhood. It also mattered more to them than to younger people that the path from their block to the exit from the estate should be as direct as possible, not, as was noted in one case, requiring some 124 unnecessary paces. The paths about the estate itself might need stout handrails and if long and steep, an occasional seat. The pensioner might also be tempted to get out of doors for a breather if the estate itself was a pleasanter place. Something on the lines of a seafront shelter, a place where even in winter one can avoid the wind and catch any sun going, would cost money to maintain but would surely be worth experiment. A lavatory for the estate would be another provision that might be especially useful for older men. The value of an inexpensive cinema should not be overlooked. For some old ladies 'the pictures' may have been almost their only recreation in earlier life and socially the cinema is even less demanding than an O.A.P. club.

In discussing the pros and cons of a high flat as a home that helps the older tenant to feel *in* the community the following points are relevant. These older tenants have often come from a home which they have shared with their grown-up children or other relatives. Now they are likely to be just one of a couple, or by themselves.[1] In the Balgrayhill study, for example, 24 of these 30 older households had had more people in their previous home than the new one. Then again, the Glasgow pensioners had often lived in the old one so long that they knew many people even if only by sight. Ten of the above 30 had been in their former home for 40 years and in one case for 75. One pensioner told an interviewer who called on a Wednesday that she had not seen anyone since the previous Saturday. Another, who led an active life compared to many of the pensioners in her block, said how depressing she found it to go to bed and realise you'd not spoken to anyone since you got up. One obvious way in which to counter isolation is to help people *see* as much of the outside world as a multi-storey permits. Thus the windows of their flat should be low and not, as in some blocks (presumably to make space for furniture) as much as 5 feet from the floor. Many of the 1-person flats have no balcony, or if there is one then too often its wall is concrete or clouded glass so that one cannot see out when sitting down. Efforts to get tenants to treat the hall of their floor as

[1] The Glasgow pensioner may be unusually short of relatives since younger people moved away from the city in large numbers during the 1930s. A 1968 study of pensioners in Rutherglen, contiguous to Glasgow and not dissimilar socially, found 1 in 4 of the total sample of 1,232 old people living alone and 1 in 5 with no children, or children who lived too far away for much visiting.

a kind of common room have had little success, perhaps because there is no specific reason why one should frequent the place. Would some organisation like a Church or the W.V.S. experiment (in a block which has many older tenants) with a kind of pedlar's pack service stationed on one of the floors? By no means all pensioners have the milkman or paper boy call so that, however few the goods stocked, this service would enable them to get such things as tonight's *Citizen* or the odd tin of soup. If it could cope with things that are heavy to carry, like potatoes, that would be fine. A few seats about the place and a wall heater would be welcome. Its prime purpose would be to give the elderly, especially those who live alone, something and someone to look forward to for that day anyhow. It might even prove to be a useful alternative to voluntary 'visiting' which so often breaks down and is anyhow disliked by some tenants.[2]

Another service to lessen the anonymity of high flats is, of course, through such things as Day Centres, O.A.P. clubs, etc. At least one pensioners' club was probably within reach for most of the estates but it was not likely to be held more than once a week. "The only time we meet each other is if we are going up or down in the lift ... there should really be a place for folks to meet and talk and have a sing song," was the comment from a couple in a 10th-floor flat that was echoed by many others. The G.L.C.'s policy on meeting places for pensioners is worth referring to. Irrespective of the type of dwelling the Council, using its housing powers, provides either club rooms or common rooms for casual use. For the former almost the only requirement is that the group of old people's dwellings shall exceed 40 units. In such cases provision is virtually automatic, the premises being built, furnished and let at a very low rent to the pensioners' club on somewhat similar lines to those for a tenants' club room (Chapter 11). Should the number of dwellings be less than 40, then a common room only is built and this is rent free. In size it is the area of one flat and it has a sitting-room-cum-lounge with one corner partitioned off for tea-making.

Fellow tenants can, of course, give a great deal of neighbourly care to the pensioner. A case in point was a social club on one of the multi-storey estates which had a band of 'collectors', each of whom was responsible for the tenants on several floors in his block (Appendix F3). Unless asked not to do so he called weekly at every flat (not only those of pensioners) offering a ticket for one or another of numerous varieties of inexpensive raffle. The club's 1967 winter programme included a pensioners' Christmas party, invalids' parcels, a men's smoker, a theatre night, a pantomime, a children's party, and gifts to any tenant's child permanently confined to hospital. The relevance of all this to the older tenant was that certain able-bodied individuals were in *regular* touch

[2] *Old and Alone*, Tunstall, Routledge & Kegan Paul. 1960.

with pretty well every pensioner in their own block. Living on the spot they have more time to linger than has the visitor from a distance and since their social background is much that of the pensioner both sides can communicate easily.

However valuable this neighbourly help, the fact that in a high flat old people may have such a very isolated life means that there is more need for a professionally watchful eye than in a home of traditional type. As said earlier, there should be someone to keep an eye on things in the first few months. Care by a trained worker may also be wanted in a crisis, for example when one of a couple dies. Though individuals age at very different rates, extra care is likely to be wanted from about 75 onwards. This may be especially valuable for the kind of old person who obviously requires but rejects any offer of help. The O.A.P. club that really seeks out and caters for the most needy probably requires some full-time staff. Another important aspect of the job of the professional worker is that he can assess where existing services should be strengthened or expanded. For example, might it be possible to upgrade and train a section of the Home Help Service? Recent studies have suggested that more effort should also be made to explore fresh sources of voluntary help.[3] It would be interesting to see whether the multi-storey estate is not one of those ready to be tapped. One method of recruitment would be to offer short, simple training courses, held actually on the estate. They would include a little elementary psychology about ageing, and make known what services are available. Such a course might produce not only voluntary help but a limited number of people – ex-nurses, ex-ambulance men, capable housewives – who, with some further training, could be employed on a part-time basis for more intensive work.

To summarise. Glasgow's high flats appeared to make quite a good home for older people provided certain important precautions were observed. It was less clear whether, whatever the precautions, they were satisfactory for the pensioner who lived alone. An essential for peace of mind was that the older tenant, or anyone who was often housebound, should have some means of summoning help. It was also very desirable that full advantage should be taken of the balcony and that windows should not be placed too high in the wall. Since older people may be slow about striking up acquaintance with strangers, it was desirable that the block should contain at least a few households who had lived relatively near each other in the past. Even if they had not known each other this gave them common talking points. Whatever the type of block, it was probably sound to include some older people in its popu-

[3] *The voluntary worker in Social Services,* Aves, Allen & Unwin, 1969. *Planning and Local Authority Services for the Elderly,* Sumner and Smith, Allen and Unwin, 1969.

lation. Apart from anything else it meant that the block was less 'dead' in working hours. On the other hand the block so designed that it housed none but the middle-aged and elderly produced a concentration of older people that runs counter to today's policy of keeping the pensioner *in* the community. So many features of life in a multi-storey block make for a feeling of isolation that every care should be taken to try and counter this in the case of the older tenant who spends much of his time at home. Good physical provision is no guarantee against the loneliness that may lead to an existence that is "dead, dumpish and sour". It is unlikely that the necessary precautions will be taken to make this new type of home suitable for the pensioner unless a certain number of professionally trained staff are responsible for their care. In the case of the multi-storey population it seems probable that the work of the professional could be eased by skilful recruitment and training of voluntary, and to a lesser degree part-time paid help, from the estate itself.

Chapter 9

FAMILIES WITH CHILDREN

"My house is high up"

The children in general

Among the 18th-century tombstones in the old Gorbals burial ground and almost under the shadow of enormous multi-storey blocks is a memorial to a child. It speaks of her as "gifted with most endearing sensibility and goodness of heart". Something of this same feeling for childhood was reflected in the Glasgow tenants' almost universal comment that high flats were "nae use for the bairns". Whether the speakers were young parents or ancient grandads they seemed to feel instinctively that multi-storey life was somehow alien to the children. So did most of the Glasgow doctors, psychologists and social workers consulted in this study, and the housing officials, architects and sociologists met with here and abroad. It was noted that the literature on the social aspects of multi-storey housing mostly concentrated on the children and generally with misgivings.[1] "By far the most serious problem is to provide adequately for the recreational needs of children living in the flats" was one of the conclusions reached in *Housing Management in Scotland*.[2] Van der Eyken, writing of a high tower as an essentially anti-child environment, points out that it requires a type of behaviour which is acquiescent, silent, restrained – the antithesis of childhood.[3] He contrasts this with the normal child's delight in keeping pets and with his small joys in such things as rushing outside at the first fall of snow, or whooping round a bonfire. Play, active and imaginative, is life to the child, the means by which he learns. To pen him in so that he is short

---

[1] *Flats and Houses 1958: design and economy*, Ministry of Housing and Local Government, H.M.S.O. 1958 (out of print).
Living in flats, Central Housing Advisory Committee, Ministry of Housing and Local Government, H.M.S.O. 1952 (out of print). *Two to Five in High Flats, op. cit. Children's Play on Housing Estates*, Hole, H.M.S.O. 1966. *0–5: A report on the care of pre-school children*, Yudkin, National Society of Children's Nurseries, 1967. *The Springburn Study, op. cit. High Living, op. cit. Children and Planning*, 'Town and Country Planning', Oct.–Nov. 1968. *Planning for Play*, Lady Allen of Hurtwood, Thames & Hudson, 1968. *Children's Play*, Holme and Massie, Michael Joseph, 1970.

[2] *Op. cit.*

[3] *The Pre-School Years*, Van der Eyken, Penguin, 1967.

Plate 10. An estate composed almost entirely of high flats. Red Road, Glasgow.

of experiences and challenges is a serious deprivation. Bertrand Russell argues that the thwarted child runs the risk of becoming an unhappy adult, one who aims at distraction not satisfaction.[4] The special quality of these initial years and their flying hours also needs to be borne in mind. In adult life a particular situation, for example a love affair, can generally be repeated; the childhood years are irrecoverable. One wonders what sort of an "I remember, I remember" picture of his early life in a multi-storey will be drawn by the man who writes his autobiography in the 2020s? Despite the fears, little hard statistical evidence has been obtained in this country or elsewhere about the effects of this new type of home on children, nor has this Glasgow study added much. There were certainly no overt signs that their health suffered. Indeed parents stressed the advantage of the sunny, clean and warm home though of course modern low-rise housing can provide such things equally well.

The main sources of information on the children were as follows. Numerous questions related to them were asked in the interviews of the initial and main 5% samples. This brought in material from about 1,000 households. Even when not directly connected with children, most of the minor studies included some material on them and certain ones concerned them specifically. These studies were undertaken at a number of the estates and at several of the near-by primary schools. As regards the under-5s, a good deal of information came from small discussion groups with mothers held at the 5 selected estates and from 18 months' observation of how the mothers at one of them, Royston, tackled the setting up of a playgroup. Practical problems connected with the estate's children cropped up continually at tenants' associations, and casual talk with people at their homes nearly always came round to the children, if not their own then those of their estate. Other information came from children themselves. Even when no great shakes at writing they had definite ideas on what makes a good place to play.

The basic facts about the multi-storeys' child population were as follows. The July 1968 sample of households showed the 143 blocks to contain some 6,700 children under 15. This was 20% of the total multi-storey population as compared with the 26% in the city as a whole (Census 1966). The blocks' under-5 population, 2,400, was 7% compared with the 9% of the city (Table 6). Thus the popular image of the high-flat child as one not yet old enough for school was mistaken. As regards household structure, there was marked difference between that of the flats and of the Corporation's tenants in general as found in 1965.[5] In the flats there were 175 households, 27% of the total sample, which had 1 or more children aged 0–15 inclusive. Forty-seven of the 175 had 1 or more aged 0–4 inclusive, and 42 had all their children of

---

[4] *Conquest of Happiness*, Russell, Allen & Unwin, 1930.
[5] *A Profile of Glasgow Housing*, op. cit.

this age (Table 14). *A Profile of Glasgow Housing* (to draw some comparison) showed that 46% of the total of the Authority's households had 1 or more persons aged 0–5, and 19% had 3 or more children of this age.[6] In the 5 selected estates the proportion of the child to the adult population differed markedly (Table 29). At Wyndford about 1 in 8 of the population was aged under 15; at Red Road (in the blocks then occupied) the figure was 1 in 2·5. Figures for the sample as a whole indicated that each of the 4-year cohorts of the 0–19 population was of roughly equal size. This was interesting since it showed that this new type of housing had not the distortion, e.g. the 16% aged 15–19, shown in much of Glasgow's postwar housing.[7] As regards where the children lived in the block, 79% had their home above the fourth floor (Table 30, Diag. 4).

The official provision for outdoor play, normally not less than 20–25 square feet per person,[8] varied so much from estate to estate that generalities are misleading. It may be more useful to quote as example what was available on one of the 5 selected estates (Albion) where the estimated child population of its 3 blocks was 155. As recorded by a social studies student in March 1967, the children had the run of the following – a paved area under each of the blocks (20 × 10 yards); an asphalt approach to garages (100 × 50 yards); an official playground from which equipment had been removed (20 × 10 yards); a red blaes football kickabout (20 × 15 yards). Dismissing for the moment the under-5s and the over-11s where in general did the intensive players, those of primary school age, play? Seven-year-olds from Royston, asked to write about this, mentioned "out on the veranda or on the landing", "enterance", "I play on the ground floor", "at a pinch", or even "We don't play in our block of flats". Playgrounds with static objects like tunnels, climbing frames, etc. in concrete and metal were not particularly well used, except in the case of slides. When school was out any equipment that moved was nearly always busy. So were the boys' kickabouts. A sad little "They have taken away the swings" occurred in one form or another in many of the children's writing. There is a strong case for including some movable play things on pretty well every estate. On the whole more activity probably took place around the estate in general than on the official playgrounds. To the casual observer there seemed a great deal of what looked like just rushing about or, at the other extreme, of doing nothing at all. The preponderance of boys and the absence of toys was noted. Maybe the

[6] *A Profile of Glasgow Housing*, op. cit.
[7] *Time of One's Own*, Jephcott, University of Glasgow Social & Economic Study, Oliver & Boyd, 1967.
[8] *Homes for Today and Tomorrow*, Ministry of Housing and Local Government, 1961

children are not so keen on taking something like a doll's pram down to ground where, with few grown-ups about, it can easily be filched or damaged. It is also a bother to the child and may be a nuisance to adults in the lift.

The children aged 5-10

As said earlier (Chapter 3) it had not been intended to do much work on the children but in the event it proved unrealistic not to consider the innumerable problems they raised. Thus their needs were borne in mind throughout the study though the only detailed investigation was one in which an honours psychology graduate examined the population of a primary school at which 47 of its 257 children lived in high flats. She was in close contact with both staff and children, and used written and verbal tests, drawings, tape recordings, etc. Though there were many weaknesses in the study (e.g. the children from the low-rise homes were living in particularly bad housing and the numbers in the two sets were unequal) she was confident that the multi-storey group did not show any retardation. The staff's own assessment of the two groups was that in health and attendance, academic attainment, and social development the high-flats children were rather superior. On the other hand they came from better-off families as was shown in the fact that just one of the flats' children was receiving free meals compared with 80 from the low-rise homes. The comment of this school on its attendance figures was borne out by those from three primary schools in other parts of the city where record was kept for six weeks. This showed little difference between the children from the high flats and those from traditional-type homes.

Before discussing some of the play problems connected with the children of primary school age (which in general meant those connected with their outdoor play) it may be useful to bear in mind the following points. (*a*) Today's children are taller, heavier and more robust than those of earlier generations which may well mean they are harder in terms of wear and tear on the environment and the amount of noise they are liable to make. (*b*) Now that families are smaller they have fewer domestic jobs in the home, and in high flats the really big family is rare. (*c*) Urbanisation is continually restricting the areas available for their play and limiting what they may legitimately do. In multi-storey housing their play is hedged in by negatives – you mustn't play in the hall, chalk on the pavement, make a see-saw on that wall, cycle on this path. Moreover, the places where the child plays are becoming more exposed to public view. Parents contrasted the relative privacy of their old backcourts and 'our street' with the openness of the estate which had few defined spots to which their child had his own right. (*d*) The

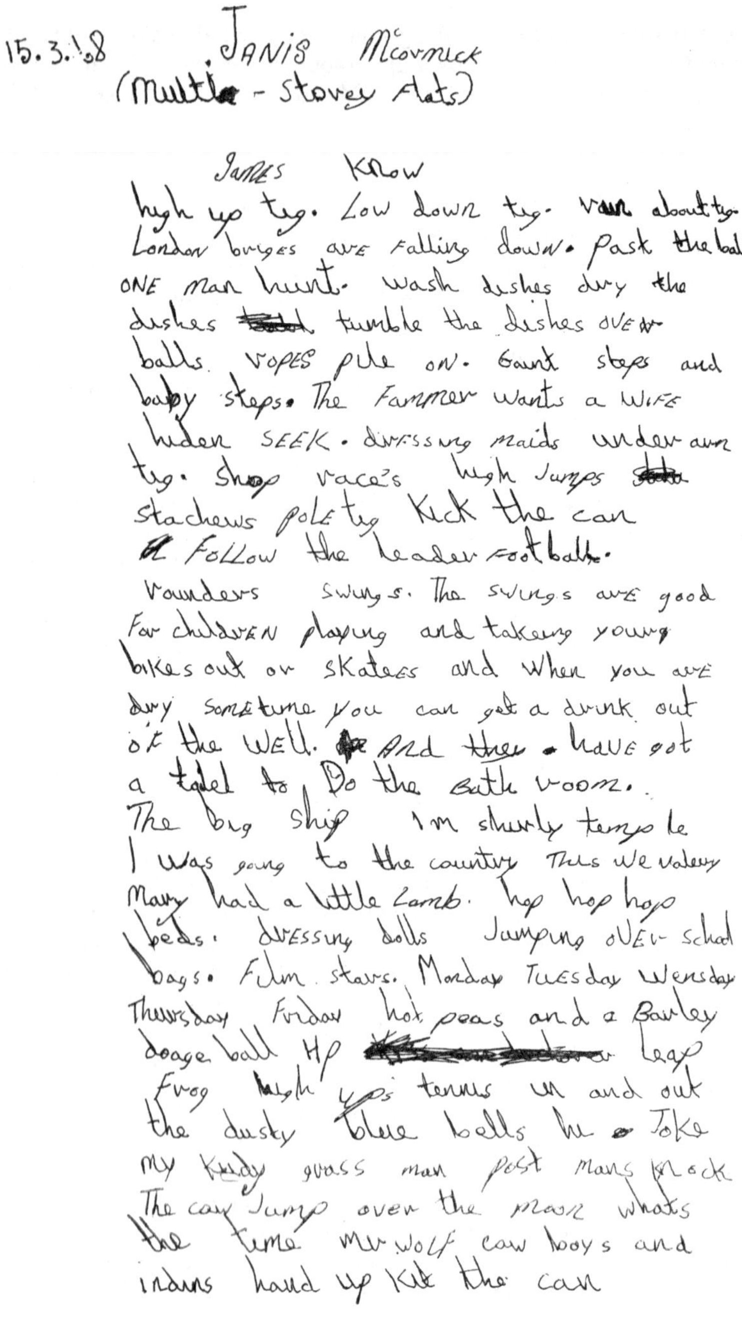

15.3.68 Janis McCormick
(Multi - Storey Flats)

James Know
high up tig. Low down tig. Van about tig.
London bridges are falling down. Pass the ball.
One man hunt. Wash dishes dry the
dishes tumble the dishes over
balls ropes pile on. Giant steps and
baby steps. The Farmer wants a wife
hide n seek. dressing maids under arm
tig. Shop races. high jumps
statues pole tig kick the can
Follow the leader football.
rounders swings. The swings are good
for children playing and taking young
bikes out or skates and when you are
dry sometime you can get a drink out
of the well. And they have got
a toilet to Do the bath room.
The big ship I'm shirly temple
I was going to the country this we value
Mary had a little lamb. hop hop hop
beds. dressing dolls Jumping over school
bags. Film stars. Monday Tuesday Wensday
Thursday Friday hot peas and a Barley
doage ball Hp legs
frog high ys tennis in and out
the dusty blue bells he Joke
my Kndy grass man post mans block
The cow jumps over the moon whats
the time Mr wolf cow boys and
indians hand up kick the can

Fig. 7.

multi-storey estate demands a setting that is spick-and-span and this is what the adult longs to maintain since he has so often come from a down-at-heel area. The children are unconcerned with such niceties. What they need is a place and things they can *use*. (*e*) The open, tidy estate makes a most inferior setting for play compared with the variety of the street, its passages, old walls, derelict buildings, culs-de-sac, stairways, unexpected corners. Children are natural foragers but where, on a multi-storey estate, is the flotsam and jetsam which is treasure-trove to the child – an old door, a cardboard carton, a plank, a bucket, a length of rope?

Since play is an infinitely subtle affair and one about which grown-ups know little, it may be useful to hear what children themselves had to say. Written comment was culled from primary school children who lived in various types of housing. 'Games I know' produced lengthy lists even from those no great shakes at writing (See Fig. 7.) Their views on what makes a good place to play ranged from that of the romantic who opted for "a misterous maze or a gosht train", to that of the mild little girl who said "I just like sitting down and getting sunburnt". A place with no glass or gangs was judged good. They rated parks highly, enjoyed being able to dig there, talked about the trees, ponds and ducks and appreciated that "you can move around in all the space". Their constant reference to "ornary grass" emphasised that, compared with grown-ups, children are more often in direct contact with the ground. Dangers from traffic were often mentioned, "You mite get nocked down" wrote one, and "Don't play in the raod'" warned another, driving the moral home with a sketch of a child, a rolling ball and an approaching bus. Here are further views:

> What my ideal playground would be to have swings a chute sand games and swimming. I wish all these thing were in a park. The most thing I like best is swimming we never have any good games to play. I think they should have things for the small ones to like a castle and boats to go in the ponds. It would make a change for the parents to have the children out so that they can get on with there work. They should have a race track to so when you go in you pay sixpence to get on it. Down at the flats they only have a football field, and a monkey puzzle but we are getting a grass football field and swimming baths and tennis courts but even thats going to take a lot of time and hard work. And thats what I think would be my ideal playground.

> I would like to play with pepol that are frendlay and dont fight with each other and dont talk scrufy I lik places that are tiddy and not all papers about I like to play with my mums dresses and high

heels and my other frends do that a well I woul ofen play at houses with them.

A good place to play is a church were I go with my mother and my sister becuse isside the church thare are a big room were are toys big one's and small toy's.

I think the railway is a good place to play. This is why I think it is a good place to play. I like to play with my scooter up at the railway. I like to go under the tunnel too. Some times I like to take my pram up at the railway. Sometimes I take my bike up too the railway.

I like football but when you stay in the high flats you cant get playing football, because all the big boy's dont let you play they like to take your ball of you and play with it. Why dont they do it to boy's the same age as them, I hope we can get grass pitches for boy's of eight and eleven, and we all hope that the goals will have nets. We all like playing football but if the big boy's would leave us we would enjoy it but if they dont we will not enjoy ourselfs. Some of the girls like to play tennis if they got tennis courts for the girls that would make them happy, and we all hope they get the little children swings and a sand pit for them that would keep them happy.

Where I live there is no where to play, except for a long stretch of concrete, a hill that leads to the other block and a number of other things. We are not even allowed to play on the grass, that means we cant get a good game of football without getting chased of. A few children sit on skates and go down the hill. But the passing people say noisy little brats. I think the grass should be open for the public use. The corporation should find some workers who will make swings and make a decent football pitch and things for the girls as well as us boys. The sheds have signs saying NO LOITERING and NO FOOTBALL. I agree with the first sign. But not the second. There should be a chute, swings a grassy place and the signs should be taken down. Just now there is a play group for children up to five. I don't think this is right, my young sister goes but she is almost five. She has only been going a few weeks. I think that the corporation should send a few more people to take the older ones. It will cost money but I think the public would give some money as it will be for their childs sake. I also think that the caretakers should help. If this is done the flats would be pleased. The football pitch or the red ash is good but you cannot dive if you did you would hurt yourself the attendants should make good sized goalposts and take the banana skins of and the glass.

What problems do high flats give rise to for the children of 5–10 and what action might be helpful? As regards outdoor needs, one problem that produces many others is that this new form of housing segregates the generations and cuts off the child from his home. In traditional housing dozens of reasons lead him to make brief appearances there. He runs in to shelter from a squall, to fetch a toy, to go to the toilet, to wheedle 2p when he hears the chimes of the icecream van – all of which mean that he is fairly often in touch with his grown-ups. In a high flat this is less likely because of the bother of the lift. The adult is equally reluctant to have to use it. And as regards anybody having a glance now and then to see he is all right, the child can slip under the block, round the corner and vanish from sight more easily than in a street. Nor can the grown-up admonish by a tap on the window and administer justice, "who slapped who?" The child's casual contacts with people other than those of his own home have also lessened. No-one leans on a sill or pops out to look at a pram, no couples have a half-hour's blether at the gate, no father mends a fence, no gran sits on the step minding a toddler but also available for talk with the 8-year-old. A 5-minute count at Red Road on a summer evening showed 17 or so adults about the place compared with about 120 children. Most of the grown-ups were rapidly making their way into a block, going off in a car, etc. while the children looked as if they were there for the evening. A similar count at Castlemilk showed 90 children and not half a dozen older people. It is, of course, educationally valuable for children to have grown-ups' activities going on around them and it also means they are less likely to become a law unto themselves. By and large this new type of housing certainly increased the children's freedom from most types of adult supervision. On the other hand they did have to contend with one new aspect of control, that of the caretaker. And in a minority of cases, e.g. the family where the parents were unusually nervous about safety or unusually keen to raise the children's standards of behaviour, they probably got less freedom in that they were kept indoors for a large proportion of their day. Certain children who had moved from a low-rise home to a high flat themselves commented on the above point.

It is perhaps not irrelevant to mention here a suggestion put forward that a tall tenement, the traditional Glasgow home, may conceivably be associated with the Glasgow boys' reputation for physical violence. In low-rise housing the small child can whip back home for safety when street life gets too hot for him. In the tenement this is less easy, so to survive he must learn to be tough and aggressive. Should there be anything in this theory, the moral for high flats is plain enough.

Another of the troubles associated with play which high flats aggravate is noise. Perhaps the extra-confined home makes the children extra exuberant when outside it. Moreover noise can funnel up a high block in a quite remarkable way. If the flat's balcony door is open a 30-minute session of 'Nuts in May' by half a dozen small girls can madden the adults on a 16th storey. A street normally has several focal points so that the children spread themselves out: the multi-storey has only one, its base. This is where the comings and goings to the block take place, where the mobile van stands and where the children can get some shelter from rain and wind. It likewise has walls for balls. The thud, thud, thud of just one 10-year-old battering his football against the side of the block can be distracting for the homes in the vicinity. The stairs make another handy spot for play and here again the noise, "see how many steps you can jump", can bother old people, those on shift work, etc. Attempts to keep children away from such spots, the Corporation's "No loitering", "No ball games", "No cycling" (supplemented by some wag's "No breathing") are ineffective and, in view of the shortage of suitable play places, hard on the children however desirable for adults. Even with the official playgrounds their noise is a continual problem. Youthful jollity is all very well but a concentration of high-pitched shrieks, wails, the rattle of tin wheels on concrete, can make a confounded din when 40 or so children crowd on to the 200 square yards of a playground proper. Careful siting of playgrounds in the original plan would lessen the likelihood of ructions over noise between those families which, having children, see the kids' case, and those without, who long for tranquillity. Sunken play areas and ones screened off by tallish shrubs and trees might help since this disperses the children. The value of rulings as to where they may or may not play might be increased if the Authority decided these in consultation with the tenants and older children. Should this be unworkable in the early days of an estate, then make it clear that the decisions are temporary and will be re-discussed when views have crystallised.

Untidyness, as distinct from vandalism, is another problem that is a particular irritant on the multi-storey estate. It is obviously not one that will be solved by more rubbish bins though some really mammoth ones might be a help. After all some children, the well-drilled Brownie for example, have been known to use them. A far more effective measure is to have a free-flowing landscape with not too much formal mown grass. Provided there are plenty of trees, rough grass can absorb a lot of litter and hard use. Though the children's constant reference to grass in their writings showed how much they valued it they don't need the trim variety. If measured by capital costs, mown grass is a cheap

Plate 11

Mrs. ...... Her one-person flat is on the 19th floor.
Wyndford, Glasgow.

form of ground cover. But when that of maintenance is added, especially in the estate with a lot of children, it can, to quote an architect, "become as expensive as marble". Heather-planted areas stand up well to children, and rhododendrons make the good hiding places that the typical estate so lacks. In terms of all-the-year-round use, conifers, with their thick furry texture, are more useful than deciduous trees. It would be useful on some estates if a wild area, "a big bite of spare ground" as one child pleaded, was set aside for really rough use, the very active play that boys of 8–11 need. A place of this kind would give children the chance to burn the discarded couch, have their three shots to break the bottle, dig to Australia, etc. None of the above precludes the case for Adventure Playgrounds proper but they, of course, need staff.

Warmth was something to which the children referred more often than had been expected. Perhaps their centrally heated and wall-to-wall carpeted homes emphasised the chilliness of the estate. One does not want to molly-coddle, but there is a limit to the amount of bad weather children can stand and Glasgow gets its fair share of blustering winds and driving rain.[9] Moreover if mothers knew the children could get to some form of shelter they might be more willing to let them play outside which, by and large, is especially desirable for these children whose homes so limit active play. Some kind of shelter, a 'child-port', would seem to be an exceedingly useful provision. If it was slightly raised it would be drier underfoot than the concrete and tarmac of the estate which tend to get awash. It probably ought to have one side well open otherwise the question of supervision arises. And it should offer more than just bare walls. Perhaps it could have a central pillar with a seat around it and some pattern in the floor. If it could also be given some form of foolproof heating, that would be an enormous asset. The builders say it would be easy to part-enclose one of the semi-open areas at the base of many types of block, but could the noise problem be solved? Should an experiment of this kind be made it would be a suitable time to explore the possibility of putting in a lavatory. Mothers would welcome this and health visitors point out what bad training it is for the small child to get accustomed to being dirty.

[9]	Rainfall		Temperature at sea level		Hours per day bright sunshine	
England and Wales	38·7 ins.*		50·5°f.*		4·1*	
Scotland	59·3 ins*		47·7°f.*		3·3*	
	Aug. 67	Feb. 68	Aug. 67	Feb. 68	Aug. 67	Feb. 68
Glasgow	2·8 ins.	2·2 ins.	14·2°f.	0·9°f.	4·7	2·7
London (Kew)	1·6 ins.	1·9 ins.	17·3°f.	3·4°f.	6·0	2·3

*Annual averages.

If boredom, the root of half the trouble that play causes, is to be staved off, the child needs a wide variety of situations in which to play. An estate so planned that it is intrinsically interesting has more potential than one where play areas are tacked on. Variety in the levels adds interest. This means plenty of hummocks and places that take no harm when climbed up or slid off. Some version of the broad stone steps that are built into the tall Scottish field walls would offer all sorts of opportunities. So would a wall with 'windows' of different sizes and at different levels. Crannies and semi-sequestered spots make the child feel safe and provide bits of territory that are his own for the time being. They also increase the chance of the unexpected which is half the fun. If encircling walls, fences, etc. are of different heights and built of different coloured and textured materials this too gives variety. The Dutch use tough, tallish shrubs to define play areas. Things like elder, thorn and willow seem to survive the ravages of children on, for example, derelict railway banks. Could not this kind of screen be used around the visually boring kickabouts and the unsightly rough areas referred to earlier? Could there not also be strategically sited objects, an extra big seat or a lamp post, to use as 'home', the gathering point that many games demand. The ubiquity of concrete, asphalt and metal on certain of the multi-storey estates cries out for objects with tactile variety – water, sand, earth – and the tree trunks and boulders that, presumably, are to be had for the asking within a few miles of Glasgow. Another useful material, and tougher than wood, is moulded plastic. The ancient, seasonal nature of children's games suggests that it might be possible to introduce variety on these lines too, perhaps merely by moving some pieces of equipment from one estate to another. In planning for variety the landscape architect and the artist are especially useful because their training teaches them to cater for choice. Some authorities (Skelmersdale Development Corporation is one of them) appoint artists to their staff. (See Plate 13).

The schoolgirls' play needs were poorly met. The boys could enjoy their football almost anywhere and they also had their kickabouts. It might be useful to give the girls a hard surface area with a netball stand together with a couple of posts plus rope for bat-and-ball games. Some of the Continental estates visited provided places for roughish versions of croquet, clock golf, etc. One feature that seemed to distinguish the play of the girls of 8–10 or so from that of the boys was that they were more prone to enjoy chattering with each other and also with grown-ups. Perhaps outdoor play places may be less useful for them than group provision, through junior youth organisations, etc. Girls and quiet children in general might respond to a simple arts centre as is being tried out for Gorbals children in Glasgow and for middle-class ones at a Young People's Arts Centre in St. Albans. Younger girls, those of 4–8 or so, need pleasant little corners for their pretend 'houses', 'nurses', 'school', etc. and for the brides and space-ladies of their dressing-up games. The amount of quiet, sociable sitting-down play that takes place at the entrance to traditional housing suggests that the estate needs plenty of places where children can sit around. Perhaps a few pieces of solid furniture, a bench or table, could be brought out in the day time to humanise the barren corners at the base of the block.

Another valuable provision would be to give the children of all ages more opportunities to get to know something about the animal kingdom. Except for the occasional high-flying gull they rarely see any birds from their home; there are no spiders, daddylonglegs or bumble bees about the flat; and the 100 or so households of the child's own block may not have a cat or a dog between them. Children are, of course, fascinated by living things. Infant lore e.g. *Puss in Boots, The Three Bears, Benjamin Bunny*, is steeped in animals. The Authority's ban on dogs and cats is probably sound merely in terms of the animals' welfare, but these children miss a great deal now that pets have been whittled down to budgies and goldfish, neither of which can be handled. It would be sad to think that high flats were producing children whose immediate reaction to any animal was "Shoo it away". And what about compassion? Would children who had a dog in their home have thrown one (as they did) from the block's roof? It would be delightful to see a pets corner, as provided on a Bristol multi-storey estate, or a small children's zoo, as was seen at Tcharnergut in Switzerland. Youth organisations working with high flats might make a speciality of arranging outings to the country, and evening and weekend expeditions to Glasgow's parks, some of which are so spacious and rural.

All the evidence from places visited which were doing useful work on children's play and the situation in Glasgow itself strongly suggested that staff is the main key to intelligent provision. The relative absence of adults about the place, and the separation of child from home, make it especially desirable not to stint on staff, paid and voluntary. They are needed as preventers of trouble in the early months of an estate when no playgrounds may be ready. And they may be permanently needed at any estates with large numbers of children and where there is a complex of problems as, for example, at Red Road. A good many abortive efforts by tenants to set up youth clubs might have been avoided had they been able to turn to staff knowledgeable about ways in which the Youth Service can adapt itself to meet the new situation posed by multi-storey estates.

It may be useful to refer to one or two interesting examples of play provision that were met with in the course of this study. Not all were specifically connected with high flats but they could possibly be adapted. At Milton Road in Haringey use was made of garages for play areas. They included a lavatory and a kitchen. In North Kensington a group of voluntary workers connected with Notting Hill Social Council has drawn up a scheme for using 25 acres under the Western Avenue Extension as a recreational space for all ages. It will have an adventure playground near a supermarket, an exhibition wall for school paintings near a pensioners' club, a self-service laundry opposite a mothers' club, and seats with fixed concrete chess tables near a pensioners' club. The provision for children's leisure that was seen on the Continent was particularly comprehensive in Stockholm. It included kindergartens, day nurseries, after-school centres, clubs for the 12–14s and delightful play parks. The municipality runs 127 of these, the normal standard being one park to 5,000 population. They are staffed by some 400 people trained at various levels and most of them working full-time. Children of all ages use these parks for group and free activities. At Bredang, on one of the days this estate was visited, 7-year-olds were putting on and forming an audience for a puppet show in the ground-floor flat of a high block alongside the play park. This flat was given over permanently for children's use. Other attractions included an open shed for carpentry, an open-air concrete surface for table-tennis, and a delightful set of Wendy houses, one of which a child could book for a set period. In Zurich the Authority left the actual running of play provision to *Pro Juventute*, a large voluntary organisation. Half the finance came from the Authority, the other half being raised by the organisation, largely from a tax on stamps sold by the state. At the Heureid estate the organisation had a Robinson (Swiss Family?) building ground, a village of tree houses put up by the children with their leaders and parents. A child could buy a house through paper money earned by doing chores.

The little children

It is common knowledge that families with small children tend to have a load of problems if they live in a high flat. This is what one wife had to say (see Fig. 8) and she, it will be noted, was only three floors up. She was 27, had three children and had been in her flat for three years.

As said before, the sample showed the number of children under 5 in the 143 blocks occupied at July 1968 to be 2,000, some 760 of whom were living above the 4th floor. Spot estimates of the numbers in this

FIG. 8. (facing)

"This is what one wife had to say" . . . .

When we moved in to our third floor flat, Brian was about eighteen months old and Alison was six months. At this time I couldn't do any travelling with them as I couldn't manage two babies on and off buses. The only time I saw my mother was on Tuesdays, when she and my sister came over to visit me. I knew no one in Castlemilk but I resolved to make some friends among my new neighbours. I discovered that meeting people in a multi-storey block is not easy. Each house is rather like a warm, comfortable, isolated cell. When I wanted to do some shopping I would put both children in the pram, go out into the landing and press the lift button to descend. During the first few weeks the lift seemed to be constantly out of order or being used by removal men shifting furniture, so as often as not I had to push the pram down the three flights of stairs. I shudder to think how the poor mothers up in the eighteenth floor managed. However, on reaching ground level, off I would go to the nearest shops which, incidentally, are some distance from the flats, which means that on really bad days its difficult to do shopping with small children.

Having done my shopping I would return, pull the pram up all the stairs again and back into the flat. All of which would be accomplished without my having glimpsed a neighbour far less having a word with one. I used to go out to the chute room, as we call it, to empty the rubbish in the hope of seeing some other living soul but invariably there was just no one.

At this time I began to feel the loneliness was unbearable and I felt like a prisoner, tied to my children. I longed to go over to a neighbour's door and invite her in for a cup of tea but I never could pluck up the courage. I suppose I was just afraid of a rebuff. If only I had known then that we were all feeling much the same. Anyway, after a couple of months, I made friends with a girl on the same landing, and through her, with her immediate neighbours. It was a tremendous relief to have someone to talk to during the day. I don't mean by this that we were always in each other's houses but just to know I could run for a neighbour in an emergency helped me greatly.

Three years later I have still not made any more friends although I am on nodding terms with quite a few people. I don't know whether this is due to my own shyness or to the fact that it isn't easy to meet people in this type of housing. At the beginning I was terribly pestered by door to age group at three of the five selected estates, taken at various dates, showed the following: 65 at Wyndford (5 blocks); 56 at Royston (3 blocks); 108 at Red Road (2 blocks and part of a third). Figures for a single block, one of those at Castlemilk, showed where these small children were located. Floor 1 had 2 children under 5, 2 (2), 3 (8), 4 (8), 5 (8), 6 (9), 7 (3), 8 (6), 9 (5), 10 (2), 11 (2), 12 (4), 13 (4), 14 (4), 15 (1), 16 (5), 17 (1), 18 (4), 19 (0). When assessing the block's needs it is necessary to remember that the above figures relate to *all* the children under 5. The real baby may even be advantaged by life in a high flat since the balcony makes a safe and sunny stand for his pram.

An officer of the Glasgow Corporation's Health and Welfare Department, Dr. Katherine Scott, kindly offered to test, using the Griffiths Mental Development Scale, a few children aged 2 and under, though in view of their age she did not expect different results from tests given to children in housing of traditional type. The estate chosen was Royston where just 9 children were found to be eligible. The only unexpected characteristic which the test showed was lack of the appropriate response, in terms of the child's age, when faced with the 'stairs' used in the test's locomotor section. The doctor found no evidence that health was suffering.

The flat's shortage of space was one of the problems for the small and active child. House size being tailored to that of the family, there was rarely a spare bedroom and it was an unusually lucky little chap who, as seen at one home only, had the run of an unslept-in room (complete with mini swing). The utility cupboard that most flats possess was sometimes turned over to the children, but as the main storage place for the home it was awfully cramped. The balcony was 'out' on grounds of safety and so was the lift hall on the child's own floor if just one of the other households was crotchety about noise and extra cleaning. Lack of a doorstep, the safe world that is half in and half out of home, was a major loss. These small children reacted to extra space dramatically. Watch them, the moment their door opens, spill out into the hall like a flurry of mice; or listen to the screams of a 3-year-old when, after seeing someone off, the remorseless door clicks to; or notice how the child new to a playgroup just rushes up and down for mornings on end. Sheer shortage of space means the child is liable to be nagged at for precisely what, at that age, he should be doing. Lack of space also means that there is no room for hoarding the innumerable treasures that, given the chance, children use for imaginative play. And they may not get out of doors long enough to play with sticks, pebbles, leaves, puddles, earth, etc. They are also short of things to look at. Unless living on one of the very low floors there is no point in the child scampering to the window the moment he gets out of bed since no amount of climbing will enable him to see anything much but the sky. 'A view from my home', as drawn by a child who lived in a high flat, was a blank page except for a little round sun in the top corner and a line of small cars at the very bottom. Even the child's trips outside the flat, the daily shopping expedition, have limited value. They are adult affairs, done at the wrong pace for the child and involving a lot of bundling on and off buses and hustling about in crowded shops.

Some of the problems due to shortage of space would be eased by having a small and pleasant play space close to the blocks and/or near the places which mothers frequent – shops, clinics, laundrettes, etc. Some form of lowish enclosure is helpful because then the child knows where he is expected to stay, "you don't go outside this". It also keeps off older boys and their footballs. If this fencing must be wire or a wall, soften it with shrubs alongside. Seats, some of them sheltered from wind and the odd shower, are important. So is grass since little children tumble a lot and their feet and hands are tender. Alongside this it is useful to have a piece of hard surfacing for damp days. A hillock to roll down is fun, so are little plank walks and stepping stones (see Fig. 9). Sand pits are so valuable for the child's development and give such endless pleasure ("He's never out of it") that they really ought to be used much more frequently in Glasgow despite the maintenance problems. The Continental countries seem to have mastered these. Stockholm, for example, has hundreds of sandpits, mostly quite small but dotted all over the city. Its Parks Department require *in the direct vicinity of the entrance to the dwelling* 13 square metres of free area for play for every

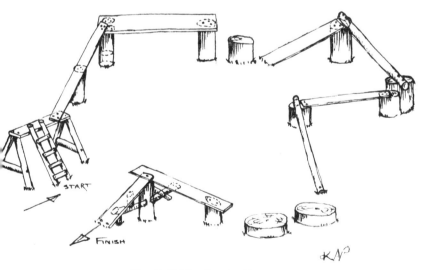

FIG. 9. Children's catwalk.

municipal flat containing children. Most of these places contain a sand pit. It normally has a wooden frame with an overhanging lip about a foot wide which helps prevent the sand being spilled out and makes a seat-cum-table. It is often fenced off which, among other things, prevents trouble from dogs. One small town visited near Stockholm had its own dog lavatory, a semi-enclosed bit of grass with posts. In Amsterdam the sand pits have to be watered, drained regularly, and renewed every three months. Some useful points on toddlers' play places were those in the following extract from a report of a conference held by the Space for Youth Foundation in Rotterdam.[10]

> A communal garden should comprise, at a maximum distance of 100 metres from the dwelling, playing facilities for toddlers and infants, including at least the following:
> a) A combined sand-box for toddlers and infants.
> b) A small, paved area with some static playing appliances and some seats for the mothers; total area of the facilities mentioned, depending on number and size of the dwelling, approximately 250–400 square metres per 100 dwellers.
> c) Playing lawn, not intended for ball games.
> d) Near playing facilities for toddlers and infants, if desired, a play-pond at most a few centimetres deep but having an area of approximately 20 square metres.
> These playing facilities must be within view of the dwelling.

Another handicap of the high flat is that it so restricts the child's social contacts. The absence of large families means relatively few siblings so he is mostly minded by adults, not by older brothers and sisters with *their* circle of child friends. As said before, he gets no doorstep play with all the chances of other children's company that this normally affords. Tenants fairly often referred by name to a child in their block who was exceedingly shy or the one who would not stay with anyone but his mum or, more often, to a child who only saw another kid about once a fortnight. Teachers from a school with many high-flats' children noted them as reluctant talkers and oddly uncurious about each other. They also thought that, compared with other children of their age, they were short of general information, a point to be expected. The research staff themselves gained the impression that the small children they encountered in the flats were unusually quiet and less liable than normal to interrupt adults' talk. All told it would seem that life in a multi-storey runs counter to what the psychologists say about the child's social needs, viz. that it is important for his development that he should meet plenty of people, grown-ups as well as other children.

[10] *Yeugd en Woonmilieu*, Report No. 11, Space for Youth Foundation, 1966.

Unless he does so, and at a quite young age, he is not talked with enough which means he does not learn to express ideas or form concepts. Biologists, too, stress the case for rubbing shoulders. Morris, quoting experiments with young monkeys, argues that "the child that has been severely sheltered from social contacts as a member of a playgroup will also find himself badly hampered in his adult social reactions".[11]

As regards research into the effects of high flats on small children, Dr. F. H. Stone and Dr. I. F. Sutherland of the Department of Child Psychiatry, Royal Hospital for Sick Children, Glasgow, have suggested a research technique which could be set up quickly. This would be one focused on the development of social competence and a project that could be used as an indicator between different aspects of this competence. The prediction would be that children moving to a high flat would be less competent in relation to other children and less independent than those living in more ordinary flats (unless they attended a playgroup or a nursery school). There might be a second group in high flats whose mothers allow them out and who *are* competent with other children but less able in speech and areas of social development for which the child depends on the adult (unless he attends nursery school or playgroup). The Vineland Social Maturity Scale might be suitable for this project and in addition a vocabulary scale such as the Peabody. The extension scales of certain developmental tests might be used to supplement the Vineland. It would be necessary to examine children before the move was made and, since many children would have some temporary reaction to the new home, again on two occasions after the move. One would need to compare three groups of children aged 2–4: (*a*) those moving from a traditional low-rise home to a high flat, (*b*) those moving to a flat on the ground or 1st floor, (*c*) those living in a traditional low-rise home.

The problems were not confined to the children. "Infants clam'rous whether pleased or pain'd" make a testing situation for any mother. The restrictions of life in a high flat mean that she and the child are seldom more than seventeen or so paces apart so that his chatter, patter, bangs and tears are never out of earshot. One of the discussion groups illustrated the point. Five mothers with seven small children installed the latter in one of the flat's bedrooms, putting another child, a baby, on the couch in the living-room. The children's voices were a noisy back-cloth to the discussion, two's and three's of them constantly erupted into the living-room, the baby had bouts of crying and the mothers almost shouted one another down with all the things they sensed wrong with their current life but felt powerless to put right. They criticised themselves as being so tetchy with the children, and teachers

[11] *The Naked Ape*, Morris, Cape, 1967.

at a school which had many pupils from high flats noted that they talked a good deal about their mothers being cross. But the mothers had so many problems. There was the anxiety about the balcony. You could trust your own two but what about their friends? And any play outside the flat itself was a worry. With every stair and floor alike, the small child has no landmarks even inside the block. Having to use a lift means there is no quick rushing home for solace when things go wrong. The mothers agreed with the health visitors' advice that it improved tempers to take the children out at least once a day. But it was such an effort. You had to manœuvre pram and baby, toddler and toy, yourself and shopping bags into the lift and if crowded you and yours were only too obviously a nuisance. You might then have to negotiate a steep ramp and/or steps. You faced similar difficulties on the return plus the nagging anxiety that the lift *might* be off.

The position as regards play groups and other provision for social contacts for the under-5s in high flats was roughly as follows. No figure was obtained as to what number were in any kind of group but it was believed to be minimal. By July 1968 only 2 of the 49 estates had managed to set one up. The Royston story, referred to in Chapter 3, is worth elaborating. In 1967 the research staff held a few small discussion groups with mothers from the Royston blocks who seemed to feel vaguely that something ought to be done about the small children. But the dismal history of the estate's tenants' association had sapped their confidence and they were scared to have a go at anything. They probably also sensed that they lacked the ability to run a group. With six months of quiet backing by a knowledgeable graduate they got something started. There was no question about the children's reactions. As reported by one mother, "First thing he asks when he wakes is whether it's the play-room today." But the group ran into problems and rows over who should hold the cash and it would have floundered time and again but for support from various sources, a Councillor, Corporation officials, the Pre-School Playgroups organisation and a grant from the Bellahouston Bequest Fund. Its future was precarious until, in July 1969, the Save the Children Fund took it over. The other group was at Red Road. Run by the mothers, it took a long time to get started and was only able to make limited provision both as regards the group's programme and in relation to the number of children on the estate. In other words experience showed that in Glasgow anyhow one could not depend on the tenants themselves meeting this type of need.

As estimated in July 1968, Glasgow's overall provision for its children under 5 showed that the number being catered for by both statutory and voluntary agencies was about 5,000, or 10% of the 55,000-odd children aged 2, 3 and 4 (Census 1966). National financial stringency and the city's own economic problems make it most improbable that official services such as nursery schools will be extended to any considerable extent. The answer – or part of it – lies in an expansion of the voluntary groups. The argument that these do not cater for the child as competently as does the nursery school is fair enough but is this so important provided that voluntary provision does not fall below the standards approved by informed opinion? In the present plight half a loaf is not to be despised. There is no doubt about the demand for provision and contacts with the mothers in high flats suggested they were prepared to pay towards it. The growth of the Pre-School Playgroup movement illustrates the demand. In 1967 Glasgow had hardly any such groups. By April 1969 they had risen to 21, with 8 others waiting to start. But this movement and the Glasgow Playgrounds Association and the Save the Children Fund all spend an undue amount of their energies in money-raising. They must have cash if they are to help finance the groups which otherwise could not get started, to keep an eye on them at an early stage, and to train the numerous people who appear to be available for both voluntary and paid work. Any major advance in the work done by the voluntary bodies would seem to depend on a dynamic lead from the Corporation.

Before finally leaving this question of the under-5s in high flats, it may be useful to refer briefly to examples of provision which were seen in London and Edinburgh. The G.L.C. is very flexible in its approach to provision for play. It runs a variety of play services itself for children of all ages and it supports the work of voluntary organisations through grant aid for running costs and personnel. Its own One O'clock Clubs are particularly interesting. They have four great merits. Available from 2–5 p.m., they are open all the year round and from Monday to Saturday; they meet in parks in simple but fenced-off premises so that the children get a whiff of the open air; they are very definitely mother-cum-child provision (the mother has to be there the whole afternoon); and they are permissive affairs. On the other hand paid staff are responsible for the club so that though the mothers help they also get a little relaxation with other adults. Examples of G.L.C. policies on estates with high flats were seen at the Pepys estate in Deptford (4,000 population) and at Brandon (6,000). At the former a ground-floor flat had been converted for use as a play centre which was then run by the Save the Children Fund. At Brandon a play group organised by the London Council of Social Service met in a hall provided by the Building Industry Youth Trust. In Edinburgh the Corporation's Health and Social Services Department make an annual grant (£5,359 in 1968/9) to an old-established body, the Voluntary Health Workers Association. This runs some 36 toddlers play centres, 7 of them in multi-storey estates. All told, the Association caters for over 1,000 children and has a waiting list of another 1,000.

The conclusion of the research staff as regards high flats and families with young children was that they were quite unsuitable and that even when the children were of school age many and often expensive safeguards were required. On the other hand it is only fair to say that, though almost invariably disparaging the high flat as a home for children, the tenants themselves appeared to think that the physical assets outweighed other things. Minority opinion was mostly confined to families which themselves had two or more small children. With this type of family certain ones shirked balancing the flat's physical advantages against the children's all-round needs. There was no question that this type of housing added to the mothers' problems and also that the presence of children created problems for the estate. As regards compensatory measures the following points stood out. It would be valuable for the Authority to have on its staff at least one person with special responsibility for the recreational needs of children living in high flats and for the Youth Service to make a special study of this subject. It should keep an eye on the needs of girls of 8–12. High flats should have priority in any extension and co-ordination of the city's services for the pre-school child. Any multi-storey estate with family flats should have a fenced-off toddlers' play area with some form of sheltered seats. This ought to be ready by the time the first block is occupied. The desirability of a semi-sheltered structure for the use of school children should also be explored. Finally there should be more attention to the idea that children's play is a family affair, not something that necessarily separates adult from child or the little ones from older children.[12]

[12] Cf. *The Playground in Modern Danish Society*, Sigsgaard, Danish Foreign Office Journal, No. 54 October 1965.

Chapter 10

OTHER TYPES OF HOUSEHOLD

One type of household which seemed particularly content with life in a high flat was that of the middle-aged couple whose children had now left home. Though no exact figures were obtained, it was believed that the multi-storey population had a high proportion of such households. It was, for example, known that 34% of the total population in the flats was aged 50 and over, that 23% was aged 50–64, and that 32% of the *households* were two-person units (Tables 5, 12). This couple, with the children off their hands and old age not yet a threat, had reached an enjoyable stage, what the old-fashioned mum used to call her "nice time". The fact that the flat was so easy to run meant the wife could go out to work without much strain. This gave her company which lessened the flat's loneliness. Its lack of space did not hamper the couple's activities since their interests were no longer family-centred. The second income meant they could probably run a car, go to things like the works' dinner dance, and get a holiday in Spain. And they might also involve themselves in the voluntary jobs so obviously needed on a new estate. The above Glasgow finding was supported by views expressed elsewhere, for example those of a senior official of the Housing Department in Utrecht.

Other contented households were those whose interests were centred on job, friends and leisure rather than family. They included the self-supporting, not so young unmarried and youngish individuals who had lost their spouse or had been divorced. All these were likely to appreciate the smart-looking home, and the isolation of multi-storey life did not bother them since they made their friends through work and at clubs and pubs. They particularly welcomed the fact that a high flat is more likely than other types of local authority housing to be centrally situated. This made for easy access to transport and to the leisure-time facilities of the city centre. Another household that benefited from a central situation was that which had a single earner who was responsible for a dependant, e.g. an unmarried daughter with her invalid father, or a single woman in her 40s looking after an adult but crippled nephew. As workers they could not afford time or money for much travel and their housebound dependants welcome the pleasantness of the flat. Another type of suited household met with abroad (though not in Glasgow since it was ineligible for the housing list) was that of a set of students, or of those in their early 20s whose career took them away from home but who were not yet at the stage of wanting to build one up.

A rather unexpected household which a multi-storey home suited was that containing or comprising someone who was seriously disabled. Glasgow has 16,000 such adults on its occupational therapy books, and 9% of the sample households contained someone with a major physical disability. A social studies graduate student contacted 12 such people living on 9 different estates. Ten of them liked the place. A lady crippled with arthritis thought it "the best thing that ever happened to me"; a man who had lost both legs found it ideal for himself and his wife; and a muscular dystrophy invalid, a young man in a wheelchair living with his parents, was delighted with this home. The two who did not find the flat satisfactory were a middle-aged mother with polio who found that the doorways and sills prevented her managing her chair properly, and a seriously crippled man who could not negotiate the steps at the base of the block. The absence of steps inside the flat, the lift (for those not housebound) and the comfort of the place were blessings. These disabled people had no strong preferences about the height at which their flat was situated except that, for the sake of security, they preferred not to be too near the ground. It was also important to avoid a site near a noisy playground, a lift head, or a busy parking lot. The view was very important. "It makes you feel nearer freedom" said a crippled lady of a 16th-storey flat that looked on to busy crossroads and then across to shipyards. As in the case of pensioners, everything possible should be done to exploit the view. One lady (not among the above 12), both of whose legs were amputated, had to be hoisted out of her chair and on to a box if she was to see anything of the outside world. The least understandable of the problems connected with these people who were so greatly disadvantaged was that such a tiny minority of the rest of the households in their block appeared ever to give them a thought. The student's notes referred to lack of contact with the neighbours in 8 of the 12 cases and read as follows on three of them: "She had made no friends"; "Hardly ever saw neighbours"; and "Did not find neighbours particularly friendly (too proud to ask for help from them)". Despite this, the student's' summing up was as follows:

> For an oldish not very mobile disabled person who has no desire to get out much, high-flat living is really ideal. These people love the view (provided they can see it); they like the size and layout of their flats (once again as long as they can get round them with ease); they feel secure; and they like the knowledge that they are not alone in an old building. The lifts are another

important factor as they cut out the steps of a tenement building. It is for the more mobile disabled person that most of the problems arise.

A household which did *not* suit multi-storey life was the expansive experimentally-minded family which thrived on outdoor life, valued amplitude, preferred space to privacy, spontaneity to order and perhaps quantity to quality. Essentially makers and growers, they were more irked than most by the flat's physical restrictions. For example, they could do nothing about altering the place like adding a porch or a shed. The trim, constricted interior allowed little opportunity of making things even on a small scale. There were no working surfaces, no storage places for bulky objects, no rooms where noisy tools or mess or smell could be tolerated.

The family's level of sophistication was perhaps the most important factor in how it reacted to this new type of home. The household which could be described as socially rather 'below average' could find the life particularly difficult. This did not necessarily mean it was the kind of family which was liable "to do a moonlight" or "one that doesn't go in for paying up". But it did not bother much about bettering itself or perhaps it was just too poor to cope.[1] Families of this kind are presumably those chiefly responsible for the total of court actions (17,325 in 1968) brought by the Corporation against its tenants in general, together with the abscondings (1,056) and the ejections (212). That the multi-storey population was only marginally involved in such things was suggested by the 1967 figures from the 5 selected estates. Only 22 households, under 1%, were involved, though the trouble was concentrated, 15 of these families living on one estate (Appendix B). Any household which was very untidy and very noisy was particularly liable to be in trouble in a high flat. Impatient of regulations and perhaps semi-literate, it disregarded admonitory notices and thus got at loggerheads with the caretaker and other tenants. The wife took the shared job of cleaning the hall in the same casual way as she ran her home. She probably came from a society which only recognised obligations to people who knew each other well. Her care of the children could be minimal. She might, as was known on one estate, send them out of the house early and late, her sole contact with them being the bag of crisps she chucked down from time to time.

Another family that found this new type of home a strain was the young one which had grown fast. This had enabled it to move up the housing list quickly and the offer of the super flat was an enormous

[1] Figures from the Child Poverty Action Group describes 12% of families renting their home from the Local Authority as having two or more children and being very poor. *Poverty*, No. 4, Autumn 1967.

temptation. But having young children this mother found it difficult to go out to work so she was extra hard put to meet all the new costs. That the babies in this family had come so rapidly suggested that the parents did not do much planning in any field, including that of foreseeing the extra expenses of multi-storey life. The above household tended to have several children, and every additional child in the block is something of a threat to it. Apart from their propensity to misuse the lift, their pushchairs and wheeled toys reduce its serviceability, always a potential source of bad relationships. Life up high also makes it that much more difficult to keep an eye on children, a fertile source of illwill between households. Another thing that tells hard on the 'below average' family is the loneliness. In her old home this mother was probably accustomed to rely fairly heavily for mutual services and companionship on her mother and known neighbours. But if the rest of the households on her floor look on her askance she fails to build up the personal relationships that, with her limited range of interests, mean a lot to her. Thus domestic troubles get bottled up, with risk of eventual explosion. It is easy to argue that the 'below average' households should be excluded. But can they, and in any case is it fair not to give them the opportunity to share in the good things going? And maybe some of these hail-fellow-well-met families have a warmth in their human relationships, a willingness to stand and listen, that is valuable in a population which, as consciously on the rise, is not inclined to have much time for other people. Possible action on the part of the estate itself to help the less sophisticated family to adapt to life in a high flat is discussed later (Chapter 12).

There is some ground for thinking that this new form of home suits women better than men. It is the woman, not the man, who benefits from the easier housekeeping. Whereas the latter cannot use such tools as hammer, saw or shovel, the flat imposes no ban on such feminine interests as sewing and knitting. But apart from car-tinkering somewhere outside the block, what masculine-type hobbies can the average man possibly pursue if he lives in a wall-to-wall carpeted flat? Even in terms of children's leisure, small boys make more claims on space than girls. The problem also shows up with men who have recently retired. With no coal to get in, no steps to sweep, no outside repairs to be done, the man's small jobs about the home have gone. The Melbourne study quoted a wife as saying that "men forget the things they used to do".[2] And another study, referring to the rare occasions on which the father is able to do anything constructive in the presence of his wife and children, likened his role to that of the star boarder.[3]

[2] *op. cit.*
[3] *Housing and Social Standards*, Wallace, Philadelphia Housing Authority, 1952.

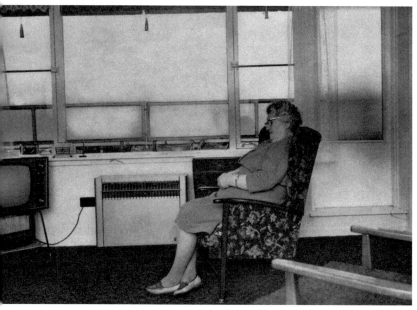

Plate 12   Miss ……, of Wyndford

and the view she cannot see from her chair.

To sum up. The households most likely to make a success of a multi-storey life were those whose interests did not centre on their home; who had plenty of personal resources; and were relatively well-educated and well-off. Would it, perhaps, be a fair assumption that 'living high' caters best for the household and individual who, in very broad terms, prefers order to growth?

Chapter 11

HIGH FLATS AND SOCIAL CONTACTS

"They're nice enough but not what you'd call neighbours"

"That new baby in the flat at the end of our corridor, he was six months old before I ever set eyes on him." Remarks such as this epitomised what was generally agreed by the tenants, viz. that multi-storeys were socially chilly and tended to cut one off from that topic of inexhaustible interest, human nature. Outsiders thought the same. Health visitors, for example, found it far more difficult than in low-rise homes to get information from neighbours on such a thing as whether a family was on holiday, and probation officers said that domestic rows were less likely to be common knowledge. The kind of society where, when anything of interest happened, the street had the news the same hour is of course on the way out and some of the high flats' alleged anonymity is less due to a new kind of housing than to changes in social conditions. Decline in household size and less sharing of homes means that fewer people come in and out of the home. Less child bearing and easier housekeeping give the non-working housewife more time in which to be conscious of loneliness. The increase in married women's employment enables the wife to share much of her shopping and interests with others beside her neighbours. Better education means that people find it easier to talk with relative strangers, and the increase in holidays away is another thing that has enlarged the circle of acquaintances from which friends are drawn. Affluence, too, has reduced the economic significance of neighbours. When families were very dependent on mutual support they literally could not afford to isolate themselves from those living near-by. A tenant, contrasting life in a multi-storey with what he remembered of his boyhood in the early 1900s, wrote:

> When I recall my home I picture 6 closes in Lawmoor St. (452 to 470) and two in Naburn St. round the corner, 8 in all, a closely knit Community where everybody knew their neighbours' business. We knew who was expecting, who was dying, who had a fancy man. After a mother had her baby we all hung round the close waiting to see who would get the Silver Christening Piece, a silver 3*d* or 6*d* placed between two biscuits or cake and if the baby was a girl it was given to the first male and vice versa.

When a person died we all went up and paid our respects no matter what religion they were.

You got your messages on tick from the wee shop round the corner, every Saturday some of us went to the Pawnbrokers to redeem Dad's suit or Mother's coat if she had one, then it was taken back on the Monday to pay the rent! I reckon about 80% of the Working Class Population lived this way.

Reference to the loneliness of multi-storey life was common. There was the pensioner who never failed to wave to another tenant as the latter went off to work, the younger woman affirming that this tiny contact, "someone cares", made the older one's day. Or there was the lady in her 70s who burst into tears when one of the research staff called – "It was just hearing my bell ring". Younger people, too, could find themselves affected, e.g. the wife whose husband was working abroad for six months, or the mother tied by a couple of small children. The sheer scale of the block was offputting. One could conceive of the 30 or so people in one's old tenement as neighbours, but it was different when they numbered 300. Living nose to tail with so many potential acquaintances perhaps makes anyone who does not easily make social contacts feel there is something odd about him or, more likely, herself. While none disputed that multi-storeys were anonymous, an unexpectedly large number of tenants stressed the value of the privacy they afforded. Some may have equated this with physical security but mostly they contrasted it with the rows, noise, and borrowings to which the old type of home was so often exposed. Many felt there had been overmuch neighbouring in the past and were glad to be rid of the "inescapable togetherness". You could have good neighbours without wanting to see a lot of them. A recent study by Dutch sociologists[1] emphasised the value now attached to the home's privacy and it was frequently mentioned in papers contributed to a CIB Symposium in Stockholm.[2] Some forms of neurosis are thought to be associated with lack of solitude[3] and it has been suggested that the modern emphasis on the desirability of privacy may reflect unconscious biological demands.[4]

It was difficult to obtain or evaluate the facts about anonymity since this whole thing was presumably so tied up with the relative newness of the multi-storey population. It was difficult to frame questions

[1] *Wonen aan een woonpad.* Onderzoek naar de waardering van het wonen in woonpadsystemen. g.h. jansen, j.b. burie, Ytrecht, 1967.

[2] 'The results of sociological research carried out in the flats and blocks of flats and their application in practice', Mackova, Research Institute of Building and Architecture, Czechoslovakia. CIB Commission. Symposium, Stockholm, 1967.

[3] *Housing Welfare Problems in High Flats*, Skone, Public Works Municipal Congress, 1962.

[4] *Community and Privacy*, op. cit.

in the formal interviews that could really establish how far such an amorphous matter as social contacts had been affected by the move to a multi-storey home. Only 114 of the 641 households in the main sample gave a clear-cut reply to a question on whether they wanted more social contacts. Of those who had been in the flat for under a year over half said "yes". The figure had fallen to 11% in the case of those there for 3-4 years.

Since no one much likes to admit to actual loneliness it was not judged wise to ask bald questions on this. But it was noted how often they said they thought others found the life lonely. Most said that moving to this high flat had not affected the extent to which they met relations and friends, though if a change had occurred the contacts had generally decreased. Another problem was how to distinguish those alterations due to "multi-storeyness" from the ones derived from changes in household size. For example, the initial sample showed that when there had been this change, as happened for a third of those interviewed, then the size had generally fallen. However none of the figures on this subject were judged to reflect the speakers' attitudes so closely as their chance comment in casual talk. Here it was noticeable that nearly all types of household were conscious that life in a high flat had an aura of its own and one that was somehow lacking in human warmth. This feeling of being sealed off from life was particularly sensed by those who lived alone, by individuals who had suffered some emotional shock, and by those who (to the lay eye) appeared likely to have personality problems.

The influence of building form on social contacts was noted at the new Balgrayhill estate where a comparison was made between 20 households living in the estate's high flats and 10 in its deck access dwellings. They were all 1-bedroom homes, the occupants mostly pensioners and relative newcomers in that only 18 had been there for as long as a year or so. Six of the 20 households in the flats, but only 1 of the 10 in the deck access homes, had not yet made any friend on the estate. Such tiny figures obviously prove nothing but the flavour of the comments was markedly different. Whether those in the deck access homes criticised or praised the setting as noisy, fine for the children, draughty, etc., they consistently agreed that it was a place where you met folks. The other set referred to the peacefulness of their high flats but the very absence of sound made them feel cut off. They also said they lacked the casual sight of known faces, whereas the deck access people did not refer to this. And those in the high flats used a wealth of phrases about isolation – terms and words that never come out in the talk with the others. A spot check taken by one of the research staff (in a 7-minute walk along the deck access corridors) showed that 55 people were passed compared with just 6 during a similar time spent around the flats.

One matter that adds its mite to the anonymity problem is the difficulty of locating addresses.[5] This has serious implications for fire and medical services and is an irritant and waste of time for the public. Tracking down an address on some of Glasgow's multi-storey estates can have the frustrations of a bad dream. A block, for example, may be built on roughly the site of a former street and have a street name and number for its address: but if the street as such has vanished where does one begin to look for its nameplate? Moreover, the block's address is based on what was roughly the street number of the original house in which the new building stands but the change of scale makes it difficult to locate the spot. At one large estate, for example, the first block encountered when entering from the main road is No. 60, the second No. 10. At another estate where the blocks are quite near each other their street numbers are 9, 65 and 104. Instances could be multiplied. One also frequently has to hunt about for the plate that gives the block's address in terms of its street number. This is not necessarily in any consistent position and being the same size as that used for an ordinary house (5" × 4" for a two-figure number) it is lost on the massive expanse of the multi-storey. In some of the more recent Corporation blocks the address has now been placed above the main entrance. This is fine. The S.S.H.A. uses really bold figures for street numbers on its blocks and often adds a name, both of which are helpful and increase the dignity of the building. There are further difficulties, viz. how to locate a flat within the block. As said before, in many instances there is neither name board nor consistency between blocks in the instructions beside the lift as to which floor and flat it serves. Even the basic terms do not tally, 'flat' meaning 'house' in some blocks, 'floor' in others. The following addresses, picked at random from tenants' letters, lists, etc. illustrate the confusion: Flat 30, 2241 Great Western Road; 15 Eccles Street, Flat 10c; House 31, Floor 10, Kittoch Heights; 15F. 305 Caledonia Road; 17/4, 42 Viewpoint Place; 4B, 94 Viewpoint Road. In the case of a 6/5 address the figures can easily slip into 615. In general local authorities appear to be discarding the old street numbering system for multi-storeys. The G.L.C., for example, uses only the block's name, but in very tall lettering. If matters are to be rationalised, could they include discussion on the appropriateness of using such terms as 'oval', 'street', 'terrace' and 'square' for the new type of layout associated with high flats? Perhaps, too, such insipid ones as 'development', 'scheme' and 'estate' for places that are home for thousands of citizens will be discarded and the local place name, with its evocative overtones, be allowed to stand in its own right.

[5] Cf. Scottish Development Department Roads Circular No. R.97 "Street Nameplates and Numbering of Premises", March 1963.

Another thing that makes for anonymity is that a high flat drastically reduces the visual signals that, trivial in themselves, help people to get to know about each other. There is no front window where new curtains, Mother's Day daffodils, or a schoolboy's model plane tell their day-to-day story about the people inside. With no smoke from the chimney, no line of washing being taken in and no windows lighting up, neighbours do not know if the place is empty or crammed. Nor can happenings outside the block be related to a specific household. Someone's son comes on Sunday afternoons to take his mother out in the car, but whose? High flats have also done away with the 'hing', the tenement custom of sitting comfortably at a window and having a half-hour's rake of the street below. Tenants also pointed out that the lift did not compare with the tenement stairs as a place for the odd bit of talk. In a multi-storey it is not people but a machine which determines when a conversation shall start and stop. And on some estates the lift may not get many users except at rush hours. For example, the interviewers who worked on the initial sample made 1,361 lift journeys (between 1 and 10 p.m.) and in 65% of those they were the lift's only occupant. Then again, the rigidly defined mine and thine territories of the multi-storey mean it lacks anything comparable to the close entrance, those thousands of neutral, handy, semi-sheltered spots where so much of Glasgow's social life takes place. In the traditional working-class street home the pavement below one's window is a place which, with a chair brought out on a summer evening, invites talk. But where, at the base of a multi-storey is *your* piece of pavement? In certain circles, too, it is customary to 'stand', i.e. to spend a free half-hour in a prolonged natter with one or two neighbours at some recognised spot outside the actual home. But many of those living in this new type of housing regard this as lowering the block's tone. The Corporation's 'No loitering' notices positively discourage traditional ways of making contact. There is a case for trying to provide places suitable to meet this need for casual talk. The individual block should have its own seats in relatively sheltered spots and ones where the talkers are not likely to be a visual or audible disturbance. The estate as a whole also needs to develop some focal point where there are a number of seats and where one can expect to find people at most times of the day.

Dogs and gardens are other useful socialising agents and the multi-storey has neither. The tenants did not say much about not being able to have any garden but then only 17% had one in their old home (Table 27). On the other hand, evidence from the city's peripheral estates, few of whose tenants have had any garden previously, suggests that this new interest has caught on unexpectedly well. The Authority's figures show that only 14% (of these new garden-owners) had completely abandoned the place,[6] while any walk around the estates suggests that many people are obviously finding their garden a pleasure. The arguments for just a bit of garden are many. It adds space, tempts one into the open air, and affords boundless opportunities for self expression – whether for the dedicated rose grower or the rhubarb-and-no-nonsense man. It also encourages joint activities – he cuts the privet, she scoops the clippings, their 7-year-old struggles with the barrow. It is a far better fosterer of communication, the "innocent emulation" to which Mr. Cooney refers, than are the common areas of the estate or even parks.[7] A solace for the lonely, it can be a boon to the recently retired man for whom flat life offers so few time-killers. Finally, and a point oddly neglected in the controversy over private garden versus common landscaped areas, it gives the owner a great deal of pleasure. Must the thousands of people who are going to live in high flats be automatically deprived of all this? One answer is to try and extend what was seen to be a fairly common interest among the high-flats people in Glasgow, viz. the cultivation of indoor and balcony plants. As a test of interest it might be worth getting tenants to arrange a small 'show' on one of the floors of their block. A communal potting shed or one of the modern plastic greenhouses would enable the enthusiasts to store soil, swop cuttings, etc. Another experiment would be to provide a dozen or so very small plots of ground near the base of the block for anyone prepared to look after them. Provided the plots were really tiny, perhaps only 12' × 9', they could hardly be a labour. A successful version of the extremely small bit of garden (though in both cases associated with low-rise housing) was seen just outside the front doors of some pensioners' houses in the Netherlands. And the odd one or two seemed to work at Wyndford. A really exciting experiment would be to give the estate some version of the new type of allotment, the Leisure Gardens recommended by the recent Departmental Committee of Enquiry.[8] Plots of varying sizes would be rented to the individual gardener, but the total area would be so laid out that it added to the looks and interest of the landscape. There are numerous Continental examples on some such lines. The Report recommends that those who cultivate these gardens should be encouraged to form a strong local association which might, incidentally, help overcome the seemingly eternal problem of vandalism.

Clubs and societies are, of course, another and obvious way in which to counter the isolation of multi-storey life. As far as Glasgow is

[6] *Annual Report*, 1967, Corporation of Glasgow Housing Management Department.
[7] *New Homes and Social Patterns: A Study in East London*, Cooney. 1962 (Unpublished report for the Institute of Community Studies.)
[8] *Departmental Committee of Enquiry into Allotments Report*, H.M.S.O. Cmnd. 4166. 1969.

concerned there was little evidence that the tenants were any more involved in such activities than is normal in most working-class communities.[9] Nor had they reached the stage of making their friends on a common interest rather than a territorial basis. If they were going to join an organisation at all the chances were it would be one meeting near by. Relatively few owned a car, as manual workers the men often had a physically tiring day, and so did the many wives who worked. The week-end away was not a feature of their life. Summer holidays, even if spent away, rarely last for more than a fortnight. Apart from football, the circles they moved in had not much tradition of joining leisure-time organisations. Moreover in these new communities anything that, like a club, depends on co-operative effort, has more problems to face than in a settled society. Finally allowance has to be made for sheer inertia, "the old intractable level in human nature".

No study was made of the extent of membership of organised groups but they were definitely not much in evidence. The estate's shops were singularly barren of notices about local events and high flats of course drastically reduce the number of windows in the private house that are available for handbills. None of the city's 7 community centres was sited on a multi-storey estate though, as said earlier (p. 66), the Castlemilk tenants could easily reach one by bus. Nor were social organisations connected with the churches much in evidence. No instance was met of an ecumenical approach comparable to the playgroup set up by the churches in the new town of Livingston. A tenant commented that the churches tended to push leaflets through letterboxes, not to make themselves known in person. Organisations – for good works, cultural activities, sports, etc. – that were well established in other parts of the city did oddly little about setting up branches in these new communities. One of the self-evident gaps included parent-teacher associations for these estates where many families seem to be setting higher standards for their children. It would also be useful to have some kind of social group for mothers with small children, a bit of gaiety to take their minds off higher rents, rising prices and perhaps another baby on the way. Groups for music, drama and dancing, activities that can be put on in a local display, would be useful as helping to break down the anonymity of the multi-storey estate.

Apart from churches, by far the best known organisations were tenants' associations. Though by no means all the estates had one, in June 1969 as many as 22 of the 34 associations believed to be active in the city were in areas containing multi-storeys. A study was made of 13 of the associations, 11 of which drew all or most of their 7,000 members from high flats (Appendix F1). They normally met once a month in

[9] Voluntary Association membership of American adults', Wright, *American Sociological Review*, October 1968.

Indoor play
Pollokshaws, Glasgow

Outdoor play, Skelmersdale.

Plate 13

schools, scout halls, etc. Most of them operated on a modest budget and all had a constitution and annual subscription, in general 12½p per family. They raised additional funds through weekly totes, socials, etc. In the above 13 associations half of their 96 office bearers were aged 50 or over, and rather more than half were men, mostly skilled manual workers. Attendances at the monthly meetings varied but were often 50 or on occasion far more. Activities were of two main types. The association nearly always came into being and continued to concern itself with tenants' complaints, e.g. improving the bus service, keeping a school playground open, battling with the Corporation about condensation in a particular flat. And it invariably fought rent increases. The other main activity was broadly connected with welfare, e.g. running an O.A.P. club, and swimming and football clubs for the youngsters. At one estate fathers organised bus trips to Saturday morning children's cinemas so as to give mothers time to shop. One typical monthly meeting, attended by about 80 people, dealt with these subjects – a report on halls and finance connected with the possible formation of a youth club; vandalism; noise from children; an abandoned car; a weekly accumulator; an O.A.P. outing; a steamer trip to Arran.

A pen picture of an association secretary, as described in *The Gorbals View*, a local news sheet, was as follows:

> He, his wife and two boys of 12 and 8 live in the 16th floor of a multi-storey. It is a very nice home and they like living there very much. He (and his mother) were born and bred near by and he has only been away for a short spell in the Air Force and at Coventry. He is an inspector in the Aero Division of a large motor works. Very hardworking, he is involved to the full in local affairs. He has an open door to all his neighbours and their problems – not to mention his keen involvement in political life. The job that takes up most time is Chairman of the tenants' association, which he helped to form over three years ago. He claims that most of its success is due to the great team spirit of the men and women on the Committee. He also takes a Youth Club at the Parish Church on a Monday night. A very cheerful fellow, he has one big grouse – lack of Youth facilities in the area, or, at least, premises where meetings concerning the community can be held FREE of charge.

However serviceable the associations they had their critics. They were said to be just a media for personal aggrandisement – "*I* did this or that" or "It was *I* got that new playground". They were ephemeral bodies, starting off with a flourish but fading away as soon as trivial problems had been solved. They set their sights too low, promoting socials and bus trips, not classes and discussion groups. Caretakers were inclined to regard them as rakers-up of grievances, aspirants to becoming a second boss. Corporation officials might dismiss them as having high falutin' ideas, no conception of administrative and financial problems, and hindering the work of the most conscientious official by sidetracking him for a Councillor or M.P. Another criticism was that, though non-party political in name, there was often a cross link between committee members and those of trade unions and municipal Ward Committees.[10] They also fought rent increases on party political lines.[11] It is easy to conceive of a tenants' association as a kind of trade union to fight the local authority and Glasgow has a strong tradition of using political action to effect social change. Another criticism was that their co-ordinating body, the Glasgow Council of Tenants' Associations, had never shaken off the communist sympathies which had coloured its early days in the politically conscious Clydeside of the 1920s. The Council's officers strongly repudiated this charge, instancing committee members who belonged to various political parties.

Assuming that on balance the associations were a good thing, what problems had they? Sheer lack of administrative know-how meant that their committees were weak, e.g. many of the letters that their secretaries wrote so laboriously and by hand asked for the impossible. A lot of time had to be spent on acquiring the factual information that would be common knowledge in middle-class circles. "We discovered that..." was a phrase which cropped up repeatedly at their meetings. They often failed to do justice to a good cause when approaching an official or Councillor because they were unaccustomed to marshalling thoughts and putting arguments forcibly and this left them feeling that they had been brushed aside. In these new estates where so few knew each other, people were nervous of delegating responsibility so took on far too much themselves and eventually packed up the whole thing. "He worked his heart out over it" was typical of the phrases used about tenants' association officers. They also lost potential help from the more retiring tenant because the only way in which they knew how to involve people was through committee work. The internal row, based on personal animosities, was perhaps their major weakness. It was, of course, the kind of problem liable to occur with people who had little experience of committee work and who, in their jobs, were short of outlets for exercising power. Once an association had cracked up, a kind of collective depression was liable to set in. This was most unfortunate since it

[10] Ward Committee. A Glasgow institution to link Councillor and constituents, set up and grant aided (£15 per annum) by the Local Authority. Non-party-political.

[11] Cf. *Political Mobilisation: A case study*, Brier & Dowse. International Review of Community Development. N. 19–20. Piazza Cavalieri di Malta 2, Rome.

was hard to revive the estate's self-confidence in communal effort of any kind.

The case for the tenants' associations, especially as meeting the needs and opportunities presented by multi-storey housing, included the following matters. Glasgow's high-flat population has a relatively high proportion of people with some leisure and these associations are in a good position to tap this new source of help for the common good. Their meetings illustrated another useful aspect of their work, viz. the amount of factual information they spread among the ordinary tenant. Then too, though the meetings might be stormy on occasion, they did give people the opportunity to let off steam and rid themselves of some of the frustrations that were inevitable when, as was so often the case, they had waited years for a better house. The associations were also useful not only as pressure groups on the Authority to make good glaring deficiencies on the estate, but to help the individual tenant get attention for his own small-scale problem. Finally, the way in which some of the tenants spoke of "Our association" strongly suggested that it was giving a sense of fellow-feeling and civic purpose.

The Glasgow Council of Tenants' Associations, hardworking and valuable as it was, had not the resources (officers with enough time to devote to the job, people with some knowledge of legal matters, clerical help, office accommodation) to give adequate support to the 30 or so associations which were scattered throughout the city. Nor had it time to study the special needs of those connected with multi-storey estates. Contact between the G.C.T.A. and its affiliated bodies was often a hit and miss affair, depending on chance encounters. One area of work about which it did nothing was to run training courses on individual estates roughly on the lines of the 'New Homes and New Neighbours' referred to in Appendix G. It would also have been a boon to association secretaries if it could have provided a quick, cost-price duplicating service for the news sheets and notices that are so valuable in helping a new community to get to know itself. Experience in other cities suggests that one way to get a competent central body is to support it with staff who have had some training in community development. London, for example, has gradually built up a strong co-ordinating body, the Association of London Housing Estates. The Greater London Council Housing Committee and the Inner London Education Authority jointly, and through the London Council of Social Service, give £9,000 per annum towards its total budget of £11,000. The Association is autonomous, membership-controlled, operates from small central offices and appoints its own staff, two of whom are trained in community development. The staff keep closely in touch with the 90 or so affiliated associations and are immediately available for consultation in the crises that are almost inevitable in bodies of this character. They also act as a link between the associations and other statutory and voluntary organisations. They regard the provision of training courses for tenants' association officers and ordinary members as one of the basic services given by the central body.

The formation of organised groups on Glasgow multi-storey estates was seriously held up by lack of suitable places in which to meet. On the assumption that a meeting place of some kind is an urgent need for a new community, what action ought to be taken for the blocks already up? While it is of course possible to redesign a floor so as to make it suitable for social purposes, this is an additional cost and likely to be opposed by those who feel that in Glasgow houses should not be sacrificed to anything else. Though many authorities have found it satisfactory to provide recreational rooms within the block,[12] Glasgow's experience about halls either in or near by has been unfortunate in the only two cases it was tried. At Royston the Corporation set aside two rooms at the base of each of 3 blocks for social use but did nothing about providing staff to advise on their use. A tenants' association got itself going, flourished for a time and then disintegrated, which meant rooms were practically unused for several years. At the Ballater Street estate, small, purpose-built rooms for social use were provided but they too hung fire for several years, again chiefly through lack of supporting staff. Just one of the estates built and managed to maintain a hall by its own efforts. There were endless examples of how groups for toddlers, school children, adolescents and adults were hamstrung by this lack of premises. An example in the case of adults was an estate where the tenants held their monthly meetings for over 3 years in the lift hall of one of the floors. There was nowhere to sit, it was difficult to hear the chairman, and the business was continually interrupted by comings and goings to the lift. At another estate the nine members of a social club committee, handling some £2,000 per annum, used a tiny, cold, unventilated caretaker's storeroom for their monthly meetings. Premises of a sort of course exist within the vicinity of most of the estates but they are often unsuitable, overbooked or too expensive. Schools by no means meet all needs. There is much pressure on them and unless the purpose for which they are needed is one under the auspices of the Education Committee the charges are likely to be prohibitive, as is shown in the following comment from the secretary of a tenants' association:

> Application was made by me for the use of classrooms etc. for the purpose of Committee Meetings, Chess Club, Dramatic Club, Over 50's and Old Age Pensioners Club and various other activities. All of these applications were granted. Then the crunch. We are

[12] *Living High*, Housing Department, Burgh of Motherwell and Wishaw, 1970.

charged £1·25 per night for Committee Meetings (once a month), £1·25 per night for Drama Club Meetings (weekly), £5 for one afternoon to hold a Children's Xmas Party, £6 per night for over 50's and Old Age Pensioners Whist Drive (we've had 3), £1·25 per night for the Chess Club (weekly); and so it goes on.

Moreover, schools are not available at week-ends or during school holidays. They also impose niggling regulations. However necessary from the school's angle, the adult user is put off by rules about no smoking, no cups of tea, and a formidable 'shut down now' bell. Even if the regulations are modernised to meet modern needs it is doubtful if school premises are the sole answer, particularly for the high density of the multi-storey estate. The city's new community centres are enormous assets but they are far too costly to be provided in more than a few areas. Moreover, as a service of the Education Authority they may not be suited to the informal, democratic control that a tenants' association would like.[13] The latter may well differ from the Corporation on, for example, the inclusion of a bar.

The experience of other cities as regards halls may be worth quoting. The G.L.C. does not make a grant for a hall to a tenants' association, but provided an estate has not less than 400 dwellings and that the funds are available to the Housing Committee, it will usually build and furnish simple premises for any association that has proved itself viable. The tenancy agreement between the tenants' association and the G.L.C. makes over the running of the premises to the association; provided that the terms of the agreement are met, the Council rarely interferes, although it has the right to bring the agreement to an end with a week's notice in emergency. In the pensioners' clubrooms the position is different; a member of the Council welfare staff and an officer from the Housing Department usually serve on the pensioners' own management committee which may also include such people as a local headmaster, vicar, etc. To have a strong co-ordinating body like the Association of London Housing Estates safeguards the Authority and it helps the association cope with problems of running a clubroom. Committee members of one of the London associations on a multi-storey estate whom the research staff met several times were strongly opposed to the provision of any hall for which they were to be responsible *before* the association had become properly established. They were also adamant that if a tenants' association was to be in control it must have support either from its own co-ordinating body or from community development staff attached to the Authority or some voluntary organisation. Most of the London associations were convinced of the need for early

[13] *Community of Interests*, Scottish Education Department, Standing Consultative Council on Youth and Community Service. H.M.S.O. 1968.

provision of some meeting place. Birmingham Corporation is another city which regards meeting places as important in promoting community development. It aims at a hall of some kind for every 2,000 of its 140,000 tenants, and in 1969 had 35 such premises. They were not elaborate, the average cost being about £15,000.

To sum up. The physical restrictions of the flat and the social isolation of multi-storey housing demand extra-good facilities for recreation and social contacts *near at hand*. This means places for informal contact, for hobbies that can be pursued alone and premises where organisations can function. In general, premises for the use of new communities will not be used to the best advantage unless the tenants can draw on the support of staff trained in community development. Some form of quite modest meeting place of its own should be provided on any estate whose population is as much as 2,000 or so. There will be other places with a considerably smaller population where special factors (isolation, peculiar siting, etc.) justify the provision of premises. In general some form of meeting place should be available within a year of the first block's occupation.[14]

[14] *Housing Management in Scotland, op. cit.*

Chapter 12

THE CASE FOR INVESTMENT IN STAFF

"They think all you've got to do is get a hall
and people come out bosom pals"

Until recently the Corporation has not paid much attention to the need for staff to deal with the social aspects of its housing. In 1967, however, and with the appointment of a very experienced Housing Manager, a vigorous change in policy was initiated. The City Factor's Office became the Housing Management Department, the number of district offices and supervisory staff was much increased and 40 members of its staff were asked to attend part-time courses for the Diploma of the Institute of Housing Management. The Department's daily load is, however, extremely heavy and with the best will in the world its officers have little time to deal with the broad social issues deriving from 140,000 tenancies, quite apart from the new type of problems and opportunities presented by high flats. It was noted that the S.S.H.A., whose multi-storey estates on the whole presented fewer social problems than those of the Corporation, had long had a policy of employing a certain number of staff with some training in housing management. It was also noted that the 1967 report of the Corporation's Housing Manager emphasised the necessity for staff with professional qualifications in the social aspects of housing, particularly in regard to the 'unsatisfactory' tenant.

As far as the day-to-day life of the multi-storey tenant was concerned, staff meant caretakers, the 100 or so men who were employed either by the Corporation or the S.S.H.A. They were married men and lived in a flat at one of their own blocks. Their previous jobs were often ones where technical skill had been needed or where they had been required to handle people, e.g. as an engineer or a chief petty officer. The ratio of caretakers to blocks was roughly two men to three, or sometimes four blocks. Official working hours, shared between two men working alternate shifts, were 8.30 a.m.–12.00; 3–6 p.m.; 7–10 p.m. Including the rent-free flat, overall earnings were about £20 per week (July 1968). The caretaker normally worked from a small office situated at the block's entrance. His prime duty was to see to the safety and efficiency of such services as lighting, boilers, refuse, and above all the lift. As the one person who, in the child's phrase, could "unstick the lift" he played a vital part in the life of every tenant. He needed to be someone who kept his head in an emergency. And he had to be fit since a lift held up on a 26th floor might involve him in a couple of fast treks up and down 390 concrete stairs. He also supervised the cleaning of shared facilities, cleaned himself, dealt with vandalism and tried to keep the children relatively orderly. He was broadly responsible for ensuring that the tenants kept to their agreement with the Authority and if driven could report unsatisfactory behaviour. The research staff's interviews with selected caretakers (p. 34) showed that they were very much alive to their responsibility for the physical safety of their tenants. "Even in bed you half listen for the lift bell. It may be urgent, you never know." Most of them did dozens of jobs other than their official stint, from repairing a switch for a pensioner to playing the piano at a Christmas party. They were also, of course, invaluable to outsiders as one of the few sources of information about the curiously hidden world of the high flat.

Since a multi-storey block must have a caretaker, the tenant willy-nilly has to deal with a new relationship. He has no say in the appointment of his caretaker and the latter has to put up with whatever tenants he is given. There are thus inbuilt sources of friction quite apart from those due to the occasional tenant who thinks the caretaker should be at his beck and call; or to the truculent one who is "not going to be told by any b - - - caretaker where *my* weans shall play"; or to the caretaker who is inefficient, cross-grained or vindictive. As a job it lends itself to petty dictatorship and a self-respecting tenant can be irked to hear a caretaker talk about "*I* don't allow" or needled at the scribbled bit of paper which says that tenants *must* not do so and so. Caretaker and tenants' association were often on uneasy terms. Though some of the men thought the association united the block, they more often saw it as a body which existed to hatch up grievances, while the association did not always allow for the fact that the caretaker's hands may be tied. Innumerable situations arose which could not be covered by any written code. Such matters, and uncertainty as to the caretaker's legitimate powers, were fruitful sources of trouble. "Has he or has he not the right to stop the boys who live on this street from standing here?" Father-figure in an emergency, policeman, someone on whom to load dissatisfaction, the caretaker has a peculiarly testing job and one that may profoundly affect the contentment of the tenants and the way in which the block's social life develops. In view of this he ought to command a good salary. The research staff were impressed by the standing of the senior caretaker at the Bredang estate in Stockholm. He had an excellent office and one which, incidentally, included in its equipment a tape recorder attached to the telephone so that tenants could leave messages at any time convenient to themselves. A proper office for every

Plate 14

"The Hing", Glasgow.

Glasgow caretaker would ease his work, add to his status and act as a small hub for the block. It might also be useful to give him regular opportunities to discuss the practical side of his job somewhat on the lines seen at the Winstanley estate in Wandsworth. There the Borough's Housing Management officer, the chairman and secretary of the estate's tenants' association and one or other of its caretakers 'walked' the estate every three months, noting problems and seeing where co-operative effort might be applied. Another suggestion relates to the job's social aspects. Interviews held with selected Glasgow caretakers showed that when asked "Is there any one quality that a caretaker in a multi-storey block needs in particular?", they nearly all referred to such things as good temper, patience, care for their tenants, a sense of humour – in other words to social skills. Short training courses might be helpful. They could cover such things as how to balance the children's rights against those of the grown-ups and the need to care for Corporation property. Is it possible for him to do this without becoming an ogre who spoils the fun? The relationship between caretaker and tenant obviously needs to be thrashed out, e.g. the extent of their rights and his own need to respect them sufficiently to stand up for himself if a brush becomes inevitable. Some very elementary psychology might help explain two things which caretakers (and tenants' association officials) felt particularly sore about, viz. tenants' ingratitude and behaviour that seemed senseless. Like social workers the world over, the caretakers might be glad of someone on whom they could unburden themselves from time to time. Finally, a course of this kind would pool information about the kind of problems that are brought to caretakers and the sort of things they get asked for. Both might be valuable clues to the deeper needs of the tenants in this unfamiliar type of housing. If it is argued that the above is asking a great deal of the caretaker one can only reply that *someone* ought to be dealing with these and many other situations related broadly to the field of social welfare and community development. As things are no one is charged with the job. The matter is regarded as so important that although the question of staff for such purposes has been touched on at numerous places in the preceding chapters it is discussed again in the succeeding paragraphs.

It may be useful to refer briefly to the work of staff at certain of the examples of multi-storey housing seen in places other than Glasgow. In London any district office of the G.L.C. (responsible for up to 33,000 dwellings) had a staff of welfare officers. They dealt with neighbourhood troubles, marital differences, rent arrears, etc. Brandon had a resident officer whose main work was social welfare and rent collection. She linked the Housing Department with agencies working in Brandon and in connection with this served on the committees of local schools, youth clubs, etc. The Winstanley estate of Wandsworth Borough had no resident welfare staff but the Estate Superintendent and the Area Assistant concentrated on welfare and had no work connected with letting or inspections. Sheffield regarded community development as the job of the Housing, not the Education Committee, and the former employed 19 women welfare officers (1967). Their work included pre-tenancy consultation, keeping in touch with families at risk and arbitrating in disputes. One other officer worked full-time with tenants' associations. The Hyde Park estate (2,300 dwellings, mostly in multi-storeys) was a good example of Sheffield's policy on community development. The plans for the estate included premises for two tenants' meeting halls. A senior welfare officer worked from the local estate offices, a centrally situated building. Five other salaried staff were employed and also a full-time youth club leader. One of the many jobs in which the senior worker was involved was a dining club for pensioners which was held at the tenants' meeting hall at Park Hill. An interesting point was that the dinners were cooked and served by volunteers, housewives from the estate and members of the tenants' association.

In the case of Glasgow's 49 multi-storey estates just what work really needs staff with professional qualifications? To take one example. It is known that the rougher type of family creates a lot of problems in the initial stages of moving to a high flat. Would it not be sound to have a worker who could hold informal meetings in any area where numbers of such families are to be rehoused? As a kind of devil's advocate he would put the case against the physical charms of a multi-storey flat and at least warn of the adaptations the family will have to make. Whatever the prospective tenants' level of sophistication, skilled pre-tenancy contact should cut down the number who, later on, get a chip on their shoulder. Preliminary contact between trained staff and tenant would also enable the Authority to open a short case-history of the household (somewhat analagous to a medical record) a copy of which would be given to both parties. Another useful type of work in the early days of the larger estate would concern temporary play provision. A worker is also needed at this stage to help pensioners, and especially those who live alone, cope with the many unaccustomed features of this new type of home.

As regards more permanent work and as said earlier (Chapter 10) it would be most valuable to have one person on the Corporation's staff with professional qualifications in the recreational needs of children especially as they are affected by multi-storey housing. He would continually assess the play needs of the individual estate and in conjunction with the Youth Service see how best they could be met. The case for staff to co-ordinate work with the under-5s relates to the city as a whole but would be especially relevant to the multi-storey homes with small children.

Permanent staff are also needed for work with the older tenant. For example, the chairman of a tenants' association said how many of the elderly came to consult him whereas what they really needed was "some woman body". Unlike their problems on moving in, the matters with which they wanted help now could not be solved by giving them an agency's address or reading an electricity meter. Concentrated and continued support may be required in the case of blocks with large numbers of old people, not just with their problems but to help them get a bit of zest from life. Among the many experiments being made in this field attention should be drawn to a pilot scheme being tried in some of Manchester's high flats. Operated jointly by the Housing Committee and the Welfare Services, it provides additional supervision and security to old people in multi-storey housing.[1]

Staff with professional training would also be useful for permanent work with the 'below average' households that cause most of the serious trouble in the block. A skilled worker might be able to involve the caretaker and sympathetic neighbours in joint efforts at forestalling trouble. Since it is often the household's children who bring it into disrepute, the worker would try to get them into nursery schools and ask youth leaders to do a bit of pressurising about the older ones joining youth groups. Another job which neighbours and caretaker may overlook but which the professional worker would not, is to see that the trouble-prone family gets fair play.

Another field where the professionally trained worker is needed is on the estate where most of the tenants have come from particularly bad housing in a socially disadvantaged part of the city and have few specialised skills or interests. An estate of this kind may well justify the full-time services of a worker for the first two or three years. He or she might follow the lines used by the late Ilys Booker in North Kensington. This is based on helping people to identify the goals they are setting for themselves. It assists them to isolate the practical problems with which they are competent to deal. Above all it aims at changing passive acceptance, "You get used to it", into confidence in the ability to effect change. A slow and unspectacular job, it may well be basic to the social health of the down-town multi-storey estate. Until these tenants have begun to cope with their many day-to-day problems, especially as these have been intensified in the move to a high flat, it is waste of effort to expect them to build up a community, join leisure-time organisations, etc.

Another type of job but one unlikely to get off the ground without the backing of professionally trained staff is to recruit self-help from the estate. As mentioned earlier, a good deal of the care needed for the older tenant in multi-storey housing could be given by local people

[1] *Annual Report 1967–68, Manchester Welfare Services Committee*

provided they had some simple training and someone to turn to when they met problems. With the whole of the geriatric services bedevilled by shortage of staff, why not see what the tenants can do to look after their own? The same applies to work with children's play, youth groups, etc. It would also be exceedingly valuable to have someone with experience in community development to work with the tenants' associations.

The Social Work (Scotland) Act, emphasising the Authority's legal responsibility to promote welfare, provides the framework through which pretty well any type of community development may be initiated and it gives the necessary powers to appoint staff. In Glasgow various Departments of the Corporation have recently been considering such appointments.[2] Those responsible for this book are obviously not competent to advise on the administrative set-up connected with the above staff but it would presumably relate to policy making at headquarters and to field work on a relatively small number of individual estates. Any *ad hoc* co-ordinating committee should probably be associated with the Planning Department since this is the one which determines the estate's physical character. The members, however, should be drawn from other relevant departments. They must be of sufficiently senior level to recommend policy, allocate resources and authorise the deployment of staff. For example, the Education Committee might second one of its Youth Service officers for three days a week to the Housing Department to advise on play provision. Working through senior officials, the Committee would analyse the demographic and social character of the existing multi-storey estates and of new ones as they come into being. On the basis of this material it would decide what social facilities the estate is likely to need for the next five years and which Departments should provide them. It would also discuss with any appropriate voluntary organisations what responsibilities they were prepared to accept. The running of training courses for both paid and voluntary staff in various aspects of community development would be one of its important functions.[3]

As regards intensive work on the individual estate, this might be desirable if it is built in a socially disadvantaged district or contains a considerable proportion of tenants who previously lived in this kind of area. On such an estate the staff would do unusually thorough pre-tenancy consultations, give short-term help in the initial stages of moving to the flat, and provide continuing support where needed. On the large estate like Red Road and Sighthill where nearly the whole of

[2] *Report by a Joint Working Party on Community Problems appointed* by the Corporation of the City of Glasgow and the Secretary of State for Scotland 1969.
[3] *Community Work and Social Change: A Report on Training.* Calouste Gulbenkian Foundation, Longmans, 1968.

the population is living in high flats a kind of modified Citizen's Advice Bureau might make a useful base for the staff's work. On-site premises would be essential but they could be small since this would be primarily a place for the germination of ideas, not for meetings. It has been suggested that, to take an estate like Red Road, students from the near-by College of Further Education might put up a small prefabricated building. With this and one full-time trained worker it would be possible to co-ordinate the sporadic bits of external help that get offered to the estate and, more important, there would be a local place and someone known to the tenants to gather in *their* ideas and *their* help. It is not envisaged that this worker would supply a vague kind of leadership but rather that his presence would create a tool for Corporation and tenants to use jointly in order to work out detailed answers to specific problems. Since local authority services related to community development are still at an experimental stage, the traditional safeguards connected with the direct accountability of the above staff are probably less important than that they should be capable individuals and given considerable freedom of action.

Chapter 13

CONCLUSIONS

A General Review

By 1968–9 local authorities in Britain had in round figures built 300,000 flats in high buildings and 79,000 more were underway. This is a very rapid introduction for a type of home which differs radically from what has been customary, and for social groups about whose problems and potentials practically nothing is known. "Living high remains a mystery and an adventure" and it is over-optimistic to hope for comprehensive answers to the questions posed by such a complex and subtle theme as a new type of home. Though the long-distance implications are as yet anyone's guess, the more immediate and obvious pros and cons of multi-storey housing as used in Western Europe became apparent fairly soon after its introduction. On the whole the findings of this present study have been in line with what was already noted. High flats are, for example, commonly approved on the grounds that they are a rapid method of meeting the urgent need for new housing; that they enable people to live in central areas and thus to draw on the resources which justify urban life; that they help to solve the growing problem of site shortage; that the blocks' setting provides a green and peaceful island in the city scene; and finally that the flats themselves, with their splendid views and communal services, are attractive and functional. In criticism, those who are suspicious of this new form of housing point to its excessively high costs and to the attrition of social life with which it is associated. More important, they say it may be exposing children to unknown risks. A flat which is 250 feet above the earth's surface is certainly alien to the dream home of the man in the street or that which the small child instinctively makes in a drawing – a little house with windows each side of the door and a garden path. Popular opinion in this country by now has set fairly strongly against multi-storey housing. On the other hand there is little evidence, here or elsewhere, that those who have actually experienced life in a high flat are in general opposed to it. Though certain 'types' of household, notably those with young children, and also perhaps some 'types' of personality, have found it unsatisfactory, they are a minority among the occupants. The key to this widespread approval appears to be the high physical standards of the flat itself. It is almost invariably light and airy which suggests that it is good for health. It is well-designed and well-fitted, which meets rising expectations of comfort. It is easy to run, which suits modern life since it gives the housewife leisure and enables her to go out to work if she wishes. And it guarantees privacy, a luxury which the working-class home has rarely hitherto been able to afford. While low-rise housing could provide some of these assets equally well, though probably at high cost, the flats have certain advantages that are intrinsic to themselves. But they are hardly major ones: and it does seem curious that the tenants' own reactions should by and large run counter to the general popular antagonism towards this new form of home. In considering what the flat dwellers themselves have to say it is worth remembering that people tend to be chary about disparaging their home. For example, a study of tenants in Oldham which was made within 6–12 months of their moving to new estates, showed 89% as satisfied.[1] And even in Glasgow, with its notoriously bad housing, Professor Cullingworth's figures for the city's households as a whole gave 31% as very satisfied.[2] In any case views on such a tender subject are less likely to be a rigorous assessment than an expression of the speaker's personality. His level of education is also relevant; it is easy to drum up an opinion on the fittings of a new bathroom, but less so to weigh up and then put into words such a nebulous matter as the influence of life in a high flat on one's social contacts.

All this indicates that no foolproof evidence has as yet emerged on the desirability or otherwise of high flats as a form of local authority housing. But before giving the conclusions of this study as regards their social implications, it is desirable to refer briefly to the current arguments for and against their use on grounds other than the social ones. Though the boundary between these and the non-social issues is seldom clear cut, such matters as the high cost of high flats, their ability or otherwise to save site space, and their impact in terms of aesthetics can be discussed in their own right.

To take the first non-social point. However administratively convenient, high flats are notoriously expensive.[3] A (1968) figure for a 2-bedroom flat was about £5,500. The Ministry of Housing and Local Government in its circular No. 36/67 comes down firmly on this matter of expense, pointing out that "two-storey houses are in general the least costly form of building".[4] Or again, "dwellings in high blocks cost some 25% more than those in blocks of 3 or 4 storeys, or 50% more than

---

[1] *Moving Out of a Slum: a study of people moving from St. Mary's, Oldham.* Design Bulletin 20, Ministry of Housing and Local Government, H.M.S.O. 1970.
[2] *Op. cit.*
[3] *Housing, Town Development, Land and Costs*, Stone, The Estates' Gazette, 1960.
[4] *Op. cit.*

equivalent houses". Though construction costs per square foot do not increase proportionately with height, they nevertheless rise steadily and can soar to almost double those for traditional housing. For example, in 1963 a Glasgow tender for a 2-apartment house in a 5-storey block was £2,474 while in a 23-storey block on the same estate it was £3,747. The steep cost of a flat meant that originally it attracted a government subsidy (£30 per annum for 60 years) which was greater than that for a similar sized house of traditional type. However, in January 1969 new regulations for costing came into force which should make the higher blocks in general too expensive to qualify for subsidy. This suggested that the Ministry was questioning the desirability of multi-storey housing and using its yardstick powers to hold down the height at which it was prepared to encourage authorities to use it. As a type of building still relatively untried by time, high flats have also proved liable to unforeseen costs. The Ronan Point collapse has involved some 50 or so authorities in very considerable expense which was entirely unexpected. A known and continuing cost and one much greater than for low-rise housing is that of maintenance. Thus the 1969–70 figure quoted by the S.S.H.A. for the average annual maintenance costs of its low-rise property in Glasgow was £8·39, while that for a high flat (which included electricity for lifts and laundries) was £21·75. Moreover on social grounds high flats often require extra generous and extra well planned physical facilities, e.g. a very tempting toddlers' playground or a meeting hall for pensioners that is really near the block. Experience proves that in many cases this provision will not be effectively used unless it is staffed. And personnel is always costly. A borough treasurer, advising his authority how its budget should be allocated, may easily dismiss such staff as a fringe service; but any councillor knows that bricks and mortar *per se* do not guarantee that improvement in the quality of life which is the ultimate aim of an authority's housing.

The second non-social feature of high flats relates to the amount of land they occupy. The happy theory that they are a sound answer to site shortage has now been generally discredited. Dr. Thomas Sharp puts the arguments clearly and cogently when he shows that a building can achieve the accepted maximum density for urban areas of about 70 rooms per acre without rising above three storeys. If higher, then "the maximum density remains and no more accommodation and population can be got on the ground".[5] In other words the site space needed for high flats is not smaller than that required for the equivalent number of low-rise dwellings unless one is (*a*) prepared to turn a blind eye to open-space provision, (*b*) willing for the additional population to become parasites on the locality's existing facilities and services. It is also questionable whether the land freed by building high – the large, open

[5] *Town and Townscape*, Sharp, Murray, 1968.

expanses of grass, concrete and tarmac which are the normal setting for towers and slabs – has much intrinsic value for the flats' own population or the community at large. It is difficult to give such places visual interest, they do not lend themselves to the casual encounters that humanise the physical scene, and the tenants cannot put them to the infinity of ingenious uses possible in their own backyard or garden however microscopic. Nor is there any shortage of practical illustrations on how to get high densities without building high. Britain now has good examples of low-rise housing in traditional-type terraces and in relatively low (8–14 storeys) building where the overall density is above that in soaring towers. For example, an estate at Haringey has achieved a density of 110 p.p.a. using 2-storey houses plus a few flats for old people. A Southwark estate built in 4-storey flats and maisonettes has achieved a figure of 173 p.p.a. On a 3-acre site belonging to Westminster City Council (Lillington Gardens, Phase 3) a density as high as 254 bedspaces per acre has been obtained through medium high building, much of it at not more than 4-5 storeys. All the family dwellings (i.e. 2-bedroom and larger) have their own, quite small garden court, about 20' × 16'. As one would expect, the cost exceeds that for a low density estate of low-rise dwellings, but the estate is built within housing cost yardstick.

The third non-social matter concerns the way in which multi-storey blocks affect the scene, near and far. Whereas the early skyscrapers, e.g. those of Manhattan, seem to have formed meaningful groups, these new ones are in general built on any site that happens to be vacant. Thus they mostly rear up fortuitously and in unrelated chunks. Traditionally too the tall, eye-catching building has not only been sited with aesthetic considerations in mind but has been an expression of the community's concept of something pre-eminent, a church, town hall, or university. Apart from deliberately introduced landmarks of this nature, buildings have mostly flowed close to the contours of the ground, a kind of brick and mortar carpet. Moreover the lofty silhouette has normally had some affinity with natural forms, i.e. it has been tapered or rounded or had broken levels. The rearing rectangular outline of the multi-storey block is hard on the eye. And it is inescapable. The only thing that can soften it is nightfall which can sometimes transmute a block into a sort of stylised Christmas tree. But nothing can disguise these towers in the day-time nor diminish the impression they give of height. They dwarf everything, important public buildings, trees, humans. They also shut off and shut in. A single block can become a giant stopper, keeping out what used to be a pleasant glimpse of the sky at the end of a dull street. Or a line of blocks may slash across a dramatic view of snow-capped hills. They also diminish the pleasantness of city parks and public gardens since their prodigious height dispels the illusion of rural things. The pastoral scenes of Pollok Park, to quote a Glasgow example, are suddenly punctured when one catches sight above the trees of a hard line of red slabs. They likewise steal the nearer sky, lessening the chance of small pleasures like a fine sunset or a new moon. And any house or garden lying alongside a multi-storey block suffers drastically from the overshadowing of this cold and concrete wing.

Assuming the general validity of the above points, is there ground for thinking that these arguments against high flats might be outweighed by certain assets as regards their social character? This does not appear to be so since they have commonly produced immediate social problems and have commonly been held to contain the seeds of longer distance ones. To take a major point. There is the question whether high flats meet the local authority's need to cater for all and sundry as found on a housing list. Practically no one disputes that this form of home is unsatisfactory for the family with small children. It is a strain on the mother and an over-restricted environment, physical and social, for the child. There are problems even for families whose children are of school age since the children's world is so cut off from that of adults. And the trim orderly setting of the multi-storey estate requires unusually imaginative provision for play if the children themselves are not to be thwarted. Another group of households which life in a high flat does not really suit are those rather below the social and educational level of the block's households in general. These tenants find it difficult to cope with the methodical habits and the self-contained existence of life in a multi-storey block, and are likely to be more of a disruptive element than would be the case in low-rise housing. Those who fit easily into life in a high flat are people who are self-sufficient and socially rather 'above average'. The wider their experience of men and affairs the more they can cope with sharing services and undertaking mutual obligations with a large number of other people. The more advanced their level of education the more likely they are to recognise the risks associated with this new type of home. And the higher their income the more they can afford to spend on compensations – a car, a seaside holiday, membership of sports clubs, etc. The Netherlands study referred to on page 3 came to this same conclusion, viz. that high flats are chiefly suitable for "a limited category of more cultured families in the middle and higher income groups".[6]

Another of the recognised social disabilities of the high flat is that it is excessively self-contained. It has none of the handy neutral areas, doorstep, yard or garden, which help people to build up their dossiers on each other without necessarily exchanging a word. And it is blind in that its windows afford no two-way link with the outside world. This turns the block and estate into eventless places, short of those goings-

[6] *Op. cit.*

on of life that tempt people out of their homes, give them shared interests and help them strike up acquaintance should they so wish. The traditional attitude to the tower as a building form is that it represents two aspects of life, isolation from other homes and a spiritual refuge:[7] and in an odd way this is how many of those living in today's towers regard them. Though they welcome the privacy, they sense the isolation; and many seem to feel that it somehow diminishes the quality of their life. The anonymity tells particularly harshly on the smaller, and in particular, the 1-person household yet these smaller households are just those which characterise high flats.

Another area of risk associated with the social aspects of multi-storey housing is that it tends to restrict the tenant's opportunities for choice, self-expression and personal freedom in small matters. It lends itself to more risk than is the case with Council housing of traditional type to the idea that "*We*, even though sanctioned by the polls, decide how *they* shall live", and to the paternalism (management) that stultifies responsibility. To take small matters. The tenant is forbidden to keep a dog or any pet of much consequence. He has no opportunity to make the small adaptations, those generally permitted in low-rise housing, to meet his fancy as regards the looks of the exterior of his home. He has no garden, which cuts out the boundless possibilities for choice that are afforded by even the smallest plot. The necessity to use a lift to some extent controls his freedom of movement and may do so seriously if the service is inadequate. He also has to accept the presence of a caretaker and whatever authority this officer is authorised to exercise over himself and his children.

The summing up would seem to be as follows. Dismissing for the moment the social implications of high flats, there is no clear case on other grounds in favour of them as a form of local authority housing. On the contrary, there are solid arguments against them, particularly because of their excessive cost. As regards social issues, they display few features which might outweigh their disadvantages in other fields and few indications that they make a home which is really satisfactory as distinct from one that is more or less all right. Indeed the evidence from this study indicated that they have positive drawbacks and may conceal actual dangers. Thus the conclusion cannot be avoided that local authorities should discontinue this form of housing except for a limited range of carefully selected tenants or in cases of extreme pressure.

REDUCING THE EXISTING DISADVANTAGES

What action should be taken about the high flats already built in Britain, the 380,000 homes with their million-odd population which are

[7] Cf. 'The Tower', *Analecta Romanica*, Heft 22, September 1969.

likely to be occupied for the next 60 years? The obvious answer is to identify the areas of need, and then to see what might mitigate the disadvantages even if the basic causes are irremovable. Before enlarging on some of the issues believed to be common to many of the areas where high flats are in use, and as exemplified in Glasgow, it is necessary to repeat a few of the facts about this city's use of multi-storey housing and the tenants' reactions to it.

In this last half-century, and by various quirks of fortune, Glasgow has taken some hard knocks especially as regards its economic life. A couple of hours' tour of the city demonstrates vividly the massive reconstruction judged essential if it is to hold its own. The most intractable matter of all is its rehousing. Dismissing such matters as the city's severe financial stringency and the Scottish tradition of very low rents, there are many additional problems. The first, the sheer scale of the need for new and reconditioned homes, means that pressures on the housing list are likely to remain high for years. While overspill policy has resettled many families in new and expanded towns, and economic decline has caused considerable emigration from the city, the backlog of congestion, and the accelerating rate of obsolescence in the existing stock of houses, are such as almost to overtake the fairly slow-moving overspill process. The constricting effect of the administrative city boundary has also greatly handicapped house building. An additional inhibition, imposed by the Clyde Valley Green Belt, has hindered consideration of Glasgow's housing problem as a regional one, and has perpetuated the belief that the Clyde Valley has an absolute shortage of building land. This is true for the city itself, even though the problem has been artificially created by the existing anachronistic boundary. It is largely because of this that the Corporation, caged within the local government territorial confines, has been driven to opt for high flats, building their first 10-storey blocks as early as 1952. The speed with which 'systems building' can be erected has also been in their favour, political and social pressures for new homes being so intense. Demands of this magnitude have tended to divert the attention of policy makers from the social implications.

In May 1969 not far short of 50,000 Glaswegians were living "up in the heights". This represented the population of 15,500 flats, in 163 blocks. At the date on which most of the statistical material of this study was based, July 1968, there were 143 blocks on 49 estates. These were scattered throughout the city in 30 distinct areas. Densities were high, a not uncommon figure being 150 p.p.a. The estates ranged in size from 2 to 40 acres. When completed, one of the largest will have a population of 7,000, practically all living in identical blocks (19 storeys). The buildings in general were tall, 40 of the 143 rising to 21–23 storeys, and three-quarters of the remainder having 11 or more floors. Nearly half of the 30 main geographical areas containing high flats had no low-rise housing associated with them. The figures for July 1968 showed that the age structure of the flats' population was not markedly different from that of the city as a whole as shown in the 1966 Census. This indicates that there has been little policy of confining this new form of home to selected types of tenant. The one distinctive demographic feature, the absence of the larger household, was due to the fact that practically none of the flats contained more than 3 bedrooms.

The typical recreation of the Glasgow tenant to his flat as such was summed up in the phrase that was heard time and again, "I love my home". Not every household felt like this and some loathed the place. But those were a minority, and by and large were confined to the families with more than one small child. On the whole the tenants were very pleased. They greatly appreciated the attractive looks of the flat, its labour-saving features, and the immense views. It was also patently good value even when, as was nearly always the case, their rent and rates had soared compared with those of their old home, being still only £9–10 per month for about half the households and less still, £6–8, for a third (July 1968). Another thing that told strongly in favour of this new form of home was that, unlike most of Glasgow's postwar housing, it did not inevitably shut one away from the heart of the city. And it was much more likely to keep one relatively near old haunts. Of the main sample, 36% had moved less than a mile from their previous home, 19% only 1–2 miles. They were also relatively near their jobs in that half (of those who were the household's chief wage earner) had a journey of 30 minutes or under.

Though studies on high flats in Britain and elsewhere seldom indicate any general hostility on the part of the tenants, the extent of satisfaction found in Glasgow did seem remarkably high. The flat was very much a new toy of course since at the date when the main sample was taken, 62% of the households had been in it for less than 2 years and only 5% for as long as 5 years or more. But within this time-scale there was little sign in the figures of a decline in satisfaction. Nor did the material from the research team's informal contacts with the tenants run counter to the satisfaction expressed in the formal interviews. Were the Glasgow attitudes perhaps strongly coloured by local conditions? A flat, and one in a 4-storey tenement, is of course the traditional home for nearly all social classes in the city and it is that which is still being built for low-rise housing. Thus there is nothing unaccustomed or socially inferior about not living in a house and not having a garden or a yard of one's own. There is also the matter of health. The city's high incidence of respiratory diseases may well enhance the value that Glasgow people place on the sunniness and smog-free air of the soaring blocks. The clinching influence is, however, probably the intense pressure for better housing. Not only is this pressure common but so many families still expect to have to wait interminably. The story of the man who claimed he had put in his original application for a council house 40 years back may be apocryphal; but the figures obtained in this study were stark enough. Of the 58% of households who provided information on this point that was precise enough to use statistically, 42% had been on the housing list for 15 or more years. The wretchedness of so many of the tenements and the sordidness of their surroundings, the crumbling fabrics, shared lavatories, and lack of a bathroom, make a fantastic contrast to the new high flat which is near enough the dream house of the Ideal Home exhibition. Under such conditions people dismiss pretty well everything except that they can be rid of the old place. "Give us a better house and to hell with any other considerations".

Details of the physical character of the flat and block appeared to be satisfactory in that no consistent complaints were noticed about such things as the flat's design, noise from neighbours or the layout of the floor. Tenants had no strong preferences as regards type of block nor, unexpectedly, the floor on which their home was situated. On the other hand social considerations rather indicated that the block should not exceed about 10 floors in height, the figure for which many cities in Western Europe seem to have settled. This is not too daunting to deter most people from using the stairs in an emergency; one can see something of what goes on at ground level; and verbal communication is just possible.

As regards the shared services and duties, rubbish disposal was satisfactory and the tenants' cleaning of common stairs, etc. not a problem. None of the various shared arrangements for clothes drying seemed to suit everyone and the more the housewife had her private facilities the better. (In Glasgow there has been little demand for communal laundries.) As yet the provision for cars was adequate.

Problems connected with the lift

The most important of the shared services, and the one that attracted a great deal of criticism, was the lift. It is essential that lifts should be adequate in number, size and speed and so efficiently serviced that people are not apprehensive about them going out of order. The occasional long breakdown is less frustrating than a nagging uncertainty about the lifts' day-to-day reliability. The need to use a lift means that this may, and in fact often does, add to the time the tenant has to allow when getting from his home to any activity taking place at ground level. Unless the high-flat population is to be seriously disadvantaged this delaying factor must be taken into account when the siting of services and facilities for the estate is being planned. In fact the standards here should be higher than average, since they are related to so concentrated a population.

Recommendations

1. The lift should be suited to the size and demographic character of the block and variations in lift type explored, e.g. high-speed lifts for upper floors, service lifts, etc.
2. A tougher and more child-proof version of the lift should be designed to meet the self-operated service of the multi-storey block.
3. Detailed records should be kept at every block of the times and length of breakdown and normal length of waiting time. To avoid the formation of stereotypes about the lift, it might be well to make these records easily available to those living in the block concerned.
4. When, as in two of the blocks at Red Road, the lifts still prove inadequate even after $3\frac{1}{2}$ years, special safeguards should be provided. This might mean an attendant and/or a resident technician on 24-hour call.
5. When planning the facilities for a multi-storey estate, account should be taken of the tenants' necessity to use a lift and the lift's unpredictability. The availability of facilities should be measured in terms of time as well as geographical distance.

Service and facilities on the estate

A recent study by the Ministry of Housing and Local Government on selected low-rise and multi-storey estates has suggested that the crucial factor in tenants' satisfaction was not building form but the general character of the estate.[8] In Glasgow the local conditions referred to earlier (p. 133) may have reversed the order, but nevertheless their estate, as distinct from their flat, did influence reactions to multi-storey life and on the whole adversely so. The unusually high provision standards of multi-storey flats probably mean their tenants are more aware of deficiencies in the services and the facilities available to them than is the case in new low-rise housing (though often enough the lack of amenities is a byword there too). Moreover the delaying factor of the lift augments the case for facilities to be near at hand, while the physical restrictions imposed by the flat strengthen the need for recreational opportunities in a larger setting.

As regards the physical pattern of the Glasgow estates, a mixture of

[8] *Estate satisfaction on six council estates*, Sociological Research Section, Ministry of Housing and Local Government, 1969 (Unpublished)

multi-storey and low-rise houses is thought to make a better environment than one confined to high blocks. On social grounds it would seem important that the size and number of dwellings on the estate should be such that it can cater for considerable internal movement to meet the needs of households as they change in size. Once having experienced the high standards and easy housekeeping of a multi-storey flat, these tenants are unlikely to be satisfied with anything but a modern home. In Glasgow in particular one cannot see them being prepared to move back to tenement housing, however good its quality. Apart from variations due to the estate's location, size and demographic patterns, almost the only services and facilities which did not attract criticism were those connected with education and to a lesser extent with health and welfare. Innumerable unfavourable comments were made about poor transport, the need to re-site bus stops and to install traffic lights and zebra crossings. Pensioners were particularly disadvantaged by poor transport and so were mothers with small children. The absence of women car drivers on the typical multi-storey estate strengthens the need for good transport. Some of the Glasgow estates had none of the shops, post office services, etc. necessary for daily needs; and relatively few had such perhaps more marginal but highly convenient things as laundrettes, shoe repairers, hairdressers, cafés and chip shops. Even in those cases where a few shops had been built, the tenants complained that they were limited in type and dearer and less convenient as regards opening hours than those to which they had been accustomed. The mobile van was regarded as a highly unsatisfactory substitute for the shop proper. On recreational provision for children, the tenants' general comment was that the boys' kickabouts were fine, that the playgrounds with static concrete tunnels, blocks, etc. were not much fun really, and that properly designed, or indeed any play places for toddlers and their mothers, were almost non-existent. It was also noted by outside observers, though less so by the tenants themselves, that no one seemed to have thought about girls' needs as regards their type of play. There was a great deal of criticism about lack of places which the tenants could use for meetings, large or small. Any new estate can absorb an almost unlimited amount of amenities and it is, of course, largely finance that sets the limits. This is especially so in Glasgow where so many brand-new communities are having to be established. In view of this would it not be sound policy for the Corporation to bring in outside agents and to encourage the commercial provider as is done on the Continent? This would increase the supply of facilities and give them more variety. A less complex matter, but one which would help offset the lack of physical and costly amenities, is to make the maximum use of the city's voluntary organisations. In their case a relatively small sum ploughed in often yields a good return, provided that there is plenty of

Plate 15 Traditional pavement conversation piece, Glasgow.

flexibility about integrating their services with those of the Corporation. The rapid growth of the New Glasgow Society and of the City's Pre-school Playgroups shows that once the ordinary citizen senses a need, Glasgow is not slow to offer help.

Long delay in the provision of even a minimum of basic facilities was a most frequent cause of tenant dissatisfaction. Additions to bus services are seldom made automatically to match an increase in population, so that the tenants themselves may have to battle for them, and maybe for several years. Similarly, playgrounds tend to be one of the last things built except perhaps for a single meagrely-equipped affair. For example, a couple of blocks with some 50 children still had no playground after $2\frac{1}{2}$ years, and 5 blocks with literally hundreds of small children had no suitable place for them and their mothers for as long as 4 years – a considerable slice out of toddlerhood. Experience elsewhere as regards amenities shows that, quite apart from their value in meeting basic needs, the more generous the supply the more likely is the community to become a cohesive one.[9] On the ground that a makeshift environment sets up undesirable social patterns (especially in the case of children), it is arguable that a fair range of community facilities should be ready before any flat is occupied.

Another matter connected with the setting of the high flat that commonly leads to problems is the estate's upkeep. With no private territory apart from that within the walls of his own flat, the tenant is perhaps unusually prone to regard the estate as in a sense his own porch or front. If it is allowed to deteriorate this reflects on himself. It is also a threat to those higher standards referred to earlier about which he may not be all that secure. To please the adult, the highly artificial setting of the multi-storey block just must be kept spic-and-span. But this cuts across the children's need for a place they can *use*, quite apart from the fact that, as the zoologists note, the offspring of *homo sapiens* are the most inquisitive and therefore the most destructive of all young animals. The situation is aggravated because broken **door** panels, uprooted shrubs, fences flattened, walls spray-painted and grass crunchy with glass are so conspicuous in the open landscape of the multi-storey estate. Moreover, in a block with perhaps 100 households, it is difficult to identify, let alone restrain, the careless tenant or the one who does malicious damage. And if the estate is in a district short of open spaces, playgrounds, etc. outsiders are very liable to flood in. The fact that there are fewer adults about the place than in traditional housing also means that misuse is less likely to be checked.

[9] *Council House Communities*. A policy for progress. Report by a Sub-Committee of the Scottish Housing Advisory Committee. H.M.S.O. 1970.

Recommendations

1. The case for encouraging outside agencies (commercial interests) to provide some of the physical facilities on the estate should be explored.
2. More encouragement, including some financial aid, should be given to voluntary organisations to undertake work on the multi-storey estates. This should not be limited to those providing welfare services but should include cultural organisations.
3. When services and facilities are being planned, full account should be taken of the delaying influence of the lift.
4. The need for early provision of services, even if only temporary, should be recognised. They should include such things as temporary changes to transport facilities, temporary toddlers' play areas, mobile libraries.
5. The initial layout of the estate should be such as to conceal hard wear, i.e. extensive use should be made of trees on rough areas, tough shrubs, screening walls, etc.
6. The concern felt by the great majority of the tenants for the looks of their estate should be exploited by enlisting their co-operation over positive improvements, not merely in trying to stop misuse.

Households which appeared to find a multi-storey home quite satisfactory

By and large and as said earlier (p. 47) the more sophisticated the household the better it could cope with the overt and hidden problems of life in a high flat. Leaving aside the question of sophistication, certain 'types' of household found it suited them much better than others. One such was the middle-aged couple whose children had now left home. If, as was likely, the wife worked outside the home, she did not suffer from the flat's loneliness and the second wage meant the couple could afford outside interests. The high proportion of tenants who were roughly at this stage in their life-cycle presumably helped to account for Glasgow's high rate of satisfaction with this new type of housing. A second, well-suited household was that of the man or woman who did not particularly want to make a settled home, but whose life revolved round job, friends and the recreational opportunities of the bright-light areas.

Pensioners and the disabled

Other people who on the whole seemed to find that a high flat made a good home were the pensioners, though this was very dependent on the provision of safeguards, especially for those living alone. It was generally agreed that the flat's creature comforts, easy housekeeping, absence of steps and stairs, brightness and splendid view, together with the quietness of the estate, suited old people and did something to mitigate "the surly advance of decrepitude", to use a Churchillian phrase. The height at which the flat was situated was unimportant except that really low floors were to be avoided as being noisy and giving less sense of security. A balcony was desirable so long as its walls were not of such material and height that it gave a feeling of being boxed in. This was the case if the pensioner could not see through or over it when sitting beside the window. Another safeguard for the pensioner's piece of mind, even if never put to use, was some easy method of summoning help. The lack of this appeared to be a real anxiety among the older Glasgow tenants, and not only those who lived alone. As regards shops, post offices, doctors' surgeries, transport, etc., the case for near-by provision (a major concern to the great majority of tenants) was much increased if they were pensioners. Official welfare services were regarded as essential if a really watchful eye was to be kept on the more frail in this cut-off type of home, and on pensioners in general at times of crisis. Very many would have appreciated unobtrusive support in the first few months after moving in. Since the needs of the elderly are so largely related to their physical care, health visitors are one of the most appropriate services. The social importance of the work of the home help also needs stressing. The Glasgow Old People's Welfare Committee provides a variety of admirable services and it might be that the able-bodied population on the multi-storey estates would prove a fruitful source of voluntary help to this and kindred bodies if it was deliberately sought out. The most serious of the disadvantages of a high flat for the older tenant is probably social isolation, leading to low spirits. *Near-by* provision of clubs, day centres and common rooms is needed and a bowling green would be a boon. But the surest safeguard is neighbourly care from the households living alongside and having the same social background as that of the pensioner. As regards disabled people, whether pensioners or not, the main need is to see that there is no neglect about minor physical adaptations to the flat. On the whole the disabled were probably better cared for, by statutory and voluntary services, than were the pensioners; but their able-bodied neighbours mostly seemed very indifferent to one of the main needs, i.e. for company.

Recommendations

1. The flat's balcony should be so designed that the tenant can see out when sitting beside the window.
2. Some method should be provided by which the tenant can summon help from inside the flat.

3. The pensioner's flat should be sited alongside those of households of varying sizes. This means that the block should not be so designed that its flats are likely to be occupied almost entirely by middle-aged or pensioner households.
4. Social provision for pensioners should be examined in terms of availability (how near, how often) and of the nature of the programmes. The needs of the more intellectual should not be forgotten.
5. A sufficient number of welfare staff should be available to give detailed attention to the special needs of the older tenant in this unaccustomed and physically isolated home.

Families with children

Of the unsuited households the most vulnerable were those with young children. In Glasgow the numbers were so considerable that they must be re-emphasised. In July 1968 about 6,700 children (0–14) were living in a high flat; 27% of the households had at least one child under 16; 20% of the population was aged under 15; and 7% was under 5. Of all the children 79% lived above the 4th floor. No hard evidence was obtained in Glasgow on the more surface and immediate effects of this new form of housing on children. A small study of adolescents and young adults who had spent most of their childhood on a multi-storey estate gave no indication that they themselves felt that living high had been any particular disadvantage. Another small study, of a primary school population, gave no sign that the children living in high flats displayed any overt signs of retardation compared with the ones from traditional-type housing. However, both these were very minor studies. Moreover, it is essential to underline that the effects noted were at no more than surface level. More serious ones may be difficult to detect or indeed may not show up until years later. It must be emphasised that the tenants themselves were almost universally agreed that a high flat was not a good home for children, and that it made problems for mothers. In this connection it may be relevant to draw attention to the fact that the health of Glasgow mothers (as shown in their high perinatal mortality rates) is not good.[10]

The immediate problem with children of school age is how to give them stimulating provision for all-weather play in this modern setting which, compared with the traditional street, lacks both the incidental interest and the care provided by adults and is far more vulnerable to damage. If this new environment is to be made sufficiently varied and challenging to avert boredom – the source of half the trouble on the typical multi-storey estate – then some risks have to be taken. Planners

[10] 'Perinatal Mortality in Glasgow', Richards *et. al. Health Bulletin* Vol. XXVII No. 4, Oct. 1969.

should work on the assumption that children should be expected to (and mostly do) show a reasonable amount of common sense.

As regards the children under school age and the possible ill-effects in after life of spending their early years in a high flat, no information could be found from Britain or elsewhere. But the whole pattern of this new form of housing is alien to what the psychologists say is necessary for the sturdy proper growth of a small child. The physical restrictions of the flat, and the fact that the child is so cut off from people other than those of his own home, deprive him of that variety of stimuli on which his intellectual development depends. Lacking a range of experiences, he fails to acquire the sense of security which encourages him to seek out further ones: rather he shrinks from them. Assuming that this kind of home almost inevitably stultifies the child's curiosity, and thus his ability in later life to experiment and explore, it could be particularly invidious in the case of Scottish society with its traditions of independence and enterprise. The immediate problem with these little children is how to introduce outdoor facilities that are accessible and attractive, and indoor play groups that are sufficiently well-run and widespread for the mothers to *use* these compensatory measures.

Before leaving the subject of families with children, brief reference must be made to the young family with several children which is rather 'below average' socially and economically. As any Sunday morning shopping crowd in Gallowgate demonstrates, Glasgow still has considerable sections of its population who bear the marks of generations of deprivation. High flats are likely to include some of such families; and it is asking a lot of them suddenly to show the self-restraint, social competence and rather nice habits needed for a satisfactory use of multi-storey housing. In pre-tenancy consultation this type of family should be noted; and if it is accepted for a high flat then welfare staff should keep in touch with it as potentially at risk.

Recommendations

1. In general families with children of primary school age or younger should not be given a high flat. If this cannot be achieved, it is desirable to try to exclude them from blocks situated in the more central and congested areas.
2. Since children already form a considerable proportion of the flats' population, and since it is anyhow undesirable to have many communities that are childless ones, really good opportunities for play are essential. Some of these will involve staff. All this is a matter for skilled advice; and the Corporation should have at least one senior member with qualifications in this field to work in co-operation with the Youth Service, schools and tenants' associations.

3. In the current national drive for more and better co-ordinated provision for children under 5, those living in high flats should receive special attention. The Corporation should appoint a second member of staff to work in this field and to give regular advisory supervision to the kind of tenant-run playgroup that ought to be a regular feature of any multi-storey estate with a considerable number of preschool children.
4. In view of the number of children under 5 (2,400 at July 1968) living in the city's high flats, research projects should be initiated without delay into (a) the immediate and (b) the longer distance influence of this form of housing. If both cannot be undertaken forthwith, the latter should take priority.

Problems connected with the anonymity of life in high flats

A striking aspect of this new form of housing is the way in which it isolates people from each other. How far would it be tolerated did not radio and T.V. provide some, if only a shadowy substitute for real-life contacts? Even such a tiny matter as lack of clear-cut methods of block and house numbering (which makes it difficult to locate an address) adds to the sense of anonymity. The flat itself is a sealed cell and the people on one floor know far less about those living immediately above or below them than would be the case were they in neighbouring houses in a street. Since household size is relatively small, this reduces the number of outsiders who visit the home, nor do the children pop in and out so much. Perhaps the fact that the move to a high flat often represents a rise in the family's social standards encourages people to keep themselves to themselves. Those met with in this study certainly set a high value on the new privacy even when they regretted losing certain features of the old intimate character of working-class society. But individuals like the mother with small children and the housebound invalid, and innumerable old people would have welcomed more companionship. Irrespective of age, those living alone, 19% of the total households, could be exceedingly isolated by the drastic way in which 'living high' cuts down contact with living things and shuts out almost all the sight and most of the sound of the outside world. This contracted existence is a classic situation for turning thought in on oneself with the unhappiness and eccentricities of behaviour to which this can lead. All this suggests that the social potentials of specific parts of the block and estate ought to be explored. The lift hall, for example, the one place where tenants cannot avoid rubbing shoulders, should not be a draughty, comfortless spot from which people want to escape as quickly as possible. Since in some queer way it is easier to get to know relative strangers out of doors than in, there should be plenty of spots about the estate that bring people together in a seemingly fortuitous way. Shops, pubs, cafés, churches and the services and facilities referred to earlier play an enormous part in all this. So do places where competitive sport takes place and those where car tinkering and gardening go on. The multi-storey estate, with its grass, trees and relative freedom from traffic, should make it a pleasanter setting for a home than the old congested street. But adults won't really take advantage of these new assets unless the estate so to speak tempts them to do so. It should also be remembered that the tenants came from very different social backgrounds and that, however laudable the efforts of certain groups to make the estate a socially superior one, this ought not to be allowed to drive out customary methods of social contact. Any community needs some spots that lend themselves to a bit of gossiping.

Another method of countering social isolation is of course through formal groups. These have the added merit for a multi-storey estate in that they provide opportunities for activities that cannot take place in the restricted confines of the flat. Though with a strongly dissenting minority, the Glasgow tenants did not show any particular enthusiasm for adults' clubs and societies. Many people had physically strenuous days and on the newer estates energy and cash were still going into setting up the home. In any case working-class society has not much tradition of joining leisure-time groups. But everywhere there was a chronic shortage of meeting places, only 3 of the 49 estates having premises of their own. Those residents who did see the case for formal groups often had ideas for joint activities which they felt would help pull the estate together. Most of these never got off the ground because there was nowhere suitable to meet. The main, or often the only premises were schools. But they were frequently overbooked, not available at weekends and during the holidays (a considerable proportion of the days of the year), and expensive if wanted for activities not directly connected with the Education Committee's own types of provision. Suitable meeting places mostly imply subsidised ones: but they are so valuable in promoting the activities which break down isolation and build up cultural life that it is shockingly false economy to be niggardly or dilatory about providing them. The typical estate (2,000+ population) could make a modest start if it had within the first year just one small hall that would seat about 80 (a figure based on attendances at meetings of tenants' associations). This is in line with a recent recommendation in *Council House Communities* for new estates in general.[11] The problem of control, often crucial, would be eased if the management was vested in a committee of tenants together with representatives from the Authority and a few outsiders, e.g. a councillor or local headmaster. Group activities would be speeded up if the tenants could draw

[11] *Op. cit.*

on the services of staff trained in community development. The Corporation's Housing Management Department is continually stepping up the number and qualifications of its staff but they are still too few and do not include specialists in welfare or community development. The new 1968 Social Work (Scotland) Act gives the authority legal responsibility to promote welfare, together with the necessary powers to employ staff in this field. Also much to be welcomed is the reference (in the Report of the Joint Working Party referred to on p. 124) to proposals for the appointment of community workers for Glasgow.[12] As far as high flats are concerned, it would be valuable if their initial work could include finding premises for social and cultural activities; co-ordinating, promoting, and supervising provision for the under-5s; and in particular stimulating self-help. This study gave a strong impression that the multi-storey population contained a considerable proportion of tenants with time on their hands. With steady and intelligent encouragement they might well be ready now to involve themselves in group activities both for good works and for educational and cultural pursuits.

Recommendations

1. A clear, detailed and consistent address method should be adopted for the multi-storey housing throughout Glasgow.
2. The opportunities offered by the lift hall as a focal point for social contacts should be utilized.
3. Sheltered seats should be provided at strategic points about the estate.
4. The near-by schools should be involved in the estate's social activities and the tenants not merely allowed but encouraged to use the schools' premises.[13] In view of the dependence of the multi-storey estates on schools as meeting places, the current regulations governing the availability of schools at week-ends and in the holidays should be re-examined.
5. A small hall should be provided by the Authority for any multi-storey estate with a population of 2,000 or more within a year of the estate's first occupation.

Relations with the local authority

One of the more nebulous problems arising from multi-storey housing is that it lends itself to restricting the tenant's opportunities for choice and adding to the control which their local authority exercises over them. Some of this is unavoidable. For example, the fact that the

[12] *Op. cit.*
[13] Cf. **Housing Management in Scotland**, *op. cit.*

Plate 16

The base of the block, Gorbals, Glasgow.

tenant has to share services with many other households means that more regulations are required than in low-rise housing. The presence of a caretaker also adds a new measure of control. This suggests that the tenant needs special bulwarks to protect him against small erosions of personal freedom and should be given the maximum of choice in non-essentials. To take a small example. It might produce oddities but would it really matter if he was permitted to re-paint the door of his home in his own choice of an established range of colours? One of the many arguments for providing the multi-storey estate with extra generous facilities for recreational and cultural activities is that these give opportunities for choice and self expression. And here it should not be forgotten that the local authority is empowered to provide facilities for individual as well as group use. A difficulty in this matter of preferences is, of course, to discover where the choices lie. The answer rests largely in good communications between authority and tenant, e.g. in plenty of consultation as to what regulations are really necessary.

As seen in Glasgow, the always contentious matter of rent was another area in which good communication between the Corporation and its tenants was particularly desirable. Though heavily subsidised, and therefore low compared to what the private landlord would charge, the rent of the high flat nearly always represented a very steep increase on what the tenant had paid previously. The rebate system, based on total, not take-home pay, was regarded as unsatisfactory. There was also a strong feeling that the Corporation had for years muddled its housing finance and that the tenant was now being asked to foot the bill. It was noted how at any tenants' association meeting the atmosphere froze the moment the word rent was mentioned. The research staff likewise found it almost impossible really to discuss the subject with the individual tenant. These reactions are almost certainly associated with memories of the depression years. As with the humiliations of the dole and the means test, any increase in rent is seen as a moral issue, one on which you stick to your mates right or wrong. But assuming that the current bargain rent for the first-class accommodation of multi-storey housing cannot go on for ever, and that low rents with correspondingly high rates reduce the funds available for the many facilities without which a high flat is not a satisfactory home, the traditional attitudes must somehow be made more realistic. The Authority might, for example, consult with the tenants on methods of rent payment and ask their priorities as to how any funds available for new facilities should be spent. But these are less important than trying to change the whole outlook. The only effective way really to influence attitudes on anything so charged with emotion is through education. Here the Authority might, to take an example, experiment with a series of TV programmes, following them up with discussion groups.

If this or similar experiments are to reach the average tenant there is a strong case for holding them actually on the estate.

Apart from the rent issue, there was some evidence that the households in this new form of home (two-thirds of whom had not previously been tenants of the Corporation) were fairly happy about the relationship between themselves and their landlord. Though individuals might fulminate against the Authority over a particular issue, "It's like trying to nail jelly to a wall", it was noted that when asked if they would prefer the Corporation or a private owner as landlord, a very considerable proportion opted for the former. They obviously expected a better service than they had been accustomed to hope for from the private landlord, an interesting change in outlook and one worth playing up. They presumably expected to stay on as council tenants, since few referred to pipe dreams about buying a place of their own. This agrees with Professor Cullingworth's findings, that Glasgow accepts the rented home as normal.[14]

Recommendation

1. The Local Authority should explore ways in which to increase the opportunities for easy communication between itself and its tenants.

COMMUNITY DEVELOPMENT THROUGH SELF-HELP

As seen in Glasgow, multi-storey housing undoubtedly presents social problems. On the other hand it appears to be pregnant with opportunities in one field, viz. that of self-help. Economically and socially its population is rather above that of the Authority's tenants in general; age and household structure is such that there is an unusually high proportion of people with potential leisure: the tenants expect to be in the flat for a long time. Moreover, living in the heights seems to have triggered off a determination to raise standards. "You feel you have got some place here." Or again, "We musn't let ourselves step back." The change to such a novel way of life has perhaps unleashed energies. Even the physical characteristics of multi-storey housing have assets as regards self-help since the estate is visibly an island, and the block an entity. In many cases each floor is neatly self-contained and often it houses just about the number of people, 15–20, which makes a good working cell for joint action. This assumption about the social potentials of the high-flat population is exemplified in the rapid growth of tenants' associations on multi-storey estates, and by the way in which most of these do not confine themselves to being pressure groups but

[14] *Owner Occupation in Scotland and in England and Wales: A Comparative Study:* Cullingworth 1969.

are concerned with community welfare. As genuinely indigenous bodies, they undoubtedly stimulate that public participation in affairs which the Skeffington Committee has recommended.[15] They also help to translate vague aspirations about neighbourliness into practice, "Our association is pulling us together". On the other hand they rarely identify themselves with more than a minority on the estate and seem unable to get support from those under 45. Many of their officers ("a lot of people having a go at things they've never even heard of before") have little experience of committee work. They also depend over-much on letter writing, petitions and deputations which too often fail to justify the energy put into them. If the associations could draw on the services of an adviser who had experience of kindred bodies, their work would become more effective and their number would increase. Such an appointment would also strengthen their co-ordinating body, the Glasgow Council of Tenants' Associations. A move of this kind might be particularly influential just at this moment when, as is generally agreed, relationships between the Corporation and tenants' associations are steadily improving. "They are coming round to the view that we are not just a nuisance."

The slightly unusual characteristics of the high-flat population suggest that in their case it might be sounder for the Authority and voluntary bodies to invest in staff whose prime work would be to stimulate the tenants' own endeavours rather than to concentrate on services as such. In this connection reference should be made to a recent analysis of the case for far more effort to be made to introduce the concept of self-help through organised voluntary service to working-class society.[16] Since the purpose of such staff, as people of vision and as enablers rather than organisers, would be to help the estate help itself, they would be largely concerned with recruiting and training voluntary (and some part-time paid) workers from among the tenants and in supporting them as needed at later stages. While admitting that staff for community development is a relatively untried and certainly an expensive type of service, it is worth recalling that a couple of generations ago it was a novel and unacceptable concept for society to provide homes for its less privileged members. Are we today hedging unduly about the need for a service (in this case staff) to speed up the rate at which the tenants can create from their unusually shut off households something like a viable community?[17]

[15] *People and Planning.* Report of the Committee on Public Participation in Planning. H.M.S.O., 1969.

[16] *Voluntary Effort in the Welfare State*, R. Huws Jones, Berl Wober Memorial Lecture, Glasgow, 1968.

[17] *Community Work and Social Change.* Calouste Gulbenkian Foundation, Longmans, 1968.

Working with Community Groups, Goetschius, Routledge & Kegan Paul, 1969.

Recommendation

1. In view of the massive shifts of population taking place in Glasgow; the unfamiliar situations posed by multi-storey housing; the isolated character of high flats; and the potentials for self-help believed to be a feature of their population, the Corporation should appoint staff with professional qualifications in a variety of aspects of community development.

* * *

Many of the above proposals involve costs which in the main will have to be borne by the Corporation. The expenditure required to meet these social needs adds yet another dimension to the unfavourable aspects of multi-storey as compared with low-rise housing. As regards the flats already built, the findings of this study indicate that considerable and recurring expenditure is required to counter the more immediate social problems to which they give rise. On the other hand, if funds spent on their social welfare are looked at in the longer and larger perspective, they might well prove an investment. Experience shows that once a new housing estate is allowed to deteriorate its decline tends to be cumulative; and for high flats, with their excellent initial physical standards, this decline could be particularly painful. Money laid out on community development might also provide a worthwhile investment in citizens as such. The argument here is that, by and large, those willing to try this new form of home seem unusually awake to the possibility of raising the quality of their own lives and that of their estate as a whole.

APPENDICES

APPENDIX A

Basic information on examples of multi-storey housing visited in areas other than Glasgow. 1968.[1]

City	London	London	Sheffield	Sheffield	Liverpool	Zurich	Berne	Stockholm	Utrecht
Estate	Brandon (G.L.C.)	Winstanley (Wandsworth Borough)	Park Hill and Hyde Park	Norfolk Park	William Henry Street	Lochergut	Tscharngut	Bredang I, II	Overvecht I, II
Dwellings	2,417	800	2,300	3,000	1,000	350	1,700[2]	3,800	8,800
Population	8,100	3,200	6,000	7,500	5,000	900	5,500	13,000 (Bredang I)	31,000
Multi-storey blocks	39	4	(horizontal street deck system)	15	6	1 (different heights)	13	14	35
Multi-storey dwellings	1,601	230	2,160	1,900	400	350	1,167	1,075	4,000
Multi-storey population	5,900	900	5,400	4,200	1,300	900	4,881	3,215	13,800

[1] In Britain as provided by the local authority. Abroad as provided by the local authority and/or other agencies.
[2] Includes figures for students and disabled persons.

All figures approximate.

APPENDIX B

Number of and reasons for tenants' movement out of 1,943 flats (25 blocks; 5 estates) as assessed by district officers of Glasgow Corporation's Housing Management Department (January 1st–December 31st 1967)

Estate	Mutual Exchange	Emigrated	Deceased	Absconded	Ejected	Given up (includes overspill)	Transfers flat needing repair	Transfers other reasons	Total blocks	Total flats	Total moves	Moves per 100 flats
Wyndford (S.S.H.A.)	6	2				2	2	4	12	497	16	3·4
Albion	3		1	1		3			3	285	8	2·8
Red Road	2			2		3	2	2	2	240	9	4·7
Royston	3	1	1	4		4		1	3	351	16	4·6
Castlemilk	4	1	3	14	1	12		2	5	570	37	6·5
TOTAL	18	4	5	21	1	24	4	9	25	1,943	86	4·8
Dougrie Road[1]	(4)	–	–	–		(2)	–	(1)	(3)	(235)	(7)	(3·0)
Moss Heights[1]	–	–	–	(1)		(1)	–	–	(3)	(219)	(2)	(0·9)

[1] Dougrie Road and Moss Heights, though not among the 5 selected estates, are included as a useful comparison since Dougrie Road is within Castlemilk district and Moss Heights were the first multi-storey blocks to be occupied.

High density estate, Lillington Gardens, London. This site is located in the top right-hand corner of the model below.

A table-top model of the scheme above.

Plate 17

Plate 18. Graffiti, Royston.

APPENDIX C

Graffiti

Tenants made a great deal of comment about the need to keep the looks of their estate up to the standard they and the architect had achieved for their own flat. One thing that much disheartened them was wall defacing, the graffiti – "YY Partick Cross", "Tongs O.K.", etc. that was liable to appear even before the block was occupied. In many, perhaps most of the estates, wall writing seemed impossible to stop. It was not merely unsightly but expensive in terms of repainting and it added to the caretaker's job.

Graffiti, it was interesting to note, did not often appear on the cars parked about the estate nor on the doors of individual flats. In other words it seemed to be associated with places that were impersonal. A good deal of it was apparently less a matter of dark design than done idly and unwittingly. One of the answers to the casual type of wall writing, as distinct from the deliberate challenging slogan, would seem to lie in trying to get it associated with old-fashioned habits and therefore one to be discredited. If things like spitting and dirty-smelling clothes have come to be regarded as socially unacceptable why not wall writing, anyhow on its present scale in Glasgow? The following paragraphs refer to an analysis of wall writing made for this study at one of the 5 selected estates, Royston.[1]

When confronted with a slogan such as the "YY Shamrock-Land" (Plate 18, facing p. 153) on the wall of their block the tenants say, "It's the gangs – they can't see a clean wall but they've got to spoil it." The estate chosen to look at graffiti was one whose three blocks of 20 storeys have been up for seven years. After the first two years' occupation their internal walls had become so defaced that they had to be repainted. In December 1968 a record was made of every one of the graffiti on the blocks' internal and external walls. They were found to number 5,301, categorised as follows: (1) Internal location, e.g. internal stairway of a block. (2) Floor level. (3) External location, e.g. a garage. (4) Size (larger or smaller than 6 inches). (5) Supporting or attaching interest, e.g. "Shamrock rule." (6) Gang or individual name, e.g. "Toi," "Jean loves Jimmy." (7) Medium, e.g. paint spray, wax crayon. (8) Surface, e.g. blue-painted plaster, rough cast. (9) Number of items of a particular type.

[1] Analysis of graffiti kindly undertaken by Mr. Tom Stewart, Department of Psychology, University of Glasgow.

Analysis showed the internal markings to be of two types.

Deliberate graffiti. This was defined as being written in marker pen or paint spray. From the analysis and from talk with two boys it appeared that this was done by people who did not live on the estate, in general by boys, and those aged between 15–18. Content was gang slogans or symbols (21%), individuals' names (65%), miscellaneous marks (15%). Quantity per floor was greatest at the top and bottom floors of the block. The writers either went straight to the top in the lift to avoid residents, or they kept to the ground floor for ease of escape.

Casual graffiti. This was defined as material written in chalk or wax crayon or just scratched on. The writers were boys and girls and ranged in age from pre-school children to late teenagers. 10% of the content was gang names, probably written by children who were mimicking the gangs proper since it was often surrounded by similar slogans in wax crayon and of different size. Individual names comprised 42%, love notices 11%, and miscellaneous marks and drawings 37%. Quantity decreased with floor height. The top floor, frequented by courting couples, had more markings than those immediately below it. The nature of the wall's surface affected the character of the markings. At Royston the stairway walls were of plaster, the lower part painted in royal blue gloss, the upper in matt cream. Wax crayon marks on the cream and scratches on the blue was the most frequent usage; marker pen was seen on both. Most items were less than six inches in size. Two of the blocks had about the same number of these internal markings, one considerably less.

Analysis of the *external* markings showed those to be most frequent in the one block which had no caretaker. Smooth surfaces like wood and concrete were heavily damaged by marker pen for small items, by paint spray for larger ones. Brick and stone suffered damage from chalk and paint spray (Plate 18, p. 153). Rough cast was practically untouched; any marks made were in paint but even so they were not very conspicuous.

Two of the names which appeared frequently were Jacky and Hedgy. The owners were eventually contacted. They proved willing to talk about their activities and confirmatory material suggested that what they said was relatively reliable. Both were aged 16 and lived about a quarter of a mile away. Hedgy claimed that most of his writing was done when he was still at school. He said he had given it up when he had joined a karate club and his mother had found out about all this writing. When they first started it the boys used to walk into the city centre on a Saturday morning and buy (it was not always possible to steal) marker pens or paint sprays from a department store. They toured whatever district they had chosen between 9 and 10 that night, writing their names as obviously and as frequently as possible. At a rather later age they joined a local gang. When it toured an area its name, "Tiny Shamrock" and symbol were written on the wall as well as the names of those present (Plate 18, facing p. 153). The purpose, for both individuals and gang, was to get themselves known and to impress girls. The slogan on their own ground showed that this was their territory, that in other areas indicated that they had invaded and hoped to intimidate and provoke. Hedgy's desire for recognition or self-expression may have been at least partly due to his lack of distinction in other fields. He was an ordinary-looking chap, rather small, one of nine children, and poorish both at sport and lessons though he had enjoyed art at school. Jacky too said he had liked art and he actually possessed paints. Hedgy did not go to dances and had no girl friend. Joining his karate club and going to his technical college may have provided alternative outlets to frustrated desires for self-expression. Asked why he had not done any writing at some blocks which were nearer his home, he said their surface, multi-coloured speckle on the stairways, would not take marker pen and absorbed spray paint. The smooth, glossy surface at Royston was ideal for both.

To sum up. The Royston graffiti were of two kinds. (1) Deliberate, i.e. written in marker pen or paint spray to intimidate, provoke and publicise the writers and/or their gang. The trouble might be lessened by using rougher surfaces such as multi-coloured speckle, 'Siporex' and rough cast. (2) Casual graffiti, i.e. written in wax crayon or scratched on just to pass the time or to impress the girl friend when winching on a stairway. It might be reduced by using rougher surfaces. Immediate repainting might also lessen casual graffiti since a few more marks don't look as if they matter much when the wall is scruffy anyhow. There should be fewer plain surfaces about the estate. Blank walls, especially when treated with a soft black surface, look much like blackboards and get treated accordingly. Poor finish too seems to attract trouble.

Graffiti. Location, size, gang name, etc.

		Number of graffiti	%			Number of graffiti	%
Internal Location	Campsie 1	985	21	External Location	Campsie	40	7
	Campsie 2	873	19		Nevis	52	8
	Nevis 1	825	17		Lomond	33	5
	Nevis 2	878	19		Houses	185	30
	Lomond 1	486	10		Garage	275	45
	Lomond 2	641	14		Play Area	28	5
Size	Large	2,089	45	Size	Large	334	54
	Small	2,599	55		Small	279	46
Gang Name etc.	Shamrock	829	18	Gang Name etc.	Shamrock	104	17
	Love Notices	426	9		Love Notices	49	8
	Names	2,079	44		Names	375	61
	Miscellaneous	1,354	29		Miscellaneous	85	14
	Total	4,688			Total	613	

Average distribution per floor.

	Floor	Number	%		Floor	Number	%
Deliberate Graffiti	Ground	57	5	Casual Graffiti	Ground	247	7
	Middle	43	4		Middle	150	4
	Top	84	10		Top	138	4

Medium used.

On white-painted plaster	Number	%	On blue-painted plaster	Number	%
Paint Spray	36	1½	Paint Spray	99	5
Paint Brush	10	½	Paint Brush	15	–
Marker Pen	760	27	Marker Pen	378	20
Chalk	52	2	Chalk	60	3
Wax Crayon	1,736	63	Wax Crayon	150	8
Scratch	159	6	Scratch	1,233	63
Total	2,753		Total	1,935	

APPENDIX D

Facilities within ½ mile radius of estate

Shopping Food	Albion/ Ibrox	Castle-milk	Red Road
Co-operative	7	1	2
Supermarket	–	2	1
Grocers & Provision Dealers	15	2	2
Butchers	9	5	3
Bread/Bakers	7	5	1
Fishmongers, Poulterers	–	1	–
Greengrocers, Fruiterers	5	1	1
Licensed Grocers	2	–	1
Dairies	7	–	3
Non Food			
Drapery and General Clothing	7	3	–
Boots and shoes	–	5	–
Furriers	1	–	–
Booksellers & Stationers	2	1	1
Government Surplus	–	–	–
Pet Shop	1	–	–
Jewellery, Leather & Sports Goods	1	1	–
Off Licence	2	–	–
Motor Car Accessories	1	–	–
Household Goods			
Furniture and furnishing	1	–	–
Radio & Electrical	3	2	–
Paints/Hardware/ Ironmonger	4	2	1
General Stores			
Department Stores	9	1	–

Other Shops	Albion/ Ibrox	Castle-milk	Red Road
Confectioner, Newsagent, Tobacconists	22	4	4
Dispensing Chemists	6	3	1
Service Trades			
Hairdressers	7	3	–
Cleaners/Alterations	4	2	–
Laundry/Laundrette	5	–	–
Boot and Shoe Repair	3	1	–
Betting Shop/ Pools Agent	3	–	1
Motor Car Showroom	1	–	–
Petrol Filling Station & Car Repair	5	1	1
Funeral Undertakers	–	–	–
Electricity Servicing	–	–	–
Gas Servicing	–	1	–
Banks	3	–	–
Builder/Joiner/ Shopfitters	5	–	–
Photographer	1	–	–
Travel Agent	1	–	–
Opticians	2	–	–
Watch Repair	1	–	–
Insurance Broker	1	–	–
Restaurant	1	–	–
Licensed Premises	8	–	2

	Albion/Ibrox	Castle-milk	Red Road
Other Shops	Number of Facilities		
Fish & Chicken Shop	3	–	2
Cafés	2	2	–
Hotels	2	–	–
Commercial Entertainment			
Swimming Pool	–	1	–
Sports Centre	1	–	–
Greyhound Racing	1	–	–
Exhibition Hall	1	–	–
Public Transport			
Underground Station	2	–	–
Main Railway Station	–	–	1
Bus Routes	5	–	–
Public Services			
Education			
Nursery School	1	–	–
Primary School	3	4	3
Secondary School	3	1	1
Comprehensive School	1	1	–
Special School	1	–	–
Further Education Centre	–	–	1
Health & Welfare			
Child Welfare Clinic	1	–	–
Ante Natal Clinic	1	–	–
Mothercraft Class	1	–	–
Child Guidance Clinic	1	–	–
Dentist	1	–	–
Doctor	1	–	–
Hospital	–	–	1

	Albion/Ibrox	Castle-milk	Red Road
Health & Welfare	Number of Facilities		
Nursing Home	1	–	–
Other Public Services			
Public Washhouse	1	–	–
Post Offices	1	1	3
Post Boxes	4	2	5
Public Telephones	4	1	4
Police Station	–	1	–
Police Boxes	2	–	1
Youth Employment Bureau	–	–	1
Ministry of Social Security	1	–	–
Civil Defence Centre	–	–	1
Cleansing Depot	1	–	–
Bus Depot	1	–	–
Recreation and Open Space Areas			
Parks	2	1	–
Children's Playgrounds	2	–	–
Sports Centre	1	–	–
Bowling Club	1	–	–
Football Pitches	–	–	2
Social Provision			
Churches/Meeting rooms	9	2	2
Community Centre	–	1	–
Youth Centre/YMCA	–	2	–
Youth Organisations	7	–	–
Further Education Centres	2	–	–

APPENDIX E

A note on lift waiting times and failures
ANTHONY WARREN

This note is based on material from two sources, a waiting time survey undertaken to assist with this study on the social implications of multi-storey housing and an unpublished study[1] on the behavioural consequences of height for high-flat residents, part of which comprised work on lift performance.

WAITING TIME STUDY

Aims

To establish how long residents had to wait on the ground level for a lift to an upper floor during the rush hour.

Definition

A measurement strategy depends on a definition of waiting time. This is taken as being the interval between an intending passenger's arrival and the departure of the next car after his arrival. A passenger is deemed to have arrived when he presses the call button or enters the area of the lift lobby with the intention of waiting. The precise moment is inevitably difficult to define but observers were able to note it consistently within the first ¼-hour recording. However, as data were subsequently grouped in 10-sec. class intervals this was not critical. A lift is said to have departed when it is seen through the lift door windows to move off.

Method

Observers stationed in the lift hall at one block on each of the five estates shown on p. 29 recorded the interval between successive lift car departures. This was done by stopping a stop-watch at this event, noting the time interval since the previous car departure, and starting the watch again for the next cycle. A series of time intervals are thus built up for the length of each cycle, from car departure to car departure. As

[1] 'Height as a determinant of satisfaction and neighbourliness in high flat dwellers', A. Warren (Unpublished thesis material). Strathclyde University 1968.

lift users appear their time of arrival since the last car departure is noted down. Thus a history of arrivals can also be built up, and by subtracting 'arrival time' from the 'cycle' time, the waiting time for each lift user is given. The data are recorded on sheets printed for the purpose, so that one cycle occupies one line.

In those situations where intending lift users do not use the first available car and wait for the next, a 'carry over' recording is used. Remaining passengers are counted and a corresponding number of noughts are marked for arrivals in the *next* cycle. Thus the waiting time for 'carry over' passengers is the sum of the interval between their arrival and the first car departure, plus the duration of the next cycle (assuming they leave on the second car to arrive).

The system records an approximation of the real situation. An accurate record of waiting times could only be kept with one observer per passenger, each individually timed. However, the approximation seems acceptable if the following assumptions are made:

1. That the lift installation provides a service of departing cars (which lift car of the two is irrelevant).
2. That intending passengers use the first available car.
3. That those left behind as 'carry overs' were the last to arrive and are first in the queue for the next car arrival.
4. That the number of people intending to use the lift and subsequently leaving the lift lobby is negligible.

Observation of the field situation suggested that the number of people not using the first car to arrive was small and that as in any case each lift served 50% of the potential traffic load in the block, this effect in one was cancelled out by an effect in the other.

The noting of 'carry overs' as first arrivals in a second queue is a normal statistical assumption making subsequent analysis a realistic proposition. This was borne out in the field, but there were a few notable exceptions, young school children and adults with large parcels or prams. For them, particularly at Red Road, waiting times were often much greater than for the majority. However, no record of their experience was possible.

The observers noted only occasional instances of residents departing from the lobby other than by lift. These were at Red Road during the worst excesses of delay.

Summing up, field observation confirmed the adequacy of the assumptions 1–4 above. It should be stressed that the data reflect *actual* behaviour. No suggestion is made as to why one lift is used in preference to the other (if this ever were the case). Similarly no note was made about the normality of the lift service. No observer reported a 'serious' lift breakdown, but this may have happened. The attempt was to produce data reflecting actual performance during a 'typical' week.

Situation

Recording took place during 16.30–17.30 for the week 9–13 December, 1968. There were no public holidays or working abnormalities. Children were still at school.

An attempt was made to record during the evening rush period as previous experience had shown this to be the busiest time of day.[2] Evidence from the unpublished study suggested the likely period as 16.30–18.00. Inevitably however peak periods varied from flat to flat as a function of distance from residents' place of work and working hours. This is reflected in the data obtained. Details of the five buildings used in the main survey and notes on the observers appear below. The estates were suggested by the staff responsible for the main study; the individual blocks were selected on a chance basis by myself.

Administration of the schedule

The observers were architectural student volunteers from the second year, and had some experience of survey design, data collection and statistical analysis. Each situation was covered by two observers, one timing, the other writing. Data were entered on special sheets and subsequently converted to true waiting times as outlined above. A one-hour recording period per day was adopted giving a total of 25 hours of data, sufficient for statistical purposes.

Analysis

The week's data for each of the five situations are arranged into distributions from which can be shown:

Mean waiting time for intending users.
Standard deviation.
Probability for a 90-second wait.
And the waiting time for 90% probability.
It is hypothesised that the five curves derived from the waiting time histograms are Negative Exponentials. They fulfil the four basic requirements of such a curve. These are:
x min. = 0.
x max. = ∞
continuous distribution of x.
that the distribution is skewed.

[2] *op. cit.*

Typically the Negative Exponential arises from a distribution of intervals between events. The study in fact measures waiting time, the interval between passenger arrival and car departure.

However to dispel doubt, the obtained and theoretical distributions for the Castlemilk data were calculated and submitted to chi square test. There was no significant difference between the two at the 1% level and the hypothesis that the curve was a Negative Exponential was confirmed. The distribution seems typical of the other four which are assumed to conform to the same curve.

In computing the probabilities for a 90-second waiting time and the waiting times for a 90% probability these were arrived at from the general formula using the Wyndford data. However as the 90-second waiting time and the 90% probability remain constant for all cases, the other four were devised from a simplified version as follows:

$$P = 1 - e^{\lambda^9} \quad \text{for a probability of 90\%.}$$
$$t = \frac{-2 \cdot 3026}{\lambda} \quad \text{for a waiting time of 90 secs.}$$

A probability level of 90% was chosen as offering a 'reasonable' level of success. A 90-second waiting time is usually taken by lift manufacturers as being a reasonable one. This is also the standard used in Design Bulletin 3[3].

Results and conclusions

Mean waiting time for all the blocks except Red Road fall within the recommended 90-second interval. However the chances of getting a lift within this time varies between 7 and 9 out of 10 times. Wyndford seems to offer the only reasonable service with a 90% chance of success. Red Road is distinctly unsatisfactory at only a 1 in 3 chance of success.

The distinctly poor service of the Red Road lift installation is by now notorious and seems to be borne out by empirical evidence. H. Parlaw[4] has suggested that door opening times considerably affect waiting times and that since the number of door openings in a trip is a function of the number of floors being served these should be kept to a minimum. "The results show that a marked improvement in waiting times is obtained with reduced door-times thus offering the first suggestion for improving lift service."

[3] 'Selection and planning of passenger lifts', Ministry of Housing and Local Government. *Design bulletin 3*, part 2, 1962.
[4] 'Lift operation and computers', H. Parlaw. *The Architects' Journal*, 23 March, 1966.

It seems significant that the Red Road installation has over double the number of floor stations that the four other schemes have (30 as opposed to 12) and that vandalism repeatedly makes the door early closing system unworkable so that a car stop takes between 10 and 15 secs. as a minimum compared to about 8 secs. on the other installations. Wyndford is only 15 storeys high with correspondingly less stations and it reveals a better performance.

However although improved car stop times would reduce waiting time there are other important factors such as the population of the block. Red Road has the greatest traffic load and percentage of children, Wyndford the least. Summing up it seems that the four systems were adequate for dealing with the traffic encountered during the survey (not necessarily rush conditions) and that the fifth, Red Road, was definitely not. A reduction in waiting times could be achieved by minimising door opening times and devising a lift strategy involving half the present number of floor stations.

Survey situations

Albion	Castlemilk	Red Road	Royston	Wyndford
Alva Court	Netherton Court	Red Road Court	Lomond House	110 Glenfinnan Road
Ibrox	7 Mitchell Hill Road	10 Red Road	140 Charles St.	
19 floors × 6 houses	19 floors × 6 houses	31 floors × 4 houses	19 floors × 6 houses	14 floors × 4 houses

Mean and Standard deviation

74 seconds	60 seconds	186 seconds	63 seconds	35 seconds
74	60	186	63	35

Chances of catching a lift during a 90 sec. wait

70%	77%	33%	76%	94%

Waiting time for a 90% chance of catching a lift

170 seconds	139 seconds	468 seconds	145 seconds	80 seconds

Lift Specifications

	Albion	Castlemilk	Red Road	Royston	Wyndford
No. of lifts	2	2	2	2	2
Programme	Simplex up and down collective	Duplex up and down collective	Duplex full collective	Duplex up and down collective	Simplex down collective
Floor-station	10 even 11 odd	10 even 11 odd	31	24	8 odd 8 even
Speed	200 f.p.m.	200 f.p.m.	300 f.p.m.	200 f.p.m.	150 f.p.m.
Capacity	8 persons 1200 lbs	8 persons 1200 lbs	8 persons 1200 lbs	8 persons 1200 lbs	8 persons 1200 lbs
Maker	A. &. P. Stevens Ltd.	Otis Elevator Co. Ltd.	A. & P. Stevens Ltd.	A. & P. Stevens Ltd.	A. & P. Stevens Ltd.

Car departures/hour

	Albion	Castlemilk	Red Road	Royston	Wyndford
M	41	35	13	50	39
T	44	28	21	38	42
W	47	37	19	29	47
T	44	42	15	52	38
F	17	42	13	50	49

Passengers/hour

	Albion	Castlemilk	Red Road	Royston	Wyndford
M	90	66	181	92	66
T	62	68	145	54	57
W	84	83	162	77	53
T	94	80	93	87	53
F	90	89	154	92	48

Mean car load

	Albion	Castlemilk	Red Road	Royston	Wyndford
M	2·19	1·94	13·92	1·64	1·70
T	1·40	2·35	6·40	1·42	1·35
W	1·80	2·24	8·52	2·65	1·12
T	2·09	1·90	6·20	1·60	1·39
F	4·70	2·12	11·79	1·84	0·98

APPENDIX F
An analysis of 13 tenants' associations, August 1968

Tenants' Associations (year started)	Office Bearers No.	No. interviewed	Length in office 0–1 yr.	2–5 yrs.	5+ yrs.	Annual Subscription F=Family I=Individual	Committee Meetings Frequency	Place	Rent	Association Meetings Frequency	Place	Rent	No. of Members
Balgrayhill (1967)	6	6	6	–	–	12½p F	1/mth	School	90p	1/mth	Hall	£1·25	100
Queen Eliz. Sq. (1967)	5	5	5	–	–	12½p F	1/2 wks	House	–	1/mth	School	75p	284
Castlemilk (1950)	7	5	2	1	2	12½p F	1/mth	Com. Cen.	75p	1/mth	Com. Cen.	75p	2,000
Cranhill (1951)	8	8	3	4	1	5p I	1/mth	Own Hall	rates	1/mth	Own Hall School	rates	1,500
Tarfside (1966)	7	7	2	5	–	12½p F	2/session	House	–	1/mth	Hall	£1	400
Ibroxholm (1965)	13	6	4	2	–	12½p F	1/mth	House	–	1/mth	Town Hall	£2·75	300
Summerfield (1966)	14	10	–	10	–	12½p F	1/mth	Caretaker's room	–	4/year	School	£1·25	400
Bute & Cumbrae (1968)	10	9	9	–	–	10p nightly I + 12½p	1/mth	House	–	1/mth	School	75p	80
Pollokshaws (1966)	11	8	5	3	–	12½p F	2/mth	School House	75p –	1/mth	Burgh Hall School	£2.50 £1.25	700
Langlands Rd. (1959)	8	3	–	–	3	12½p F	1/mth	School	75p	1/mth	School	75p	100
Potters Place¹ (1967)	6	5	5	–	–	5p dF weekly	2/mth	House	–	1/mth	Church Hall	donation	130
Blairdardie (1963)	16	12	4	6	2	10p dF	3/year	House or School	No inf.	4/year	School	No inf.	600
Knightswood (1934)	5	5	1	2	2	7½p F	1/mth	School	No inf.	4/year	School	No inf.	400
Other, e.g. social committees attached to above.	7	7	No information										

Age	M	F	Total	Education	M	F	Total	Occupation	M	F	Total
20–30 yrs	2	4	6	Public Elementary	20	30	50	Professional	0	0	0
30–50	19	15	34	Secondary	30	16	46	Non-manual and personal service	9	16	25
50+	25	22	47					Skilled manual	22	10	32
No inf.	4	5	9	Further Education, Apprenticeship, etc.	32	13	45	Semi- or unskilled manual	8	7	15
								Retired	4	0	4
								Housewife	0	20	20
									43	53	96

[1] Not connected with multi-storey housing.

APPENDIX F2

CRANHILL TENANTS' ASSOCIATION
179 Bellrock Street, Glasgow, E.3.
STATEMENT OF INCOME AND EXPENDITURE
for Year ended 30th April 1966

1965	Expenditure			1965	Income			
	Hall Expenses			£2,286	Bingo	£2,458		
£ 198	Rent and Rates	£150		2,037	Expenses	2,108		
36	Insurance	43		249			£ 350	
	Heating and			325	Teenagers	36		
120	Lighting	150		193	Expenses	7		
18	Telephone	24		132			29	
130	Repairs and Renewals	25		273	Whist Drives	127		
297	Wages	361	£ 753	178	Expenses	102		
64	Printing and Stationery		174	95			25	
51	General Expenses		12	263	Canteen	242		
	Office Bearers'			240	Purchases	149		
33	Expenses		30	23			93	
29	Donations		8		Committee Bus Run	50		
21	Audit Fee and Expenses		21	-	Expenses	44		
25	Honoraria		25				6	
12	Income Tax Schedule "D"		15	84	Theatre Night	87		
107	Old Folks' Treat		-	85	Expenses	83		
	Childrens' Treat			1			4	
190	Expenditure	252			Raffles	186		
115	Income	171		-	Expenses	71		
75			81				115	
	Dinner Dance			34	Advertising		26	
54	Expenditure	43		38	Members' Subscriptions		52	
27	Income	39		74	Hall Rents		67	
27			4	62	Sundry Income		1	
	Beetle Drive			6	Savings Bank Interest		6	
	Expenditure	4		65	Donations		62	
-	Income	3	1	458	Deficit for Year		310	
-	Dinner for Football Team		17					
	Dance							
11	Expenditure	40						
19	Income	35						
8			5					
£1,235			£1,146	£1,235			£1,146	

BALANCE SHEET AS AT 30th APRIL, 1966.

	General Fund				Property		
	At Credit 1st May, 1965	£4,785		3,647	At Cost		£3,647
4,785	Deficit for Year	310	4,475		**Furniture and Fittings**		
	Outstanding Accounts			533	At Cost		533
21	Audit Fee	21			**Bingo Equipment**		
-	Electricity	96	117		At Cost	66	
				66	Purchased during Year	45	111
					Cash Funds		
					At Bank		
				234	Current Account	4	
				257	Savings Account	264	
				69	On Hand	33	301
£4,806			£4,592	£4,806			£4,592

Report to Members

I have prepared the above Balance Sheet as at 30th April, 1966 and Statement of Income and Expenditure for the year ended on that date, from the books and accounts of the Association and from information available to me, and the Statement of Income and Expenditure properly summarises the Income and Expenditure for the year. Cash Funds at Bank are certified by the respective Banks. Cash on Hand is the Balance of Cash Account.

GLASGOW, 17th JUNE, 1966.

Chartered Accountant.

APPENDIX F3

Scotstoun House Social Club
Winter 1967-8

Application Form

Dear Member,

If you wish you or your children, or if you are an O.A.P. to participate in any of the undernoted functions, will you please fill in the part of this form which is applicable to you. O.A.P.'s are eligible for Theatre Night & Smoker as well as their Party.

"Please do not detach any portion of this form. It must be returned in its entirety"

O.A.P. CHRISTMAS PARTY	INVALID'S PARCEL
NAME................................ Mem'ship No.	NAME................................ Mem'ship No. ....
ADDRESS...............................	ADDRESS...............................
Please tick off	please tick off Lady............ Gent............
Lady............ Gent............	Please State If Permanently Confined To House or Hospital

SMOKER (Men Only)	THEATRE NIGHT Jan.
NAME................................ Members No.	NAME................................ Members No. ....
ADDRESS...............................	ADDRESS...............................
	How many subsidised tickets (Max. 2 per member) ....
PRICE 6/6d	How many full priced tickets (if tickets available)

CHILDREN

Parents Name.......................... Address............................... Mem'ship No. ....

PRESENTS	CHRISTMAS PARTY 23.12.67	Pantomime 26.12.67
Age up to 3 yrs on or after .12.67.	Age 3 yrs on or before 30.11.67 up to 7 yrs on or after 1.12.67.	Age 7 yrs on or before 30.11.67 up to & including 15 yrs if at school.
Christian Name Age	Christian Name Age	Christian Name Age
.		
.		
.		
.		

Any child permanently confined to Home or Hospital.   Up to 14 years.
Name............................... Address........................... Age .... Sex ....

N.B. FULL CHRISTIAN NAME MUST BE GIVEN FOR EACH CHILD. Only applications made on this this application form will be accepted.

Please return it duly completed to your collector <u>not later than Monday, 11th September</u> as the Chairman of each Block must have these forms at the executive meeting on Wednesday, 13th September at 8 p.m. - <u>No application will be considered after 8 p.m. on 13th September</u>. Please help us - to help - Don't wait until the collector asks for your completed form - go and give it to them!

A. BELL, Secretary

APPENDIX G

UNIVERSITY OF GLASGOW   EXTRA-MURAL COURSE

"NEW HOMES AND NEW NEIGHBOURS"

A course of particular value to members of Tenants' Associations though <u>anyone</u> interested is welcome to attend.

The course will be held in <u>two parts</u>, each of five lectures, on Wednesdays at 7.30 p.m., starting Wednesday, January 10th, 1968.

Place: 57-59 Oakfield Avenue, Glasgow, W.2.

Fee: 5s. for each part or 10s. for the whole course. Students may take either the whole ten-week course; or <u>either</u> of the five-week parts.

A typical evening will start with a lecture, illustrated when possible, followed by a break for coffee and ending with time for discussion.

Part I   <u>Glasgow Housing To-day and To-morrow</u>

1. Jan. 10th   GLASGOW HOUSING PAST AND PRESENT - THE DEVELOPMENT OF ITS CHARACTER
   Mr. W. Forsyth, Department of Economic History, University of Glasgow.

2. Jan. 17th   GLASGOW HOUSING TO-DAY AND TO-MORROW
   Mr. S. McLeod, University of Strathclyde.

3. Jan. 24th   RENTS
   Mr. I. MacBain, Department of Social and Economic Research, University of Glasgow.

4. Jan. 31st   TENANT AND LANDLORD
   Mr. H.J. Aldhous, Housing Manager, Sheffield.

5. Feb. 7th   PROBLEMS FACING TENANTS' ASSOCIATIONS
   Mr. G. Riches, Association of London Housing Estates.

Part II   <u>Social and Recreational Opportunities</u>

6. Feb. 14th   LAYOUT AND LOOKS OF TO-DAY'S HOUSING.   MULTI-STOREY BUILDING.
   To be arranged.

   TENANTS WITH PARTICULAR NEEDS : WHAT PRACTICAL PROVISION CAN BE MADE?

7. Feb. 21st   (1) THE ELDERLY
   Dr. Cowan, Medical Officer of Health, Rutherglen.

8. Feb. 28th   (2) YOUNG CHILDREN - RECREATIONAL NEEDS
   Mrs. Mackintosh, Hamilton College of Education.

9. Mar. 6th   (3) ADOLESCENTS - RECREATIONAL NEEDS; PROBLEMS OF VANDALISM
   Mr. R. Lennie, Castlemilk.

10. Mar. 13th A VIGOROUS LOCAL COMMUNITY - WHAT IS INVOLVED?
    To be arranged.

APPENDIX H

Table 8
Distance of present from previous home.

Miles	Total	%
0–1	232	36
1–2	119	19
2–4	134	21
4–6	99	15
6+	57	9
	641	

Table 9
Dwellings in relation to storey height.

	Wyndford	Royston	Albion	Castle-milk	Red Road	Other estates	Total	%
Lower ground–4th	12	4	2	5	5	111	139	22
5th–10th	17	4	4	8	5	180	218	34
11th–16th	9	4	4	9	5	143	174	27
17th–22nd	4	3	2	4	5	79	97	15
23rd–28th	2	–	–	–	6	5	13	2
29th–30th	–	–	–	–	–	–	–	–
	44	15	12	26	26	518	641	

Table 10
Reasons for moving to present home.

		Total	%
1.	Redevelopment	198	31
2.	Health	29	5
3.	House unfit	101	16
4.	Service House	2	
5.	Housing List – homeless	39	6
6.	Housing List – overcrowded	97	15
7.	Transfer	128	20
8.	Mutual exchange	16	2
9.	Other	31	5
		641	

Table 11

Length of residence.

Years	Total households	%
13+	4	1
8–13	10	2
6–8	10	2
5–6	3	0
4–5	39	6
3–4	87	14
2–3	86	13
1–2	122	19
0–1	278	43
No inf.	2	0
	641	

Table 12

Number of persons in household

No. of persons	Wyndford	Royston	Albion	Castlemilk	Red Road	Other estates	Total	%
1	8	2	2	7	10	95	124	19
2	20	6	2	4	3	170	205	32
3	11	2	2	7	–	130	152	24
4	5	4	3	4	6	100	122	19
5		1	3	3	6	15	28	4
6				1	1	5	7	1
7						3	3	0
	44	15	12	26	26	518	641	

TABLE 13
Households with dependents.

		Total	% of 641 households
Adult Dependents	1	12	2
	2	1	0
Child	1	105	16
	2	85	13
	3	25	4
	4	4	1
	5	1	–
Disabled	1	3	–
	2	0	–
No dependents		410	64
Total		646*	

* 5 households have one dependent adult and one dependent child.

Table 14
Type of Household

Household	Total	%
Adult. All members 16–65	282	44
Adult. 1 or more members aged 16+ in education	10	1
*Family. i.e. including 1 or more children 0–15	175	27
Elderly. All males 65+ all females 60+	90	14
Mixed elderly. At least one male 65+ or female 60+	41	6
Other type elderly.	2	0
Other type	41	6
	641	98

*Of a total of 175 households with children 0–15		% of 175
Several children but at least one aged 0–4	47	27
All children aged 0–4	42	24
	89	51

Table 15

Population in relation to age and sex. Main Sample, July 1968

Age	Wynd-ford M F	Royston M F	Albion M F	Castle-milk M F	Red Road M F	Other estates M F	Total M F T	%
0–4	1 3	– –	1 2	5 6	4 4	46 48	57 63 120	7
5–9	3 2	– 2	1 1	6 6	7 9	42 42	59 62 121	7
10–14	3 –	2 2	4 1	1 2	3 3	41 32	54 40 94	6
15–19	1 3	2 2	3 –	– 1	3 –	54 42	63 48 111	7
20–34	7 6	3 1	5 3	13 11	6 9	131 135	165 165 330	20
35–49	9 12	6 8	4 5	6 5	9 6	122 144	156 180 336	20
50–64	17 13	2 4	2 3	2 3	2 7	153 178	178 208 386	23
65+	5 15	5 2	3 1	3 3	– 4	51 86	67 111 178	11
No inf.	1					1 4	1 5 6	0
	46 55	20 21	23 16	36 37	34 43	640 712	759 882 1,681	

Table 16

Occupational class of adults in employment

	Male	Female	Total	%
1. Professional	3	4	7	1
2. Intermediate non-manual	21	6	27	3
3. Junior non-manual	41	106	147	15
4. Personal service workers	51	178	229	23
5. Foremen and supervisors	39	10	49	5
6. Skilled manual	230	18	248	25
7. Semi and unskilled manual	198	78	276	28
8. Farmers, own account, armed forces	3	1	4	0
Total	586	401	987	
No information, unemployed, etc.	24	299	323	
	610	700	1,310	

Table 17

Car (use of) and telephone (ownership) in relation to size of household.

Persons	Car			Telephone		
	Total	Total households	% of households	Total	Total households	% of households
1	10	124	8	18	124	15
2	30	205	15	58	205	28
3	45	152	30	57	152	38
4	44	122	36	41	122	34
5	10	28	36	9	28	32
6	3	7	43	2	7	29
7	1	3	33	1	3	33
	143	641	22	186	641	29

Table 18

Rent and rates (monthly) present home in relation to previous home. Running costs (heating, cooking, lighting). Difference between present and previous home.

Present home Rent & Rates	Total	%	Previous home Rent & Rates	Total	%	Difference between running costs of present and previous home	Total	%
£6–8	208	32	£0–2	242	38	More	267	42
£9–10	332	52	£3–4	150	23	Less	211	33
£11–12	68	11	£5–6	47	7	Same	97	15
£13–14	8	1	£7–10	113	18	No inf.	55	9
£15–17	11	2	£11–14	14	2	Previous home shared	11	2
No inf.	14	2	£15–17	1	0			
			No inf.	74	12			
	641			641			641	

Table 19
Overall satisfaction

	Wyndford	Royston	Albion	Castle-milk	Red Road	Other estates	Total	%
Yes	39	13	10	25	23	473	583	91
No	4	2	2	1	3	42	54	8
No inf.	1					3	4	1
	44	15	12	26	26	518	641	

Table 20
Satisfaction in relation to type of household

	Family h-hold with one or more aged 0–16	Adult	Elderly	Mixed Elderly	Other Elderly	Other	Total	%	H-holds with one or more aged 0–4.
Yes	157	266	85	39	1	35	583	91	46
No	16	24	5	2	1	6	54	8	41
DK/ No Inf.	2	2	–	–	–	–	4	1	2
	175	292	90	41	2	41	641		89

Table 21
Expectation. "Do you expect to be living here for a long time?"

	Total	%
Yes	551	86
No	66	10
Don't know & no inf.	24	4
	641	

Table 22

Likes and dislikes re house, block and estate (as referred to spontaneously.)

House likes	Total	%	House dislikes	Total	%
Everything/no dislikes	191	23	Expensive to run/high rent	76	15
Bathroom	148	18	Windows	70	14
Kitchen	119	14	Heating arrangements	67	14
Heating	109	13	Unsuitable for children	57	12
Easy to manage	67	8	Layout of house	44	9
Layout/space	52	6	Rooms too small	39	8
View	45	5	Poor workmanship	36	7
Soundproofing/quie	35	4	Not enough storage space	24	5
Good storage space	23	3	Poor soundproofing	20	4
Privacy/safe	22	3	Height	7	1
Well-built houses	6	1	Poor water pressure	5	1
Healthy houses	6	1	Other	48	10
Other	15	2		493	
	838				

Block likes	Total	%	Block dislikes	Total	%
			Lifts	166	24
			Lonely/isolated	98	14
Good neighbours	166	34	Entrance poor	61	9
Quiet	87	18	Vandalism	60	9
Everything/no dislikes	67	14	Inadequate washing & drying facilities	55	8
Good caretaker	50	10	Noisy	38	5
Good maintenance	25	5	Poor supervision, maintenance	37	5
Entrance	22	5	Poor refuse disposal	22	3
Balcony	16	3	Balcony	22	3
Good washing and drying facilities	13	3	Fire escape stairway	19	3
Good outlook	12	2	Too many dogs	15	2
Lift	7	1	No garden	10	1
Refuse disposal	7	1	No balcony	9	1
No garden	4	1	Outlook	5	1
No balcony	1	–	Dislike neighbours	5	1
Layout of landing	1	–	Inadequate storage	4	1
Other	7	1	Frightened after Ronan Point	3	0
	485		Other	72	10
				701	

Estate likes	Total	%	Estate dislikes	Total	%
Convenient/good transport	146	28	Need shops	104	21
Everything/no dislikes	129	24	Inadequate bus service	87	18
Area/district	85	16	No play place for children	64	13
Convenient shops	80	15	No social centre	30	6
Layout/landscaping	37	7	Don't like district	20	4
Active T.A., good social life	13	2	Situation/hilly	17	3
Near relatives	8	2	Poor landscaping	16	3
Good for children	8	2	Windy	15	3
Good maintenance	6	1	Poor parking/garaging facilities	14	3
Convenient for school	5	1	Too many children, noise, etc.	13	3
No children here	2	–	Need telephone kiosk	13	2
Other	10	2	Too far from school	5	1
	529		Other	94	19
				492	

Table 23
Overall satisfaction in relation to length of residence.

Length of residence	Satisfied	Not satisfied	No inf.	Total	% Satisfied	% Not satisfied
5+ years	23	4		27	5	7
4–5 ,,	30	8	1	39	5	15
3–4 ,,	82	5		87	14	9
2–3 ,,	78	8		86	13	15
1–2 ,,	114	8		122	20	15
0–1 ,,	254	21	3	278	44	39
No inf.	2	0		2	0	0
	583	54	4	641		

Table 24
Satisfaction in relation to storey height.

	Total	%
Yes	564	88
No	75	12
Don't know & No inf.	2	–
Total	641	

Table 25
Informant's satisfaction with lift and his assessment of other people's satisfaction

Informant's satisfaction Satisfied	Total	%	Other people's satisfaction Satisfied	Total	%
Yes	400	62	Yes	234	37
No	219	34	No	331	52
no inf.	22	3	no. inf.	76	12
	641			641	

Table 26

Previous home – nature of tenancy

Nature of tenancy	Total	%
Owner occupier	56	9
Rented L.A., S.S.H.A.	201	31
Rented privately	377	59
Other	6	1
No inf.	1	0
	641	

Table 27

Previous home – garden or other outside area (private or shared).

	Total	%
Garden	112	17
Other area (private or shared)	505	79
None	20	3
No inf.	4	1
	641	

Table 28

Pensioners in relation to storey height.

Storey height	No. of pensioners (65+)	%
Lower gd.-4th	45	25
5th–10th	70	39
11th–16th	40	22
17th–22nd	22	12
23rd–28th	4	2
29th–30th	0	0
	181	

Table 29
Dependent children in relation to age.

Age	Wyndford M	F	Royston M	F	Albion M	F	Castle-milk M	F	Red Road M	F	Other M	F	Total M	F	%
0–4	1	3			1	2	5	6	4	4	46	48	57	63	32
5–9	3	2		2	1	1	6	6	7	9	42	42	59	62	33
10–14	3		2	2	4	1	1	2	3	3	41	32	54	40	25
15–19	1								1	1	15	12	17	13	8
19+											2	4	2	4	2
	8	5	2	4	6	4	12	15	15	16	146	138	189	182	

Table 30
Dependent children (all ages and age 0–4) in relation to storey height.

Height	Wyndford M	F	Royston M	F	Albion M	F	Castle-milk M	F	Red Road M	F	Other M	F	Total M	F	%	Age 0–4 Total
Lower gd.–4th	3	–	–	–	–	–	–	2	3	2	33	35	39	39	21	9
5th–10th	3	3	1	2	1	3	3	5	1	4	52	34	61	51	30	15
11th–16th	2	2	–	2	4	1	9	8	2	2	35	50	52	65	32	16
17th–22nd			1	–	1				6	3	22	19	30	22	14	6
23rd–28th									3	5	4	–	7	5	3	1
29th–31st																
No inf.																
	8	5	2	4	6	4	12	15	15	16	146	138	189	182		47

Table 31
Work situation in relation to sex and marital status.

	Working (full or part-time): M	F	Not at work M	F	Retired M	F	Un-employed M	F	No inf. M	F	Total M	F	% M	F
Single	121	100	2	4	9	8	4	2	2	2	136	116	22	17
Widowed	18	46		73	12	4		3			30	126	5	18
Married	366	228	7	202	42	3	16	2	9	5	440	440	72	63
Divorced	3	10		7				1			4	17	1	2
No inf.				1								1		–
	508	385	9	286	61	15	21	7	11	7	610	700		

APPENDIX J

To fling a 'piece', a slice of bread and jam, from a window down to a child in the street below has been a recognised custom in Glasgow's tenement housing. Since the children living in Glasgow's high flats have played a considerable part in this study we think that they should have the following and final word.

The Jeely Piece Song
by
ADAM MCNAUGHTON

I'm a skyscraper wean, I live on the nineteenth flair,
An' I'm no' gaun oot tae play ony mair,
For since we moved tae oor new hoose I'm wastin' away,
'Cos I'm gettin' wan less meal ev'ry day.

Refrain
Oh, ye canny fling pieces oot a twenty-storey flat,
Seven hundred hungry weans will testify tae that,
If it's butter, cheese or jeely, if the breid is plain or pan,
The odds against it reachin' us is ninety-nine tae wan.

On the first day ma maw flung oot a dod o' malted broon,
It went skitin' oot the windy an' went up instead o' doon,
Noo every twenty-seven hours it comes back in tae sight,
'Cos my piece went intae orbit an' became a satellite.

On the next day ma maw flung me a piece oot wance again,
It went and hit the pilot in a fast low-flyin' plane,
He scraped it aff his goggles shoutin' through the intercom
"The Clyde-side reds have got me wi' a breid an' jeely bomb".

On the third day ma maw thought she would try anither throw,
The Salvation Army baun' wis staunin' doon below,
For "Onward Christian Soldiers" wis the tune they should have played,
But the "oom-pah" man wis playin' a piece in marmalade.

We've wrote away tae Oxfam tae try an' get some aid,
We've a' joined thegither an' formed a "piece" brigade,
We're gonny march tae London tae demand oor Civil Rights,
Like "Nae mair hooses ower piece flingin' heights".

[Courtesy of Scotia Kinnaird]